100 THINGS
IOWA FANS
SHOULD KNOW & DO
BEFORE THEY DIE

T0095927

100 THINGS IOWA FANS SHOULD KNOW & DO BEFORE THEY DIE

Rick Brown

TRIUMPH
BOOKS

Copyright © 2016 by Rick Brown

No part of this publication may be reproduced, stored in a retrieval system, or transmitted in any form by any means, electronic, mechanical, photocopying, or otherwise, without the prior written permission of the publisher, Triumph Books LLC, 814 North Franklin Street, Chicago, Illinois 60610.

Library of Congress Cataloging-in-Publication Data

Names: Brown, Rick, 1953 November 30– author.
Title: 100 things Iowa fans should know & do before they die / Rick Brown.
Other titles: One hundred things Iowa fans should know and do before they die
Description: Chicago, Illinois : Triumph Books, 2016. | Series: 100
  things...fans should know
Identifiers: LCCN 2016035330 | ISBN 9781629372730 (paperback)
Subjects: LCSH: University of Iowa—Sports—Miscellanea. | BISAC: SPORTS &
  RECREATION / General. | TRAVEL / United States / Midwest / West North
  Central (IA, KS, MN, MO, ND, NE, SD).
Classification: LCC GV691.U54 B76 2016 | DDC 796.04/309777655—dc23
LC record available at https://lccn.loc.gov/2016035330

This book is available in quantity at special discounts for your group or organization.
For further information, contact:
  Triumph Books LLC
  814 North Franklin Street
  Chicago, Illinois 60610
  (312) 337-0747
  www.triumphbooks.com

Printed in U.S.A.
ISBN: 978-1-62937-273-0
Design by Patricia Frey
Photos courtesy of AP Images

To my mother, Nan, my biggest fan

Contents

Foreword

My father, Charles, grew up in Norman, Oklahoma. He attended the University of Oklahoma during the Bud Wilkinson era. My father loved the Sooners, and he loved college football.

I was born in Norman but was raised in Wheaton, Illinois. One fall Saturday, when I was a junior in high school, my father and I were driving around and running errands. We came across an Iowa football game on WHO Radio (out of Des Moines). It was 1979, Hayden Fry's first season as coach of the Hawkeyes. My dad said, "You know what, Chuck? I like this Hayden Fry hire they made at Iowa. I think he's going to do something special." It was out of the blue. After that, we didn't talk about it again. In December 1980 Iowa started recruiting me. Maybe my dad had had a premonition.

I signed a letter of intent to play quarterback for Coach Fry and the Hawkeyes, and the timing was perfect. Iowa had an active string of 19 consecutive nonwinning seasons when I arrived on campus in 1981. Going to Iowa and building a program from the ground up was special.

We made an instant splash in 1981, winning a share of the Big Ten title and going to the Rose Bowl. I wasn't playing, with the exception of a brief appearance in two games, but it was a magical season, and all of a sudden, Iowa was on the map. The block of time I was at Iowa, from 1981 to 1985, was the resurgence of Hawkeyes football. It was fun to be a part of that era and an exciting time to be on campus.

I was fortunate to be a first-team All–Big Ten selection three times, and honored to be named the league's most valuable player in 1985, the same year I was also a consensus All-American and finished second to Auburn's Bo Jackson in voting for the 1985 Heisman Trophy. I will always be grateful to my teammates and coaches for the honors I received. One of my greatest memories is beating Minnesota in my last game at Kinnick Stadium. The victory locked up the 1985 Big Ten title and another trip to the Rose Bowl.

My experience at Iowa, academically and athletically, helped prepare me for my professional career—first as a coach, and now as executive director and chief executive officer of the Iowa Sports Foundation.

I've always felt loyalty to Iowa and its fan base, because they were always loyal to me. As I've grown older, people have grown older with me, and they like to go back and talk about the good times.

Signing to play at Iowa was a game changer for me...a life changer. Everything I'm about today comes from what I learned and experienced growing up. I learned how to deal with people from my father. He was a people person. Coach Fry was right there with him. I'd say those two men were my biggest mentors. I learned from watching the way my father ran his household and I learned from watching the way Coach Fry ran his program. They both definitely shaped my life. As it turns out, coming to Iowa to play football was one of the greatest decisions of my life.

I hope you enjoy this book. It was fun to be a part of Iowa history. I have great memories of my days as a Hawkeye. And my father was right: Coach Fry did something special.

—Chuck Long

Executive Director/CEO, Iowa Sports Foundation

1985 Heisman Trophy Runner-Up

Introduction

I've had the same pair of socks for 49 years. Let me explain.

I grew up in Fort Dodge, Iowa. I idolized Tom Chapman Jr., the All-State star on the Fort Dodge High School basketball team. Chapman went on to the University of Iowa, where he played for Coach Ralph Miller; he was also an outstanding golfer for the Hawkeyes.

I was 13 years old when my father took me to Iowa City to see Chapman and the Hawkeyes play Wisconsin at the Iowa Field House on February 18, 1967. I remember two things: One, Iowa lost in triple overtime. And two, Chapman gave me his game socks when I visited him in the locker room afterward. I still have them. Chapman scored 19 points in that game. I watched every move he made that day, but I was oblivious to the big picture.

Iowa entered that game against the Badgers holding a share of the Big Ten lead, as well as a 21-game home-court winning streak. But the 96–95 loss I witnessed was a crushing one. It was the first of three gut-wrenching defeats in a four-game stretch for the Hawkeyes. They also lost at Minnesota by a basket and by three points to Purdue at home. Iowa finished 16–8 overall and third in the Big Ten at 9–5, one game behind Indiana and Michigan State.

I still have a picture my father took of me, standing in the locker room after that loss. I was standing next to Chapman and shaking hands with his teammate Gerry Jones. Chapman was smiling, masking the disappointment of the bitter defeat he'd just had to swallow.

As I got older, I started to get a better picture of the thrill of victory and the agony of defeat. Eventually I got paid to try and describe those games as a sportswriter and then columnist for the *Des Moines Register.*

I took an old-school approach to my profession, working hard to establish relationships with coaches and athletes that opened the door to future stories. I was fortunate to pick up keen insight on the games, and the outcomes, from those who trusted me to tell a fair and balanced story.

I picked up that approach from watching my father, Bob, work the craft in his four decades as a newspaperman for the *Fort Dodge Messenger*. I witnessed the respect coaches and athletes had for him. I hope when I retired from the *Register* in December 2015, the coaches and athletes I covered held me in the same regard.

I saw my share of great victories and crushing losses in almost four decades of covering games. The unexpected victories were always the most fun to write about, when passion about performance flowed from the mouths of coaches and their players.

I said good-bye to my career by covering Iowa football's 12–0 regular-season ride. Twelve straight weeks of good stories and happy coaches and athletes, who got to celebrate success while establishing plenty of school history along the way. An added bonus was spending time around Iowa coach Kirk Ferentz, an outstanding football coach and even better human being.

Thank you to all the coaches and athletes who put up with me—maybe even humored me—along the way. Some of your stories are told in this book. I don't know how many trips I made to Iowa City to cover games at Kinnick Stadium or Carver-Hawkeye Arena. Not to mention trips for weekly news conferences and interviews. I can tell you all the exit numbers between Des Moines and Iowa City on Interstate 80.

It was my profession. It was also my passion. A good journalist is inquisitive by nature, and I asked my share of questions. Iowa basketball coach Fran McCaffery would say to me every time I approached him, "Another question. You've always got another question." I asked. He answered. And I told my readers what he said. Thanks, Fran. Thanks, everyone.

I hope you enjoy *100 Things Iowa Fans Should Know & Do Before They Die*. Writing it has been a labor of love. And doing research for the book has reminded me of the Hawkeyes' rich athletic history.

I received two degrees from Iowa, and Iowa City has always felt like a second home. I've seen my fair share of games too—even triple-overtime games when hero worship was more important in a 13-year-old's eyes than winning or losing a Big Ten title.

1 The Ultimate Sacrifice

Nile Clarke Kinnick Jr. was almost too good to be true.

The 1939 Heisman Trophy winner was a student-athlete in the truest sense. He was a Phi Beta Kappa scholar and president of the senior class at the University of Iowa. The grandson of former Iowa governor George W. Clarke, he appeared destined for a political career. Kinnick had passed on a pro football career, and a $10,000 offer from the Brooklyn Dodgers, to attend law school at Iowa.

Believing that war was imminent, Kinnick joined the Naval Air Corps Reserve in August 1941. He reported for duty on December 4, three days before Pearl Harbor. But the conflict had been on his mind for years.

When he gave his Heisman Trophy acceptance speech in December 1939, Kinnick touched on the realities of life and war. "I thank God I was warring on the gridirons of the Midwest and not on the battlefields of Europe," Kinnick said. "I can speak confidently and positively that the players of this country would much more, much rather struggle and fight to win the Heisman award than the Croix de Guerre."

Less than four years later, those were haunting words. Kinnick, 24, became a casualty of World War II. A navy pilot, Ensign Kinnick perished on June 2, 1943. During a training maneuver, he was flying a single-seat fighter over the Caribbean Sea, off the coast of Venezuela, when it developed an oil leak.

The deck of the USS *Lexington* was a busy place, with pilots and planes preparing for takeoff. Instead of putting others' lives at risk,

"The Acme in Recognition"

After Iowa's Nile Kinnick won the 1939 Heisman Trophy, his acceptance speech captivated the audience. That speech has become a rich piece of Iowa football history. A portion of that speech is played at home games in Kinnick Stadium, right before the National Anthem. Here's is Kinnick's December 6, 1939, speech:

"Thank you very, very kindly, Mr. Holcombe. It seems to me that everyone is letting their superlatives run away with them this evening, but nonetheless, I want you to know that I'm mighty, mighty happy to accept this trophy this evening.

"Every football player in these United States dreams about winning that trophy, and of this fine trip to New York. Every player considers that trophy the acme in recognition of this kind. And the fact that I am actually receiving this trophy tonight almost overwhelms me, and I know that all of those boys who have gone before me must have felt somewhat the same way.

"From my own personal viewpoint, I consider my winning this award as indirectly a great tribute to the new coaching staff at the University of Iowa, headed by Dr. Eddie Anderson, and to my teammates sitting back in Iowa City. A finer man and a better coach never hit these United States, and a more courageous bunch of boys

Kinnick attempted a water landing instead. His plane went down four miles from the carrier. A search turned up neither Kinnick nor his plane, only an oil slick. Kinnick was one of 407,000 Americans who lost their lives in military service during World War II.

It was devastating news back home. Dr. Eddie Anderson, who had been Kinnick's coach during his senior season at Iowa, issued a statement that spoke for a stunned state. "Nile was a grand young man whose qualities of citizenship, leadership, and all-around worth matched his outstanding ability as an athlete and competitor," Anderson said. "I feel a deep sense of personal loss. He was loved by everyone who knew him. His kindness and consideration for others stamped him as a typically ideal American.

never graced the gridirons of the Midwest than that Iowa team of 1939. I wish that they might all be with me tonight to receive this trophy. They certainly deserve it.

"I want to take this grand opportunity to thank collectively all the sportswriters and all the sportscasters and all those who have seen fit, have seen their way clear to cast a ballot in my favor for this trophy. And I also want to take this opportunity to thank Mr. Prince and his committee, the Heisman award committee, and all those connected with the Downtown Athletic Club for this trophy, and for the fine time that they're showing me. And not only for that but for making this fine and worthy trophy available to the football players of this country.

"Finally, if you will permit me, I'd like to make a comment which, in my mind, is indicative, perhaps, of the greater significance of football, and sports emphasis in general in this country, and that is, I thank God I was warring on the gridirons of the Midwest and not the battlefields of Europe. I can speak confidently and positively that the players of this country would much more, much rather struggle and fight to win the Heisman award than the Croix de Guerre.

"Thank you."

In the uniform of his country, he gave everything—that was the only way Nile Kinnick knew how to play the game."

Kinnick's Heisman Trophy sits in Iowa's Hansen Football Performance Center today. His No. 24 was retired. And in 1972 Iowa Stadium was renamed Kinnick Stadium. Nile Kinnick was a part of the charter class of the College Football Hall of Fame, inducted in 1951.

When Kinnick died, *Des Moines Register* sports editor Sec Taylor wrote, "His death is like that of a member of one's immediate family."

Today a 20-foot-tall bronze statue of Kinnick, erected in 2006, stands outside the south end of the stadium. Iowa players

Nile Kinnick remains one of the most revered players in Hawkeyes history.

and coaches walk by the likeness of Kinnick on their way to the locker room on game days and touch a helmet at the foot of the statute for good luck.

Ralph's Six-Pack

Before returning to his home in Pennsylvania for the summer, Glenn Vidnovic rented an apartment near the University of Iowa's Finkbine Golf Course for the fall of 1968.

Vidnovic had been a starting forward on the 1967–68 Hawkeyes basketball team that had been upset by Michigan and Rudy Tomjanovich in the season's final game at home, a 71–70 loss that cost coach Ralph Miller's team an outright Big Ten title. Iowa lost a playoff game against Ohio State, 85–81, with a chance to go to the NCAA Tournament on the line. The Hawkeyes went home, and the Buckeyes went to the Final Four.

When Vidnovic returned to campus in the fall of 1968, he had a surprise waiting for him. "Coach Miller called me in. I see this guy with a floppy hat, and I'm thinking, *Oh, no*," Vidnovic said. "Coach Miller said, 'Do you have a roommate?' I said, 'No.' He said, 'Here, take him.' But it turned out good. He was a great guy."

The guy in the floppy hat was named John Johnson, a junior-college transfer from Northwest College in Powell, Wyoming. Johnson, a forward, had an immediate impact on a mediocre 12–12 team. He averaged a team-high 19.7 points.

Miller returned four starters for the 1969–70 season: Vidnovic, Johnson, Chad Calabria, and Dick Jensen. Also back was Ben McGilmer. Miller needed to replace guard Chris Phillips. He filled the void by signing Fred Brown out of Burlington Junior College. And the Six-Pack was born. All that offensive potential meshed into one of the greatest teams in school history.

Iowa had averaged 84.4 points a game in 1968–69 but allowed 79.9. Miller, a defensive specialist, knew those numbers had to change. "I'm satisfied we will be a good offensive team again," Miller said. "If this team plays good defense, we will have a good season."

But this wasn't an overnight success story. Iowa turned it over 27 times in a 73–67 loss at Southern Illinois, which both Brown and Jensen missed due to illness. The Hawkeyes went on to lose four of their first seven games. And that doesn't include an overtime loss to Submarine Forces Pacific in a consolation game of the Rainbow Classic in Hawaii. That was considered an exhibition game and didn't count toward Iowa's record.

Next was the Big Ten opener against Purdue on January 3. The Boilermakers, with sharpshooting guard Rick Mount, were the league favorite. Illinois and Ohio State were considered the top challengers. Iowa, Michigan, and Northwestern were three teams "that could knock on the door."

The Hawkeyes broke that door down. Mount scored 53 points in Iowa Field House in that opener, but Iowa posted a 94–88 victory. The next game was at Michigan, and that was problematic. Iowa had failed to win a Big Ten road game in the previous season. But Miller's team walloped the Wolverines 107–99 as Johnson scored 34 points, Calabria 24, Brown 23, and Vidnovic 18. The team never looked back.

Iowa finished 14–0 in the Big Ten, three games clear of runner-up Purdue. The Hawkeyes averaged a Big Ten–record 102.9 points a game and reached the century mark nine times.

In five of those games, four different players scored 20 points or more. For the Big Ten season, Johnson averaged 31.8 points, Brown 20.7, and Calabria and Vidnovic 18.4 each. Johnson was a first-team All–Big Ten selection, and Brown and Vidnovic were named to the second team.

Iowa looked poised for a Final Four run in 1970, when the tournament field consisted of 25 teams. The seventh-ranked Hawkeyes, with the nation's longest winning streak at 16 games, drew No. 4 Jacksonville in Columbus, Ohio. The Dolphins had a front line of 7'2" center Artis Gilmore, who had made a recruiting trip to Iowa, and 7'0" Pembrook Burrows III. Gilmore had averaged 27 points and 23 rebounds per game in regular-season play. The Dolphins averaged 98.8 points in the regular season.

Gilmore finished with 30 points and 17 rebounds against Iowa, but he fouled out with more than eight minutes to play.

Brown rebounded his own miss and scored with 18 seconds remaining for a 103–102 Iowa lead. Then the Hawkeyes defense forced guard Vaughn Wedeking to launch a deep desperation shot. The ball hit the back of the rim. "All it had to do was bounce up in the air, and time would have run out," Vidnovic said. "But the ball got trapped. I've never seen anything like it. Then there was this big hand above the basket, and that was it."

Burrows tipped in Wedeking's miss with two seconds left and Iowa lost 104–103. "I can see it like it was yesterday," Vidnovic said.

Iowa made just 19 of 31 free throws in that loss. Two days later, the Hawkeyes ended the season with a 121–106 romp past Notre Dame in the consolation game, as Calabria and Johnson both scored 31 points, and Vidnovic had 24.

"They wanted to be there less than we did," Vidnovic said.

The Fabulous Five

Iowa basketball coach Bucky O'Connor was excited about his 1952–53 freshman class. So excited, in fact, he predicted they would be a championship team someday. Skeptics called O'Connor a dreamer and an optimist. The freshmen's names were Bill Schoof, Carl Cain, Bill Logan, Bill Seaberg, and Sharm Scheuerman—four of whom were from Illinois. The other, Logan, was from Keokuk. History tells us that O'Connor was right. All five players had their numbers retired after a loss to San Francisco in the 1956 NCAA title game.

They became known as the Fabulous Five. They were Big Ten runners-up as sophomores and won the league title the next two seasons. Both those 1954–55 and 1955–56 teams also made the Final Four.

"He was a good recruiter," Seaberg said of O'Connor. "He knew what he wanted and who he wanted, and he got the talent. Then he made sure the fundamentals were pointed out in practice."

The game that launched the Fabulous Five came in 1953–54. After losing 74–51 to Illinois at home on February 20, O'Connor decided to start Cain, Logan, Schoof, Seaberg, and Scheuerman in a game at defending national champion Indiana two nights later. Iowa stunned the Hoosiers 82–64.

"These guys were great basketball players, and we beat them on the road and we beat them handily, and I think for the first time we thought, *Maybe something is going on*," Schoof said.

Iowa finished 17–5 overall and 11–3 in the Big Ten, good for second place behind Indiana.

With senior McKinley "Deacon" Davis joining juniors Cain, Logan, Seaberg, and Scheuerman in the starting lineup, Iowa won the Big Ten title in 1954–55 with an 11–3 record and went 19–7 overall.

The Hawkeyes represented the Big Ten in the NCAA Tournament and reached the Final Four by defeating Penn State 82–53 and Marquette 86–81. A LaSalle team led by All-American Tom Gola knocked Iowa out in the semifinals, 76–73.

Then came a 1955–56 season that some consider the best in the program's history. Schoof replaced Davis in the starting lineup, and the season got off to a rocky start. Iowa was 3–5 at one point, losing consecutive games to Washington, Stanford, California, and then Michigan State in the Big Ten opener.

But the Hawkeyes ran off 14 straight regular-season victories after that to win the Big Ten title. All five starters averaged in double figures, led by Logan. The center scored at 17.7 points a clip. Cain was next at 15.8, followed by Seaberg (13.9), Schoof (10.8), and Scheuerman (10.1).

"You never knew who was going to have the hot hand," Seaberg said. "It was Logan or Cain or myself. It just worked out great. We didn't have one outstanding offensive player. It just kind of moved around."

Seaberg said O'Connor had a great feel for his team. "He knew that we knew what we were doing," Seaberg said. "He let us play."

Seaberg said the cohesiveness of the team off the floor matched their level of play on it. "We knew each other pretty well, on and off the court," Seaberg said. "We knew where the other person was going to be, or who had the hot hand that night. We knew the best way to use our talent."

Iowa returned to NCAA Tournament play and handled Morehead State 97–83 and Kentucky 89–77 to reach the Final Four again. Then the Hawkeyes took care of Temple 83–76 to set up a championship game meeting with San Francisco.

The Dons had K.C. Jones and legendary center Bill Russell, who had 26 points and 27 rebounds in an 83–71 victory over Iowa.

"To me, [Russell] was the best basketball player that ever played the game," said Logan, who had 12 points and 15 rebounds as the Hawkeyes finished the season 20–6.

Logan was a first-team All–Big Ten selection for the second straight season. Cain, who would help the United States win an Olympic gold medal later that year, joined Logan on the first team. Seaberg made the second team. Logan and Cain were also All-Americans.

When Iowa released its All-Century team in 2002, Logan, Cain, and Seaberg were included on the 20-man roster. "That made us feel pretty good," Seaberg said.

4 Gable's Record-Setting Good-Bye

Dan Gable grew up in Waterloo, where he fell in love with wrestling and became an international icon in the sport. Gable ended his coaching career right next door in Cedar Falls. And what a good-bye it was.

Oklahoma State entered the 1997 NCAA wrestling championships the favorite, but Gable's Hawkeyes demolished the field in record-smashing style. "We all knew this was something special for Coach Gable," said Mark Ironside, one of Iowa's five individual champions in 1997. "It was where he began his wrestling career and would more than likely end his wrestling career. We wanted to do our part in making sure that it ended on a high note for him. That was a big motivational factor for us."

Iowa turned the UNI-Dome into its own personal playground. The Hawkeyes scored an NCAA-record 170 points, erasing the previous mark of 158 they had set in 1986. The five individual

Gable Accepts Bronze?

Dan Gable's place in the sport of wrestling is not up for debate. Neither is the symbolism of the Gable statue that sits outside the main entrance to Carver-Hawkeye Arena.

The bronze likeness of Gable—he joked at the dedication in 2012 that it's the only bronze award he'd ever accept—depicts him motioning for a referee to call stalling. Not competing at your absolute best has never been in Gable's playbook.

Engraved at the bottom of the statue are highlights of some of Gable's greatest accomplishments, along with these words: [No] STALLING...EXECUTE...CONTRIBUTE FOREVER...IN SPORT AND IN LIFE.

Gable said those words are "what it is really about. It's not about history. It is about future history. It is about people who want to be about something great in the future."

champions in 1997—Jessie Whitmer at 118 pounds, Ironside at 134, Lincoln McIlravy at 150, Joe Williams at 158, and Lee Fullhart at 190—matched the five individual champions the 1986 team had. Iowa finished 56.5 points ahead of Oklahoma State.

"It's pretty cool to have been on a team of Coach Gable's that set the record," said Ironside, who finished the season with a 30–0 record. "Any time you are a part of history, it becomes more meaningful as time goes on."

It was the 15th NCAA title in Gable's 21 seasons as head coach. Though many thought it would be his final season, he didn't make it official until after the championship. "I was hoping to win it, but to win in this fashion is mind-boggling," Gable said. "If anything, this makes my decision more difficult."

Iowa came close to having a sixth champion, but 126-pounder Mike Mena lost 3–2 to Eric Guerrero of Oklahoma State in a tie-breaker. Mena won the coin flip and elected to ride Guerrero, who escaped five seconds later to win in overtime.

"Even with running away with it, there were still some heartaches," said Tom Brands, an assistant to Gable in 1997 and now

Before he was a coach, Dan Gable was an NCAA wrestling legend and an Olympian.

the Hawkeyes' head coach. "That team wasn't even picked to win it, but we won 20-some matches in a row and just got rolling. You start rolling, and things start to pile up in a good way."

Ironside, McIlravy, and Williams finished that season with a combined 81–1 record. It was the third NCAA title for McIlravy, who was named the outstanding wrestler of the tournament.

"There were multiple things that made our team click when it counted most," Ironside said. "One, Gable prepared us for zero hour. Two, we all knew what we were capable of doing, and what needed to be done. And three, with the tournament in Iowa and having so many great Hawkeye fans there, that contributed to our surge."

That 1997 team had eight All-Americans overall and was enshrined in the Glen Brand Wrestling Hall of Fame of Iowa in 2014. Like other teams before them, they used Gable's iconic standing in the sport as added motivation. "To be able to look over into your corner and see the legendary Coach Gable sitting there was one of the most motivating things a wrestler could ask for," Ironside said. "Who would want to let a guy like that down? You did all you could to make him proud and do it right. It was respect."

California, Here We Come

Iowa football coach Forest Evashevski challenged his team with these words, posted on a wall in the locker room: YOU HAVE 60 MINUTES TO PLAY THE GAME SATURDAY—AND A LIFETIME TO REMEMBER IT.

Mighty Ohio State was coming to Iowa City for a pivotal game on November 17, 1956. The Buckeyes were the muscle in the Big Ten. The Hawkeyes were the new kid in town.

Ohio State, ranked No. 6, was playing for an 18th consecutive Big Ten victory under Coach Woody Hayes, and a third straight Big Ten title. Iowa, ranked No. 7, was 6–1.

It went down in history as a day for the defenses. There was just one touchdown scored, a 17-yard pass from quarterback Kenny Ploen to Jim Gibbons in the third quarter. On a second-and-7 play, Ploen faked a handoff to Don Dobrino and found Gibbons, who had gotten past Ohio State's Frank Ellwood.

"We had our sweeping Wing-T Offense, and I just bootlegged off that same type of action," Ploen said. "Gibbons ran an excellent pattern and beat his man."

Gibbons said he ran the route just as Evashevski had designed it. "The catch was probably the biggest thing that ever happened to me in college because it meant so many things," Gibbons said.

That touchdown reception completed a 10-play, 63-yard drive on Iowa's first possession of the second half. Bob Prescott missed the point-after kick, leaving the score 6–0. It was his first miss of the season.

Iowa's defense made that precarious lead stand up. Ohio State never moved the ball deeper than Iowa's 32-yard line the entire game. The Buckeyes completed just two passes, for 18 yards. And a week after rushing for a then-conference record 465 yards against Indiana, Ohio State managed just 147.

The victory gave Iowa its first Big Ten title in 34 seasons, and earned the Hawkeyes their first trip to the Rose Bowl. Afterward, jubilant Hawkeyes fans brought down the goal posts, which were sunk in six feet of concrete, and roses bloomed in Iowa's locker room. Sixty minutes of work produced a lifetime of memories.

After crushing Notre Dame and Heisman Trophy star Paul Hornung 48–8 in the regular-season finale, Iowa packed its bags and headed to California. Ploen quarterbacked the Hawkeyes to a 35–19 victory over Oregon State in Pasadena and was named the game's most valuable player. He was also the Big Ten's MVP that season. Iowa finished the season 9–1 and was ranked No. 3 in the final Associated Press poll.

The Duke

Iowa renamed its football stadium after Nile Kinnick in 1972. Kinnick, who won the 1939 Heisman Trophy, lost his life in World War II. But before Kinnick was honored with the name, another former Iowa athlete was given consideration. His name was Fred "Duke" Slater, the first African American from Iowa to be named to an All-America team. That happened when he was a sophomore in 1919.

Slater, who attended high school in Clinton, Iowa, actually wanted to quit high school and get a job. So his father got him one—cutting ice on the Mississippi River in the winter. Suddenly Slater decided school didn't sound so bad.

Nicknamed Duke—after the family dog—Slater lived in Chicago until he was 13, when his father got a job as the pastor of a church in Clinton. Slater arrived at Iowa in 1918, where he was a star tackle on some outstanding Howard Jones–coached teams. With eligibility standards suspended because of World War I, Slater was able to play as a freshman.

Often playing without a helmet, Slater burst into prominence as a sophomore in 1919. He was a first-team All–Big Ten pick and was a second-team All-American.

Fritz Crisler, who played against Slater when he was at the University of Chicago before going on to fame as a coach and athletic director at Michigan, said of Slater: "[He] was the best tackle I ever played against. I tried to block him throughout my college career, but never once did I impede his progress to the ball carrier."

Slater was a first-team All–Big Ten choice again as a junior, setting the table for an incredible senior campaign. Iowa went 7–0 and never trailed in a game all season. The Hawkeyes celebrated their first outright Big Ten championship ever. The best-remembered game from that season was a 10–7 victory over Notre Dame and coach Knute Rockne on October 8; it was the second game of the season. That ended a 20-game winning streak for the Irish. And that victory was the fifth in what would become a 20-game winning streak for Iowa that ended in 1923.

Slater was a first-team All–Big Ten pick for the third time as a senior, and an All-American as well. Also a standout in the shotput, discus, and hammer throw, Slater helped the Hawkeyes finish third in the first NCAA Track and Field Championships in 1921. He finished third in the hammer, fourth in the discus.

Slater became the first African American lineman in NFL history when he joined the Rock Island Independents in 1922. He played for the Independents for five seasons before finishing a 10-year career with the Chicago Cardinals. He started in 96 of 99 career games.

Slater also found time to return to Iowa during his professional career and received a law degree in 1928. He was a lawyer and judge in Chicago after his football days ended.

Slater's football legacy at Iowa is unmatched. He was elected to the National Football Foundation College Football Hall of Fame in 1951. Slater is also a member of the National Iowa Varsity Club Hall of Fame. He has a spot on the Hawkeyes' All-Time team, selected in 1989 in conjunction with the program's 100th season. And he is a member of the elite Kinnick Stadium

Wall of Honor, and his name and number appear on the Paul W. Brechler Press Box.

Slater, who passed away in 1966, also has a campus dorm named after him. When it comes to Iowa football history, Duke Slater is a giant.

7 Olson, Gable, and Fry: A Winning Trifecta

Iowa athletic director Chalmers W. "Bump" Elliott was on a roll. He hired Lute Olson as his men's basketball coach before the 1974–75 season. It didn't take long to realize Olson was going to be a home-run hire. Then he hired Dan Gable to be the Hawkeyes' wrestling coach in 1976. A season later, Gable's team won the first of 15 NCAA titles under his watch.

And then in 1978 it was time for Elliott to hire another football coach. He'd hired Frank Lauterbur in 1971, and three seasons and four victories later, he'd hired Bob Commings in 1974. Commings was not much better, netting the team 18 victories in five seasons, so Elliott was in the market for a new football coach again. And he knew he had to get it right.

"Any time you're looking for a coach you feel pressure, because that's a responsibility you can't avoid," Elliott said.

Elliott called his brother, Pete, then the athletic director at Miami of Florida. "They had been in a search the year before," Elliott said. "And Pete said the one person who...stood out that they interviewed was Hayden Fry [from North Texas State]. I had known Hayden. So I called him, he came up for a visit, and away it went."

Elliott got it right. Fry, one of seven men interviewed for the job, inherited a program that had strung together 17 consecutive nonwinning seasons. "It's great to be in Hawkeye Country," Fry said at halftime of the 1978 Iowa–Iowa State basketball game, two days after he was hired. "I had an opportunity to meet with the football team, ladies and gentlemen, and we are going to win."

Fans had greeted Fry with chants of "Rose Bowl! Rose Bowl!" as he took the floor that night. An outlandish pipe dream of a chant, it seemed.

But Fry took Iowa to a Rose Bowl in his third season, and two more after that. His teams went to 14 bowl games in 20 seasons, and won or shared three Big Ten titles. Fry stepped down after the 1998 season as Iowa's all-time winningest coach with a record of 143–89–6. Iowa's record the previous 20 seasons had been 67–129–5.

Fry used discipline and psychology to create a winning environment at Iowa. "Coach Fry always had the ability to motivate," said All-American tight end Marv Cook. "I'd sit in a staff room or team room, and there'd be 115 or 120 guys in there. I thought he was talking right to me. He had a unique ability to get right to the point and make everyone feel like he was talking to them. And he knew how to motivate. In my opinion, there's no one who has ever done it better than him."

The red-letter day for Elliott came on November 21, 1981. Ohio State's victory over Michigan and Iowa's 36–7 thumping of Michigan State sent the Hawkeyes to the Rose Bowl.

"That was a great day," Elliott said.

* * *

On paper, prying Olson away from Long Beach State had been an uphill climb. "People didn't go from Long Beach to Iowa, they went from Iowa to Long Beach," Olson joked many years later. "I thought, *Well, I'm just going to break that trend.* I saw an opportunity."

Olson inherited a basketball program that had limped through three losing seasons in the previous four. In the nine seasons he was coach, Olson's teams won at least 20 games six times and earned five NCAA Tournament berths. That includes a Final Four appearance in 1980 and a share of the Big Ten title in 1978–79.

"Lute rarely swore," said Kevin Boyle, who played for Olson from 1978 to 1982. "But if he said something bad, you knew he was upset. He just did a great job. He knew how to get guys that had talent, and guys that were blue-collar, and combine them."

* * *

Gable gained fame as a collegiate wrestling star at Iowa State. He won a gold medal in the 1972 Olympics while not surrendering a single point. Many figured Gable would end up coaching at his alma mater, where he had compiled a 117–1 record during his collegiate career.

But Iowa's Gary Kurdelmeier hired him as an assistant coach in 1972. And three years later, Elliott hired him as the head coach. "He was here, I knew him, and that made it easy," Elliott said.

That 1978 NCAA title was the first of nine straight under Gable, and 15 overall. His dual-meet record was 355–21–5 when he stepped down following the 1996–97 season. His teams won 21 consecutive Big Ten titles. He coached 152 All-Americans, 45 national champions, 106 Big Ten champions, and 12 Olympians.

One of those Olympians, 1996 gold medalist Tom Brands, is now Iowa's head coach. "The best compliment I can give Gable is that we got better without knowing we were getting better," said Brands, a three-time NCAA champ.

A statue of Gable stands outside Carver-Hawkeye Arena, honoring the wrestling icon. "You see that statue out there, and you think it's automatic," Brands said. "You say, 'Oh, he's a legend, he's an icon, he won all those national championships, it was easy.' But it was unbelievably hard."

Striking Gold with Evy

It remains one of the greatest rags-to-riches stories in the history of Iowa athletics. And it was engineered by a Michigan man.

Forest "Evy" Evashevski earned fame as a football player under Fritz Crisler in Ann Arbor. He was the triggerman in the Wolverines' single-wing attack, and his blocking helped make Tom Harmon an All-American running back.

Eleven years later, Evashevski left Washington State to become the head football coach at Iowa for $15,000 a year. Evashevski inherited a second division Big Ten program that had enjoyed just three winning seasons in the previous 16, and transformed the Hawkeyes into a national power.

From 1952 to 1960 Evashevski's teams were 52–27–4, won or shared three Big Ten titles, won two Rose Bowls, and finished in the top 10 of the Associated Press poll five times. The Football Writers Association of America declared the 1958 Hawkeyes national champions.

This was not a magic act. Evashevski created this turnaround with his coaching and motivational skills. "Simply put, recruiting was No. 1," said Bump Elliott, who was on Evashevski's first Iowa coaching staff and later succeeded him as athletic director in 1970. "And No. 2, great coaching. Evy was an outstanding coach."

His first four Iowa teams were a combined 15–19–2. But Evashevski made a program-changing gamble before the 1956 season. He installed the Wing-T formation, the brainchild of Dave Nelson of Delaware. Evashevski added his own wrinkles. "I had wanted to go to the Wing-T before, but we didn't have the personnel to do it until 1956," Evashevski said.

A Notre Dame Sweep

Not many college quarterbacks can say they played for a team that beat Notre Dame three times. Randy Duncan was an exception to the rule. But that shouldn't come as a surprise. Anyone fortunate enough to get to know Randy Duncan will tell you he is an exceptional human being.

Duncan was a backup to Kenny Ploen in 1956, when Iowa smashed the Irish 48–8 in Iowa City. Duncan started in a 21–13 victory over Notre Dame in South Bend in 1957. With Iowa holding a 14–13 lead, Duncan put away the game in this duel between top 10 teams with a 16-yard touchdown pass to Don Norton in the fourth quarter.

Duncan also led Iowa to a 31–21 victory over the Irish in 1958 in Iowa City, throwing a pair of touchdown passes.

Duncan's senior season ended with a Big Ten championship and a Rose Bowl victory. He was also the Heisman Trophy runner-up after leading the nation in passing percentage, yards passing, and touchdown passes thrown.

He was also the Big Ten MVP, earned the Walter Camp Player of the Year Award, and was a consensus All-American. Duncan was the first player selected in the 1959 NFL Draft, by the Green Bay Packers.

He opted for the Canadian Football League instead, where a more lucrative contract awaited with the British Columbia Lions. Two seasons later he played for the Dallas Texans of the American Football League but ended up returning to his home in Des Moines to get a law degree from Drake University. Duncan became a highly respected lawyer in his hometown. And he would bring up his glory-filled football career only when asked. "When I got through playing football, I knew one thing," Duncan said. "I didn't want to be one of those jocks that couldn't get the roar of the crowd out of their ears."

Iowa went 9–1 in 1956, won the school's first Big Ten crown since 1922, beat Oregon State in the Rose Bowl, and finished third in the final rankings.

The Hawkeyes went 7–1–1 in 1957 and were ranked sixth in the final poll. Then came an 8–1–1 mark, another Big Ten championship, a No. 2 national ranking, and a Rose Bowl victory against California. That team featured playmakers on offense such as quarterback and Heisman Trophy runner-up Randy Duncan and running backs Bob Jeter and Willie Fleming.

"He was a great motivator of men," Duncan said of Evashevski. "And he was an innovator, unlike most coaches. He was also a tough taskmaster. Everybody who played for him feared him. I still can't talk about him without my knees knocking. It's like a private going back to talk to his general."

A share of another Big Ten championship came in 1960, when Iowa finished 8–1 and No. 3 in the final poll. When he resigned after that season at 42 years of age, Evashevski had coached 22 All–Big Ten players and 13 All-Americans at Iowa.

"Had he stayed on, there's no telling what he would have accomplished," Duncan said. "He probably would have been in the Bear Bryant category."

Evashevski, who was inducted into the College Football Hall of Fame in 2000, passed away in 2009 at 91 years of age.

"When you stop and think about the history of football, you've got to include Evashevski as one of the great ones," Elliott said.

A Rosy End to a Streak

Gordy Bohannon grew up playing baseball on a field next to the Rose Bowl in Pasadena, California. But it took a trip to Iowa for him to get through the gates of one of college football's iconic venues.

Bohannon was one of the first players Coach Hayden Fry recruited after leaving North Texas State and taking over a dormant Iowa program in 1979. It took a few zigs and zags for Bohannon to end up in Iowa City.

He didn't get any offers from major college recruiters as a senior at South Pasadena High School. He ended up at Cal State–Pomona, a Division II program. There, he met wide receiver Keith Chappelle, and the two made a productive passing combination.

But when their coach said he was switching to a wishbone-style attack the following season, Bohannon and Chappelle packed their bags. They landed at Glendale Junior College in Glendale, California.

Bohannon became the nation's third-leading junior college passer. Chappelle was the national leader in receptions. Bohannon signed with Iowa. Chappelle was headed for Missouri but decided at the last minute to join the Hawkeyes program as well.

Bohannon played for the Hawkeyes in 1979 and then sat out the 1980 season. Iowa went 4–7, the school's 19th consecutive non-winning season, even though Chappelle led the Big Ten and was second nationally in receiving with 64 catches for 1,037 yards and six touchdowns.

And then everything changed in Bohannon's senior season. Instead of seeing Iowa's streak of nonwinning seasons grow to 20 in

1981, Iowa finished the season with a Big Ten championship ring and a trip to the Rose Bowl.

"It was a great experience for all of us, and certainly a magical time in Iowa football history," said Kirk Ferentz, who had been hired by Fry as Iowa's offensive line coach that summer and would go on to replace him as head coach in 1999.

Bohannon went into his senior season expecting fortunes to change. "That was our goal, to win the Big Ten championship and get to the Rose Bowl," he said. "So that wasn't by accident."

Iowa had not won a Big Ten title since 1960, or had a winning season since 1961. And the opening game that season was a daunting task—against No. 7 Nebraska at Kinnick Stadium. But Iowa stunned the Cornhuskers 10–7, a victory that was sealed with Lou King's interception in the final minute. "I've had some great victories at SMU and North Texas State," Fry said. "But today, this is the greatest victory of my life."

Enthusiasm was tempered with a 23–12 loss at Iowa State the following week, but that was followed by a 20–7 upset of No. 6 UCLA. That was Fry's 100th victory as a college coach. And the belief in the locker room grew. "We knew we had a really good shot of doing what we wanted to do," Bohannon said.

Iowa won its first three Big Ten games of the season, none bigger than a 9–7 upset of Michigan in Ann Arbor. It was Iowa's first victory in Michigan Stadium since 1958. It was also a top 25 duel—the Wolverines were ranked fifth; Iowa was No. 12. And Coach Bo Schembechler's Michigan team had been a two-touchdown favorite.

By then an Iowa defense led by All-American end Andre Tippett, end Pat Dean, and linebacker Mel Cole was the strength of the team.

Bohannon was the No. 1 quarterback, with Pete Gales getting some snaps as well. "They both played at a really high rate in

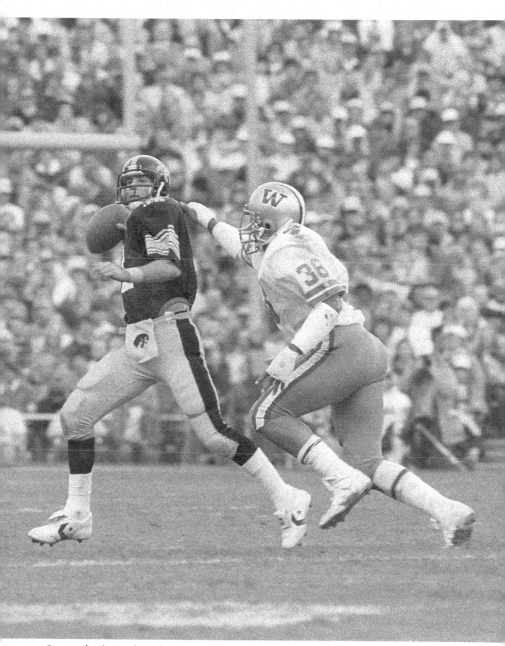

Quarterback Gordy Bohannon tries to outrun Washington's Mark Stewart in the 1982 Rose Bowl.

1981," Ferentz said. "Both those guys did a great job. But we were more of a defensive football team at that point."

Iowa's first four-game winning streak in 20 years started Rose Bowl talk and moved the Hawkeyes up to No. 6 in the Associated Press poll. But Minnesota came to Kinnick Stadium and offered up a 12–10 sobering dose of reality. And when Iowa lost 24–7 at Illinois the following week, the Rose Bowl dream was seemingly gone.

But a victory against Purdue the next week was monumental. It gave Iowa a 6–3 record, assuring its first winning season since 1961. And it ended a string of 20 consecutive losses to the Boilermakers.

When Iowa extinguished Wisconsin's Rose Bowl hopes the following week in Madison 17–7, the dream was alive. If Iowa beat Michigan State at home the following week and Ohio State beat Michigan in Ann Arbor, Iowa would share the title and go to the Rose Bowl.

My Four Sons

Gordy Bohannon's four sons found a different way to earn college scholarships. Instead of taking snaps and throwing passes, they all excelled at basketball. Which isn't totally out of character. "I was a point guard at South Pasadena High School," Gordy said.

Bohannon's oldest son, Jason, was Iowa's Mr. Basketball as a senior at Linn-Mar High School in Marion, Iowa. Jason played at Wisconsin from 2006 to 2010, scoring 1,170 points and ranking in the top five in Badgers history for three-pointers attempted and made.

Zach, a 6'6" forward, started his career at Air Force but transferred to Wisconsin after two seasons. He played in 70 games and ended his career in 2014.

Matt was a 6'4" guard at Northern Iowa, where he also cracked the 1,000-point career scoring mark and ranks in the top five in Panthers history for three-pointers attempted and made.

The youngest, Jordan, is a 6'0" guard who signed a letter of intent to play at Iowa in November 2015.

"We knew we had a shot," Bohannon said. "All we had to do was take care of business and hope the Ohio State–Michigan game worked out the way it did."

The game in Ann Arbor started 90 minutes earlier than Iowa's game.

Fry often had Bohannon drop back and take the snap in what is now called the shotgun. "He called it Bohannon's Cannon," Gordy said. "I would go under center and then pop back to the shotgun. He told me the reason he did that was I was so slow, and they needed a couple of seconds more for me to make a decision."

Bohannon remembered stepping away from center and hearing the fans roar. "I thought they were excited we were going to the shotgun," Bohannon said. "It turns out Ohio State had just beat Michigan."

Iowa put the finishing touches on a 36–7 victory over Michigan State, and roses fell from the sky.

"We didn't really have any superstars," Bohannon said. "A couple of them developed, like Andre Tippett. We were just a bunch of guys that had average and ordinary abilities on the outside and extraordinary desire on the inside. We all came together. We had great chemistry."

Iowa's amazing season also got Bohannon onto the field at the Rose Bowl. A 28–0 loss to Washington ended the season, but it's still one of the most remarkable ones in school history.

"Our goal was to get to the Rose Bowl," Bohannon said. "The problem was we didn't talk about *winning* the Rose Bowl."

10 The Ironmen of 1939

A nickname was born from one sentence in a newspaper article the week of Iowa's 1939 football opener against South Dakota.

Dr. Eddie Anderson, an Iowa native, had been brought in to coach the program out of a significant rut. The Hawkeyes had been 1–7 and 1–6–1 the previous two seasons and won just one Big Ten game over a three-season stretch. That victory came against Chicago, a school that had already announced it would drop the sport after the 1939 campaign.

Anderson had an 85-man squad for practice that spring, but only 37 of them would return in the fall of 1939. A *Des Moines Register* story the week of the South Dakota game stated, "a set of iron men may be developed to play football for Iowa."

They became known as the Ironmen, a team led by a Heisman Trophy winner. A team that became legendary after an unexpected 6–1–1 record.

It cost just $21 to attend all four games played at Iowa Stadium that year. No one dreamed they'd get their money's worth like they did.

Iowa won that opener 41–0, thanks to another nickname. Nile Kinnick was known as the Cornbelt Comet. He ran for three touchdowns, passed for two more, and dropkicked five extra points in the season-opening victory. Small in stature, at 5'8" and 170 pounds, Kinnick was on his way to becoming a gridiron giant. When Iowa defeated Indiana 32–29 the following week, it was the school's first home victory over a Big Ten foe since 1933.

Powerful Michigan, with future Iowa coach Forest Evashevski blocking for All-American Tom Harmon, ended the Hawkeyes' fast start with a 27–7 victory in Ann Arbor. But Anderson's team bounced back, winning at Wisconsin by a 19–13 margin. Kinnick threw the winning touchdown pass, to William Green, in the fourth quarter. Five Iowa players—Kinnick, Mike Enich, Charlie Tollefson, Wally Bergstrom, and Max Hawkins—played the entire game. The following week, when two safeties were good enough to win 4–0 at Purdue, eight players went the distance. The legend of the Ironmen grew.

Every big season has a signature moment. Iowa's came the next week, when Notre Dame came to Iowa Stadium and left with its national championship hopes in ruin. Iowa won 7–6 as Kinnick scored Iowa's touchdown, following the lead block of Enich, then added the winning point-after dropkick. Kinnick also punted 16 times in that game.

The *Des Moines Register*'s Bert McGrane wrote, "An amber landscape in Iowa Saturday received the remains of Notre Dame's 1939 championship hopes.

"Eddie Anderson's wonder team—Nile Kinnick and his iron mates—took over the opportunists' role held through the years by the Fighting Irish, forced the great Notre Dame array to make a single, glaring mistake, slammed across an Iowa touchdown and won a titanic triumph, 7 to 6.

"With a solid human embankment of 46,000 viewing every move of the crackling, reverberating battle, Iowa's 'heroic handful' stood off every savage thrust through 60 chill-choked minutes to do what teams from many a section couldn't do with something like twice that number."

Iowa went on to beat Minnesota 13–9 at home, scoring all its points in the fourth quarter, and tied Northwestern 7–7 to finish off a season for the ages. Iowa was ranked ninth in the final Associated Press poll.

That season, Kinnick played 402 of a possible 420 minutes, was involved in 107 of the 130 points scored, and set 14 school records, including his eight interceptions. That led to an awards windfall.

Kinnick was a consensus All-American, won the Chicago Tribune Silver Trophy that went to the Big Ten's most valuable player, and took home the Walter Camp and Maxwell trophies as well. He was later named the Associated Press Male Athlete of the Year, over the likes of Joe DiMaggio and Joe Louis. Team captain Erwin Prasse, an outstanding receiver, was also an All–Big Ten choice and an All-American. Enich was a first-team All–Big Ten player. And Anderson was Coach of the Year.

When the Ironmen were honored in 2009 on their 70th anniversary, Iowa coach Kirk Ferentz called it "a legendary story about a team led by a legendary player."

11 Ozzie and Floyd

Floyd of Rosedale, the bronze pig that annually goes to the winner of the Iowa-Minnesota football game, wouldn't exist if not for Ozzie Simmons and the color of his skin.

Simmons was a star running back for the Iowa Hawkeyes from 1934 to 1936. He was one of the few African American athletes playing college football at the time. He was also one of the best backs in the game.

Simmons was unorthodox but electric. He gripped the ball palm-down, often waving it as he ran. When President Ronald Reagan worked at WHO Radio in Des Moines, he saw Simmons play. In an interview with his former station, Reagan described him this way: "Ozzie would come up to a man, and instead of a stiff-arm or sidestep or something, Ozzie—holding the football in one hand—would stick the football out," Reagan said. "And the defensive man just instinctively would grab at the ball. Ozzie would pull it away from him and go around him."

Simmons, a two-time All–Big Ten running back, played a major factor in the birth of Floyd of Rosedale.

In an October 27, 1934, meeting with Minnesota in Iowa City, Simmons left the game in the second quarter. Some reports claimed he was knocked out three times. The Gophers, a national power at the time under Coach Bernie Bierman, left town with a 48–12 victory. But controversy followed them back to Minneapolis.

Some Iowa fans felt Minnesota had used a deliberately rough style against Simmons. The prevailing opinion was that the color of his skin had something to do with that. Bierman downplayed the allegations, claiming Simmons was treated like every other player on the field. "I really had the feeling they were after me because I was good," Simmons told the *Minneapolis Star Tribune* in 1988, 13 years before he passed away. "Oh, I think me being black added a little oomph to it."

The teams were scheduled to meet in Iowa City again on November 9, 1935, and bad feelings from the year before lingered. Bierman, who had received many letters from Iowa fans voicing their disapproval over what took place in 1934, requested special police protection when the team got off the train in Iowa City. The coach also threatened to end the series if there was an incident.

Rumors flew. One story said fans planned to storm the field if Simmons was treated unfairly. The day before the game, Iowa governor Clyde Herring put out a statement that read: "Those Minnesotans will find 10 other top-notch football players besides 'Oze' Simmons against them this year. Moreover, if the officials stand for any rough tactics like Minnesota used last year, I'm sure the crowd won't."

Minnesota attorney general Harry Peterson took exception to the governor's statement. "Your remark that the crowd at the Iowa-Minnesota game will not stand for any rough tactics is calculated to incite a riot," Peterson said. "It is a breach of your duty as governor, and evidences an unsportsmanlike, cowardly and contemptible frame of mind."

Minnesota governor Floyd B. Olson followed with a telegram to Herring the morning of the game: "Dear Clyde, Minnesota folks are excited over your statement about the Iowa crowd lynching the Minnesota football team. If you seriously think Iowa has any chance to win, I will bet you a Minnesota prize hog against an Iowa prize hog that Minnesota wins today."

Herring accepted. Minnesota won the game 13–6, without incident. Herring delivered a pig from Rosedale Farms, outside Fort Dodge, to the Minnesota governor. The prize pig, donated by Allen Loomis of Fort Dodge, was a half-brother of Dike, better known as Blue Boy from the 1933 Will Rogers movie *State Fair*.

The pig was named Floyd, in honor of Olson. He became known as Floyd of Rosedale. Olson gave away the hog to the winner of an essay contest. But Charles Brioschi, a sculptor from St. Paul, Minnesota, was commissioned to create a bronze likeness of Floyd. He came up with a trophy that weighs 98.3 pounds and is 21 inches long and 15.5 inches high. And it is a coveted prize when Iowa and Minnesota mix it up on the football field each year.

12 Trailblazer on the Mat

Simon Roberts was cut from the basketball team at Davenport High School when he was in ninth grade.

"I was told I was too short," Roberts said. "I was only 5'2" at the time."

Basketball's loss was wrestling's gain. A year later, Roberts had made the varsity lineup for Coach Jim Fox. And in 1954, his senior season at Davenport, Roberts made history. He won a state wrestling title, knocking off two-time champ Ron Gray of Eagle Grove in the 133-pound final. Davenport won the team title, and Roberts became the state's first African American champion.

"They put it on the front section of the newspaper," Roberts said. "I had a lot of people call and congratulate me. It was a big deal in the sense that I was the first. It was a real significant event in terms of my life and the things that opened up for me."

Roberts made recruiting visits to Iowa State and Iowa, and selected the Hawkeyes and Coach Dave McCuskey. "He gave me every chance to excel," Roberts said.

As a junior in 1957, Roberts qualified for his second NCAA appearance at the University of Pittsburgh. He also became the first African American to win an NCAA title when he beat Gray, then wrestling for Iowa State, in overtime.

"I wasn't supposed to win the title," Roberts said. "The guy I beat was undefeated. He was quite a wrestler at Iowa State and Eagle Grove. He was kind of a legend in wrestling in the state of Iowa."

Roberts didn't defend his NCAA crown as a senior in 1958, but he did establish another first. He became the first African American to win a Big Ten championship at 147 pounds.

Roberts won three wrestling letters at Iowa and graduated in 1959 with a degree in sociology, but he wasn't done breaking down barriers. He became the first African American to be elected to a citywide political office in Davenport, in the 1960s. He also became the first African American head varsity coach in the Quad Cities area when he was hired at Alleman High School in Rock Island, Illinois in 1966. He later became the first African American president of the University of Iowa's National Letterman's Club (now called the Varsity Club).

Roberts has been honored for his role as an outstanding athlete and trailblazer. That includes a spot in the Glen Brand Hall of Fame and the University of Iowa Athletics Hall of Fame. He was also presented a Distinguished Alumni Award by the University of Iowa in 2001.

"An ambassador of goodwill throughout his distinguished career, Roberts has shared his leadership skills and humanitarian compassion with his community and the University of Iowa," his alma mater said in a press release.

13 March Madness, Iowa-Style

Expectations? Not really. In fact, Iowa's basketball team was an afterthought heading into the 1980 NCAA Tournament.

The Hawkeyes were undefeated and ranked 13th in the nation until a knee injury to star point guard Ronnie Lester in late December took the wind out of their sails.

Iowa went into the final weekend of the Big Ten season having to win home games against Michigan and Illinois to have a shot at receiving an at-large NCAA berth. The Hawkeyes handled the Wolverines 83–67. Lester returned for the game against Illinois, a 75–71 victory. A day later, the Hawkeyes got their postseason reward.

"We were probably the last team in," said Kevin Boyle, a starting guard. "And then it was an incredible ride." The Hawkeyes, 19–8, got the fifth seed in the East Regional, drawing Virginia Commonwealth in the opening round in Greensboro, North Carolina. The Hawkeyes won 86–72, as all five starters scored in double figures. Kenny Arnold led the way with 23 points. Lester, Kevin Boyle, and Steve Waite added 17 each.

That earned the Hawkeyes a date with North Carolina State, the fourth seed in the region. "We'll be fired up for that one," said Waite, who also had 10 rebounds against Virginia Commonwealth. "The Big Ten against the Atlantic Coast Conference. Everyone wants to see that."

Again Iowa was not the favorite, and again Iowa advanced to the Sweet 16, with a 77–64 triumph. Arnold had 18 points, and Lester and Vince Brookins had 17 each. "We were not expected to make it out of North Carolina, playing North Carolina State there," said Bob Hansen, a freshman guard on that team. "I remember Vince getting hot and Kenny getting hot. And we advanced to the next weekend."

Iowa's next stop was the Spectrum in Philadelphia, Pennsylvania, for a game with top-seeded Syracuse. The Orange were a big favorite, but Lester's return had given the Hawkeyes a little bounce in their step.

"People rose up and did extraordinary things, and we just believed we could do it," center Steve Krafcisin said. "There was certainly no pressure on us."

Syracuse had Roosevelt Bouie and Louie Orr: the Louie and Bouie Show.

"No one gave us a shot," Krafcisin said. "And the East Coast writers were all making fun of us. We had this scripted *I* on the side of our road uniforms, right on the hip. And everybody thought it was a cornstalk or a corncob. But heck, we were all big-city kids. We said, 'We're going to show them. They have no clue about us.'" The Hawkeyes took out Syracuse 88–77. And again, five players scored in double figures. Brookins led the way with 21.

I'm not surprised that we're still left," Iowa coach Lute Olson said. "I think we can play with anybody. I'm not being cocky, not being overconfident, but just looking forward to the game on Sunday."

That was in the East Regional Final, against third-seeded Georgetown. And guess who played the role of underdog? "We've been underdogs for so long I'd be shocked to be anything else," Olson said. "We're the 'other' team here. Most people could name the other three but might have trouble recalling us."

Iowa trailed 42–32 at halftime, and the deficit grew to as many as 14 points in the second half. "Someone was at the line, and Bobby Hansen said to me, 'Dang it, K, let's go. We've got plenty of time left, let's win this thing,'" Krafcisin said.

And they rallied, shooting 70 percent from the field in the second half and making all 15 free-throw attempts for an 81–80 victory and Iowa's first trip to the Final Four since 1956. Steve Waite won the game with a conventional three-point play with five seconds remaining. There was no three-point basket at the time, so the Hoyas' final basket after a full-court pass was only window dressing.

A Heavy Dose of Adversity

Lester's knee injury at Dayton in the eighth game of the season wasn't the only challenge the 1979–80 team faced. The team's other starting guard, Kenny Arnold, broke the thumb on his shooting hand the week after Lester was hurt, but kept playing. Forward Mark Gannon injured his knee in a loss at Michigan January 5 and missed the rest of the Big Ten season. And then assistant coach Tony McAndrews was injured in a plane crash in the Quad Cities when he was returning from a recruiting trip.

"There were obstacles being thrown our way all the way through," Olson said. "And the old statement about what doesn't kill us makes us tougher was probably a statement that would have fit this team."

"We certainly didn't have the greatest talent compared to who we were playing against," Krafcisin said. "But we had that chemistry. We believed in each other."

The dream season ended with an 80–72 loss to Louisville in the semifinals in Indianapolis, Indiana. Darrell Griffith scored 34 points to lead the Cardinals. Two things happened that had the Hawkeyes playing uphill: First, Boyle came down with the flu the night before the game. He tried to play against the Cardinals but missed all eight shot attempts and failed to score. He averaged 11.8 points that season. "I was sicker than a dog," Boyle said. "No excuses. I remember the night before, [trainer] John Streif was throwing medicine down me. I was dehydrated. I couldn't play the way I had in the prior games. I'm not taking anything away from Louisville. They had great athletes. But it was frustrating. We were that close."

Then Lester reinjured his right knee in a collision with the Cardinals' Roger Burkman in the first half, and left the game for good.

"I remember sitting there after the game thinking, *Damn, we should have been playing in the national championship game,*" Hansen said.

Louisville won the NCAA title, beating UCLA. Iowa lost to Purdue in the consolation game, which was dropped starting in 1982.

"We had really high-caliber young men," Olson recalled during a 2015 conversation. "We had a great leader in Ronnie, even though he would say about three words a month…. It was a high-character group, a group that was really together. It was all about the team, it wasn't about individuals. That's what made them really, really special."

Lester handed the credit right back to Olson. "Under Coach Olson's leadership, we were a team," Lester said. "Basketball is a team game. If you look at the whole sum of the parts, we were a very good team."

When the team gathered for a 30-year reunion in the fall of 2009, their secret to success hadn't eroded from memory. "It's the teamwork, the camaraderie," said Vince Brookins, a starting forward. "And it's 30 years later. We were able to stick together as a team, and we pick that up whenever we meet."

14 Coaching Giant Gone Too Soon

Frank "Bucky" O'Connor was a well-known basketball figure in his native state of Iowa.

He had been a star basketball player at Newton High School and Drake University. He later found coaching success at Boone High School, where he was the boys' basketball and golf coach, and he also served as the athletic director for the town's junior college.

O'Connor came to the University of Iowa in 1948 as the varsity golf coach, a sport that was woven into his life early on. (His parents managed the Newton Country Club.) O'Connor also was the Hawkeyes' freshman basketball coach.

During the 1949–50 season, head basketball coach Pops Harrison fell ill. O'Connor coached the Hawkeyes for the final 11 games of the season. He returned to the freshman team in 1950–51, when former coach Rollie Williams stepped in to replace Harrison. But Williams announced his retirement a year later. O'Connor was named the head coach in 1951, kicking off one of the greatest stretches of success in program history.

O'Connor coached two Final Four and Big Ten championship teams at Iowa, including the 1956 national runner-up.

But tragedy struck on April 22, 1958. He was killed in an automobile accident just south of Waterloo. He was just 44 years old. "It was shocking," said Bill Seaberg, a starter on O'Connor's 1955–56 Fabulous Five team that lost to Bill Russell and San Francisco in the NCAA title game. "Unbelievable. I thought he was going to be there forever."

O'Connor had been driving to Waterloo for a golf date with some businessmen, then a speaking engagement that night with the Sports of Sorts Club. Alone and driving a state-owned car, eyewitnesses said O'Connor swerved to avoid two guinea hens in the road on US Highway 218, just three and a half miles south of Waterloo. O'Connor collided with a truck carrying a 32,000-pound load of pipe and concrete tile, which broke loose and crushed the coach in his car. O'Connor was killed instantly.

"The untimely death of Bucky O'Connor comes as a shock to all of us," said Iowa governor Herschel C. Loveless. "He long will be remembered by athletes, fans, and associates as an individual dedicated to the true competitive spirit of collegiate sports and a clean life."

Iowa athletic director Paul W. Brechler said news of O'Connor's passing "was almost incomprehensible. Bucky O'Connor was an irreplaceable man on the Iowa athletic staff. He had tremendously great influence on the athletes who played for him. His success as a coach gave Iowa high ranking in the Big Ten and [in] national basketball. I take the death of Coach O'Connor not only as a severe professional loss but as a great personal loss. He was one of my closest friends."

University of Iowa president Virgil M. Hancher said the school had lost "a teacher of character and integrity. He was a fine friend to all of us. Bucky leaves his influence upon many people. His example will live long with the young men whom he coached and has counseled far beyond the bounds of the game."

"An Inspiration to All of Us"

Dave Gunther, a junior on O'Connor's final team in 1957–58, found the news of his coach's death hard to believe. "He was an inspiration to all of us, and we're going to miss him more than I can say," Gunther said. "It won't seem the same, playing without him on the bench."

Sharm Scheuerman, who had played on O'Connor's 1954–55 and 1955–56 Big Ten championship teams and had remained in the program as the assistant coach, was named O'Connor's successor. He got the job a week after his 24th birthday.

Scheuerman, who passed away from prostate cancer in 2010, said in a 2009 interview that he was watching ESPN one day when age was the subject. "They said Bob Knight was the youngest Division I coach ever at 24 years old," Scheuerman said. "I wasn't going to argue with them, but I had to be younger. For sure, I was the youngest in the Big Ten."

Iowa struggled to a 10–12 record during Scheuerman's debut in 1958–59, but Gunther was a star. He averaged 21.9 points a game for a team that finished 7–7 in Big Ten play. Gunther had averaged 19.8 points as a junior and 12.3 points as a sophomore. He was a first-team All–Big Ten selection as a senior, moving up from the second-team honors he received as a junior.

Gunther, who was from Le Mars, Iowa, was a freshman in 1955–56. He scrimmaged against O'Connor's Fabulous Five team that was the national runner-up. "Playing against those guys was an eye-opener," Gunther said. "They played as one. It's a cliché, but they'd been together for so long they absolutely knew what each other was going to do every second of the game."

Gunther was named the Hawkeyes' most valuable player three straight seasons, and was selected to Iowa's All-Century team in 2002.

O'Connor had successfully recruited Don Nelson and Joel Novak, prep teammates in Rock Island, Illinois. They were to enroll at Iowa five months after O'Connor's death. "After [O'Connor] died, Sharm called and said he was not going to hold us to our agreement to come to Iowa," Novak said. "Both Nelson and I told him, 'No, we're still coming.'"

> Nelson started three years for Scheuerman, averaging better than 23 points as both a junior and senior and twice earning first-team All–Big Ten honors. Novak was a two-year starter. The two were cocaptains as seniors in 1961–62.
> "[Scheuerman] was truly like a second father to me," Novak said. "He was pretty young, but he took it seriously. He was a student of the game. I never heard him swear in four years. On trips, I don't remember seeing him take a drink. He was an all-American boy as far as I was concerned."

K.L. "Tug" Wilson, the Big Ten commissioner, said O'Connor's death was "a personal tragedy for all who ever knew the warmth of his personality and enjoyed his companionship." He continued, "The tragedy is only heightened by what he had to give to sports and what he had given so richly in a truly distinguished but relatively short coaching career. The conference and the University of Iowa have suffered a tremendous loss."

O'Connor's funeral was held two days later, on April 24, in Iowa City. Radio station KXIC in Iowa City broadcast the service. A crowd of 800 attended the funeral at First Methodist Church. Bill Reed, the assistant Big Ten commissioner, and several league coaches were in attendance.

"The tragedy of the death is not Bucky's," Reverend Roy Wingate said. "It is the tragedy of those of us still living whose loss this death is."

O'Connor had a 114–59 record at Iowa, including 71–41 in Big Ten games.

15 Coach with a Big Heart

If not for a discussion between Kirk Ferentz and one of his former bosses, Kevin White, Ferentz might not have been a candidate to replace Hayden Fry as Iowa's football coach in December 1998.

White had hired Ferentz, then Fry's offensive line coach at Iowa, to become the head coach at Maine in 1990. Nearly a decade later, Ferentz was the assistant head coach and offensive line coach for the NFL's Baltimore Ravens, and White was the athletic director at Arizona State.

"Kevin had been in town that fall, and he had asked me what my dream job was," Ferentz recalled. "I said I didn't really have one. And he asked me if I'd be interested in Iowa if Hayden ever retired. I said I hadn't really thought about it. I turned it on him. I said, 'What do you think? Do you think I'd like it?' Because I didn't really know. And he said, 'Yeah, I think you'd love it, and I think you'd be good at it.' Long story short, I think he said something to Bob [Bowlsby], and one thing led to another. I was kind of a late addition, I think, to the interviews."

Ferentz was the last candidate interviewed, and he wasn't leading the court of public opinion. Former Iowa defensive back Bob Stoops, then the defensive coordinator at Florida, was far ahead in the popularity poll.

But Bowlsby, Iowa's athletic director at the time, never had to select between the two. Stoops was offered the job at Oklahoma before Ferentz had interviewed at Iowa. Bowlsby felt he owed Ferentz that interview. Oklahoma moved quickly and signed Stoops.

Heading into the 2016 college football season, Ferentz and Stoops shared another distinction. They led the nation in coaching longevity at the same school.

Ferentz has had great success at a school that doesn't have some of the inherent advantages of other places—fertile home-state recruiting turf, for one, and warm weather for another. It's not easy to sustain a high level of success year in and year out. "You're going to have peaks and valleys. That's just kind of the nature of what we do," Ferentz said. "Especially if you do something long enough."

Ferentz has had five teams finish a season in the top 10 of the Associated Press poll through the 2015 season. He's won two Big Ten titles, and his team captured the league's Western Division crown in 2015. He's taken 13 teams to bowl games, including two Orange Bowls and a Rose Bowl. He's coached 14 first-team All-Americans and eight consensus All-Americans—Dallas Clark, Eric Steinbach, Nate Kaeding, Robert Gallery, Shonn Greene, Adrian Clayborn, Brandon Scherff, and Desmond King.

Clark, Gallery, Clayborn, and Scherff are joined by Chad Greenway, Bryan Bulaga, and Riley Reiff as first-round NFL draft choices.

"The importance that Coach Ferentz puts on the development of an athlete, I think that's the big thing," Kaeding said. "You come in, and he's a teacher first and foremost. And he expects that from his assistant coaches. It goes beyond learning plays and lifting weights. Coach Ferentz puts a lot of emphasis on development, teaching people about character, and doing things the Iowa way… working hard, being humble, being smart, being a student of the game."

The essence of Ferentz, Kaeding said, goes beyond winning and losing on the field of play. "He doesn't just care about you as a person because that's his job," Kaeding said. "He cares about you because he's got a big heart, and he's a good person."

During his nine seasons as a placekicker in the NFL, Kaeding talked to a lot of teammates about their college experiences and the relationships they had with their coach.

"Most of them certainly didn't have the sort of relationship with their college head coach that I was lucky enough to have," Kaeding said. "As Iowans and Hawkeyes, we're incredibly lucky to have someone like Coach Ferentz at the helm for such a long time."

16 Mapping Out Success

Athletic director Christine Grant knew she needed a home-run hire. The Iowa women's basketball program had gone 88–139 in its first nine seasons of existence. A 7–20 record in 1982–83 had been the seventh losing season.

Grant needed someone who would put the program on the map. She called coaching legends including Pat Summitt at Tennessee and Jody Conradt at Texas, looking for the right person. Funny how the same name kept coming up: C. Vivian Stringer.

So Grant reached out to Stringer, then the coach at Cheyney University of Pennsylvania in Philadelphia (which was known as Cheyney State until 1983). "I kept thinking Idaho, the potato state," Stringer said. It was a one-way conversation for a while. "She didn't know where Iowa was," Grant said. "She kept getting us mixed up with Ohio and Idaho. So I said, 'Okay, I'll come out there. We can meet.'"

Stringer, who had coached Cheyney State to the NCAA title game in 1982, agreed to visit the Iowa campus. There was a huge selling point up the street from Carver-Hawkeye Arena: University Hospitals.

Stringer's daughter, Janine, had been in a wheelchair since 14 months of age because of spinal meningitis. "They talked about

A Record-Smashing Day

When C. Vivian Stringer was introduced as Iowa's women's basketball coach in 1983, she dreamed big. She talked about filling Carver-Hawkeye Arena for a women's basketball game someday. That sounded like mission impossible at the time. Iowa had averaged fewer than 500 fans per game the season before she arrived. But it took Stringer just two seasons to pull off her goal.

On February 3, 1985, a crowd of 22,157 fans came to see the resurgent Hawkeyes take on No. 8 Ohio State.

"I wish I could turn out the lights and freeze that moment in time," Stringer said more than two decades later.

Stringer took a fast-break approach to rebuilding. Her first Iowa team went 17–10 in 1983–84, a far cry from the 7–20 program she inherited. The 1984–85 team finished 20–8. That included a 56–47 loss to the Buckeyes on that memorable February day.

The 22,157 fans who attended that game is not recognized as a Big Ten record, however, because the official paid attendance was 14,821. But the turnstile count showed 22,157 had come into the building. "They just kept coming and coming," said Dr. Christine Grant, Iowa's women's athletic director at the time. "People pleaded with us just to let them in for a minute or two to say they were there."

Once the 15,500 seats were filled, fans sat in the aisles or on folding chairs. Others stood and watched on the concourse. When the Iowa coach met Ohio State coach Tara VanDerveer at midcourt before the game, Stringer was crying. VanDerveer told her, "Oh my God. This is incredible."

Iowa didn't win the game, but it was a historical day nonetheless. "At the time, you didn't understand the significance of it," said Michelle Edwards, a freshman guard on the 1984–85 team. "It was an important day for women's basketball and for Coach Stringer's legacy."

Iowa's unofficial attendance record for a women's game at a campus arena stood until December 9, 1987, when Tennessee lost to visiting Texas at Thompson-Boling Arena before a crowd of 24,563.

Grant received a letter of reprimand from the university for breaking the fire code that day in 1985. It was a small price to pay for the statement it made.

"It was a very, very special day for our program and our state," Grant said. "So many said that people weren't interested in women's basketball, and this proved them absolutely wrong."

how they were going to take care of our daughter," Stringer said. "I was so relieved."

Stringer agreed to take the job, and rewarded her new employer with incredible success during her 12 seasons as coach. "She had an impact on our entire program," Grant said. "What she did was even greater than I had anticipated."

Stringer took a program that had experienced only 2 winning seasons and ran off 11 straight. Only an 11–17 record in 1994–95, her final season, was an exception. In a nine-year stretch starting in 1984–85, Iowa finished first or second in the Big Ten. That included cochampionships in 1986–87, 1988–89, 1989–90, and 1992–93 and outright crowns in 1987–88 and 1991–92.

Iowa went to nine NCAA Tournaments under Stringer's watch, reaching the Final Four in 1992–93. Stringer was a two-time National Coach of the Year, reeling off 10 consecutive 20-win seasons.

Stringer's coaching abilities were matched by her recruiting skills. She brought players such as consensus All-Americans Michelle Edwards, Franthea Price, and Toni Foster into the program.

Stringer was 269–84 at Iowa, and won 79 percent of her Big Ten games (169–45). She was inducted into the Naismith Memorial Basketball Hall of Fame in 2009 and the University of Iowa Athletics Hall of Fame in 2006.

"I really enjoyed it [at Iowa]," said Stringer, who left to take the head coaching job at Rutgers in 1995. "We had some very special moments."

17 The 30–5 Hawkeyes

Tom Davis left Stanford to become the Iowa basketball coach in the spring of 1986. He inherited a team from George Raveling that had gone 20–12 and lost to North Carolina State in the first round of the NCAA Tournament the year before. Seven of the top eight scorers were returning. "It was a team that people thought was going to be pretty good," Davis said. "But nobody thought it would be this good."

The Hawkeyes won their first 18 games under Davis and were ranked No. 1 in the country for a week. They got within a game of the Final Four as well, losing a 16-point halftime lead and bowing out 84–81 to No. 1 Nevada–Las Vegas. Iowa finished 30–5, a school record for victories in a season.

But some things happened before the season ever started that made the record-setting run possible. For one, Roy Marble, the leading returning scorer, contemplated transferring after the coaching change. But he had a change of heart after learning Davis coached a fast-breaking, pressing style that matched the way he liked to play.

And point guard B.J. Armstrong was looking for a new address as well. "His dad, Ben, called me and said, 'B.J. is going to transfer,'" Davis said. "I said, 'Where to?' I figured it would be some other Big Ten team or something. He said, 'He's going to transfer to Central Michigan.'"

There was still more than a month of classes remaining in the spring semester. Davis also had the luxury of 10 days of practice to prepare for a summer trip to China and South Korea.

Davis said, "I told [Ben], 'At the end of the trip I'll just tell you flat out whether he can play in the Big Ten or not. And if he can't,

I guarantee you I'll get him a scholarship at a place every bit as good as Central Michigan, if not better.' You know the rest of the story."

Armstrong, who had averaged 2.9 points per game as a freshman, had a skill set that was perfect for the Davis system. "He just fit in terms of ballhandling, and you could see he was improving rapidly," Davis said. "And I never heard from Ben again about transferring."

Armstrong's decision to stick around was magnified when Michael Reaves, the player many projected to be the starting point guard, injured a knee. "B.J. was the glue, from a ballhandling point of view," Davis said. "Especially when Reaves went down. Some of that is dumb luck. You can't give the coach all the credit."

In retrospect, Davis pointed to two players who made a big—and unexpected—contribution to the success in 1986–87. "You never would have dreamed what kind of a year we'd get from Brad Lohaus or Kevin Gamble," Davis said. Lohaus went from 3.6 points and 3.2 rebounds as a junior to 11.3 points and 7.7 rebounds as a senior. Gamble went from 2.6 points and 1.7 rebounds as a junior to 11.9 points and 4.5 rebounds as a senior.

It turned out to be a deep and talented team. "George Raveling had done a terrific job of recruiting those kids, because they were good kids, and coachable," Davis said. "Billy Jones, Kent Hill, Michael Morgan, Jeff Moe, guys like that came off the bench. Al Lorenzen. Les Jepsen was a freshman on that team. Hill was like the 11th man on that team, and he could hardly wait to get in there."

Roy Marble led that team in scoring at 14.9 points a game. "Roy was such a good team player that he made the whole thing happen," Davis said. "He was an important part of the team. But it wasn't just him." Armstrong also took a spike offensively, increasing his average to 12.4 points a game. Moe averaged 11.1 points off the bench. Ed Horton and Gerry Wright were solid scorers and rebounders inside. All the pieces fit.

Iowa's 18–0 run finished with victories at No. 8 Illinois, at No. 6 Purdue, and at home against No. 3 Indiana. Ohio State upset the Hawkeyes 80–76 at home to end the streak.

Iowa lost three more league games to finish third in the Big Ten at 14–4. The Hawkeyes were the No. 2 seed in the NCAA West Regional, and dispatched of Santa Clara, Texas–El Paso, and Oklahoma to reach the doorstep of the Final Four. But UNLV ended that dream season.

"Kevin got in foul trouble, and B.J. got in foul trouble, and we just didn't have many backup guards," Davis said. "UNLV changed its defense at halftime. They came out, got in our face, and bodied us up all over the court. And we just couldn't get it done."

The Runnin' Rebels reversed a 58–42 halftime deficit with a 24–2 second-half run. "It wasn't any fluke," Davis said. "They had good athletes at every position."

18 Emotion in Motion

Every year, when the calendar reaches January 19, Iowans stop and remember. "Nobody is instigating it," said former Iowa basketball coach Tom Davis. "It's just that somebody remembers 'This is the day and the time.' It really is a great tribute to him."

Chris Street was a gregarious, hardworking, fun-loving junior forward on Iowa's basketball team. His magnetic personality and smile drew fans young and old to him.

He was killed in an automobile accident on the outskirts of Iowa City on January 19, 1993, in the middle of his junior season. That's why January 19 evokes such an emotional pull for Hawkeyes fans who knew, watched, or heard of him.

Fran McCaffery became Iowa's basketball coach in 2010, nearly two decades removed from the tragedy. But it didn't take him long to understand the legacy Street left behind. "Everyone remembers where they were when President Kennedy died," McCaffery said. "Ask anyone in Iowa where they were when Chris Street died, and they'll tell you. It's pretty amazing."

Street played with a motor that never stopped running. He was emotion in motion, Midwestern work ethic wrapped inside a 6'8" frame.

"It's still hard for me to talk about," said Davis, who recruited Street and was his coach at Iowa, "because it just overwhelms me." Street loved to compete. He played hard. He was a coach's dream.

"He was everything that's good about sports, everything that's good about college basketball, you know?" Michigan State coach Tom Izzo said two decades after Street had passed away. "He worked his tail off. He was not an elite player. Just a man-made great player."

Street was a multisport All-State athlete at Indianola High School, but he grew up in Humeston. That's where he'd join his family to watch Iowa basketball games on a statewide television network. In other words, he was raised on Hawkeyes hoops. And he fell in love. Street committed to the Hawkeyes the summer before his junior season at Indianola.

"Of all the things he was, he was a Hawkeye basketball player," said Street's father, Mike. "That's what he wanted to be, and he was. He was living his dream."

Tragedy ended a bright future for Chris Street. His No. 40 is retired, but his memory carries on. He is memorialized on a plaque just outside the Iowa basketball locker room at Carver-Hawkeye Arena. The Chris Street Award is presented each year to "a Hawkeye player who best exemplifies the spirit, enthusiasm, and intensity of Chris Street."

A tree and a memorial to him stand just across the street from the arena. And a scholarship in his name is presented annually to a player on the team. There is a Chris Street golf outing each year to raise money for the basketball program. It is an event that Davis, who left Iowa in 1999 and retired from coaching in 2007, never misses. He is amazed guys who played before Street arrived, and others who played after he passed, come and support the event. "It's because they knew of Chris Street," Davis said. "Especially the Iowa kids."

Time and memory may slip away, but January 19 remains a day that no one in the Hawkeye State forgets.

19 Elliott's Unforgettable Legacy

They are a formidable Mount Rushmore of Iowa Hawkeyes sports figures: Football coach Hayden Fry. Wrestling coach Dan Gable. Basketball coaches Lute Olson and Tom Davis.

All four were hired by the same athletic director. His name was Chalmers W. "Bump" Elliott.

Elliott ruled with respect, not ego, during his 21 years as Iowa's top athletic official. From 1970 to 1991, Hawkeyes teams won 29 Big Ten titles in six sports, 12 NCAA wrestling titles, three Rose Bowl appearances, a Final Four in basketball, and a College World Series berth.

Elliott carries the distinction of going to the Rose Bowl in five different capacities: as a player at Michigan, an assistant coach at Iowa, the head coach at Michigan, an assistant athletic director at Michigan, and the athletic director at Iowa. "Boy, that tells the whole story of how great a guy he really was, both as a coach and athletic director," Davis said.

Elliott's experience at all those levels is why he was such a fine administrator as the No. 1 man at Iowa. "He had respect, because he had been in that arena," said Davis, Iowa's winningest men's basketball coach. "If he sat down with Dan Gable or Hayden Fry or myself or any of the other coaches and he told you something, you knew he knew what he was talking about. And he was good. He didn't overmanage. There was just a line you knew you couldn't, and shouldn't, cross."

In his autobiography, *Hayden Fry: A High Porch Picnic*, Fry wrote that it was Elliott who had made the job so appealing. "Iowa had one thing in its favor as far as I was concerned: Bump Elliott was the athletic director," Fry wrote. "Bump had a reputation as being a fair, honest, and well-liked administrator."

Gable, who was hired as Iowa's wrestling coach in 1976, remembers a meeting he had with Elliott right after Gable was hired. "I'll never forget what Bump said to me: 'Don't ask for the moon. Strive to get there, sure, but do it wisely through continuing

"Here's to What Cheer!"

Elliott was socializing with Michigan basketball Coach Johnny Orr and Michigan State football Coach Duffy Daugherty one night in the summer of 1970. During the course of the evening, Elliott was called to the phone.

When he rejoined his friends, Orr and Daugherty asked what was going on. Elliott was noncommittal at first, then could hold the secret no longer. He had just accepted the job as Iowa's athletic director, replacing Forest Evashevski.

As Orr told the story, the three men started toasting every Iowa town they could think of.

"Here's to What Cheer!" Orr said later, when telling the story, hoisting an imaginary glass into the air in a toasting motion.

to build upon what you already have,'" said Gable, who won 15 NCAA titles at Iowa. "[He said,] 'As you build, come see me, and we'll see how I can help you out.' I now call that bit of wisdom the Bump Elliott Rule, and it serves as a good reminder to keep things in perspective. Gradual, solid growth is better than any quick fix."

When Elliott came to Iowa in 1970, the athletic program was in turmoil in the wake of a bitter feud between former football coach–turned–athletic director Forest Evashevski and football coach Ray Nagel. "I wanted to make sure we all worked together and were loyal to each other, the department, and the university," Elliott said.

Twenty-one years later, the fences had been mended and Elliott left behind a department in much better shape than the one he inherited. He left behind a legacy that matched his personality— understated and unforgettable.

20 Windy City Magician

When Lute Olson transformed a sleeping Iowa basketball program into a consistent winner, Ronnie Lester was the key piece of the puzzle.

Olson recruited Lester, a gifted 6'2" point guard, out of Dunbar Vocational High School in Chicago, Illinois. "I'll never forget the day I went to watch him play [in high school]," Olson said. "Along comes an assistant from Kentucky. He asks what I thought about this Lester guy. I said I really liked him and if he could just shoot the ball a little bit better I'd be even more excited about him. Thank goodness Ronnie missed a few shots in the first half, and he [the Kentucky assistant] left at halftime."

Lester was a freshman in 1976–77, Olson's third season at Iowa, and made an instant impact by averaging 13.4 points a game.

"What made Ronnie so good was his tremendous self-pride and determination," Olson said. "He just demanded perfection from himself."

Lester averaged in double figures all four seasons at Iowa, averaging 16.9 points over his 99-game career. The Hawkeyes earned a share of the Big Ten championship in 1978–79 and reached the Final Four in 1980 with Lester at the controls. His No. 12 was retired during his senior season, when a knee injury early in the campaign limited his productivity.

When healthy, Lester was jet-quick with the ball and could take it to the rim, or rise up and hit a jump shot. "He was so good," said Steve Krafcisin, one of Lester's teammates at Iowa.

Krafcisin remembered playing an exhibition game against the Soviet National team and 7'3" center Vladimir Tkachenko. "I remember Ronnie in a full-court sprint with the ball, dribbling to the free-throw line," Krafcisin said. "Ronnie pulled up and hit a jumper over Tkachenko. Not many guys could make that shot. He could make that shot."

Lester was quiet by nature and let his game do the talking. Krafcisin started his career at North Carolina, where he played with All-American point guard Phil Ford. "Phil was pretty cocky, but not in a bad way," Krafcisin said. "He was very emotional, very vocal. I thought Ronnie was going to be like that, because Phil was one of the best ever. But you never heard Ronnie. He was an incredible talent."

Another teammate, Kevin Boyle, remembered Lester as a complete player. "He had a great first step, and he could stop on a dime," Boyle said. "Lute always used him on a high-post screen, where he would go off that screen and negotiate, either pull up or take it all the way to the hole."

An Underappreciated Star

Olson inherited Bruce "Sky" King from the previous coaching staff when he took over the program heading into the 1974–75 season. King, a 6'8" center from Dayton, Ohio, started for Olson's first three Hawkeyes teams. And he logged some impressive numbers. He scored 1,361 points in those three seasons as a starter, a 17-point career average. More impressive was his 10.7 career rebounding average. He was, for all intents and purposes, a daily double-double machine.

King still ranks in Iowa's top 10 in rebounds (852) and single-season rebounding average (13.3 as a senior in 1976–77). He was a third-team All–Big Ten selection as a junior and moved up to the second team as a senior when he averaged 21 points to go with those 13.3 rebounds.

King scored in double figures in 24 of the 25 games he played as a senior. The lone exception was a nine-point outing against Drake in the third game of the season.

King was especially productive against his native-state Ohio State Buckeyes as a senior. He had 31 points and 21 rebounds in an 84–66 victory in Iowa City. He also scored 13 points and added 21 rebounds in the rematch in Columbus, a 74–70 Hawkeyes victory in overtime.

He was also the captain of that 1976–77 team, the first of Olson's six 20-win seasons at Iowa. King was 30 years old when he died of heart-related issues in 1986.

Bobby Hansen was a freshman in 1979–80 and went on to play nine seasons in the NBA. He played against many great players. And Lester, he'll tell you, was special. "You knew you had a guy who could get a shot whenever you needed him to," Hansen said. "A guy who was almost unguardable with the basketball, and so quick. He had the ability to change directions, almost like Barry Sanders did on the football field. When I was a junior and senior in high school, watching Ronnie, it was like, 'Man, there's a player right there.' When he hurt his knee, it took a lot away from his game."

Lester was injured late in the second half of a game at Dayton on December 23, 1979. "Ronnie Lester, who was without question the best point guard in America that year, stole a pass and got free on a breakaway," Olson said. "One of the Dayton kids chased him, and as Ronnie went up to lay it in, the kid grabbed his left arm and yanked it. Ronnie went flying and landed on his knee. It was diagnosed as a severe sprain, but it was terribly damaging. Ronnie's game was quickness, and the injury just took it away."

Lester sat out the next six games, was back in the lineup for three Big Ten matchups in mid-January, then missed nine more games. He returned for the final game of the regular season, a 75–71 victory over Illinois. His number was retired before the opening tip.

The Hawkeyes rode that final regular-season victory into the NCAA Tournament, reaching the Final Four. But Lester's season ended when he reinjured his knee in the first half of an 80–72 loss to Louisville in the semifinals.

Lester was a two-time All–Big Ten selection, a three-time most valuable player at Iowa, and an All-American pick despite his injury-shortened senior season. Lester was selected in the first round of the 1980 NBA Draft and played six seasons with the Chicago Bulls and Los Angeles Lakers. He was a member of the Lakers' 1985 championship team.

21 The Improbable Catch

"I can't believe what I just saw," Gary Dolphin, the voice of the Iowa Hawkeyes, told his listening audience on New Year's Day 2005. A decade later, things haven't changed. Does he believe it now? "Not really," Dolphin said.

Jaws dropped when Drew Tate, seen here hoisting the Capital One Bowl's MVP trophy, threw a last-second touchdown pass to teammate Warren Holloway to steal victory from the jaws of defeat.

There were 70,229 eyewitnesses that day at the Florida Citrus Bowl Stadium in Orlando, not to mention those watching on television or listening to Dolphin's call on the radio.

It was an unlikely finish, but one that warms the hearts of Hawkeyes fans every time the 30–25 victory over LSU in the Capital One Bowl is brought up. Quarterback Drew Tate's 56-yard touchdown pass to Warren Holloway on the final play of the game produced the win.

The play was called All Up, X Post. The execution was out of desperation, because time was about to get away from the Hawkeyes.

The Tigers had taken a 25–24 lead on a touchdown with 46 seconds remaining. Iowa's Warner Belleus returned the ensuing kickoff to the Iowa 29. "We were playing for a field goal," Iowa coach Kirk Ferentz said.

Tate, who would be named the game's most valuable player, completed passes to Ed Hinkel and Holloway to get the ball to the Iowa 49. Tate then spiked the ball to stop the clock, but Iowa was penalized for starting the play before the referee had put the ball in play. The refs walked off the five-yard penalty, and then the clock started, something Ferentz and his coaches didn't realize. "I didn't know the rule," said Ferentz, who had two timeouts remaining. "That was my fault."

But Dolphin knew, and desperation was in his voice. "They've got to call timeout… They wind the clock… Nine seconds to play, and Drew Tate doesn't know that… The game is going to end on this play… He fires downfield."

Tate first looked left toward Clinton Solomon, then to his right, where Holloway was streaking downfield. Holloway thought the pass was intended for teammate Ed Hinkel, who was to his right, but he kept running and pulled in Tate's delivery. "I thought I overthrew him at first," Tate said.

But the pass was perfect. Holloway hauled it in 15 yards from the end zone, and Hinkel got enough of cornerback Travis Daniels to keep him from making the tackle while Holloway reached the end zone.

It was the first career touchdown catch for Holloway, a senior. And it came on the last play of his career. "It was all so improbable," Holloway said. "How many players get the first touchdown catch of their college careers on the last snap of their college careers? That just doesn't happen. But it did."

A Dozen Weeks of Perfection

When he gathered his football team in the locker room inside Memorial Stadium in Lincoln, Nebraska, Iowa coach Kirk Ferentz struggled for the right words. "I don't know what to say," he admitted. "I've never been 12–0 before."

A 28–20 win against Nebraska on November 27, 2015, gave the Hawkeyes a school-record 12th victory. It also completed the first undefeated regular season since the 1922 team went 7–0. The fact that it came on the heels of an underachieving 7–6 season the year before made it even sweeter. "It is an unbelievable accomplishment," Ferentz said.

After winning no regular-season trophy games in 2014, Iowa made it a clean sweep in 2015—taking possession of the Cy-Hawk (Iowa State), Heartland (Wisconsin), Floyd of Rosedale (Minnesota), and Heroes Game (Nebraska) trophies. Three of those four victories came on the road.

In 720 minutes of regular-season football, the Hawkeyes trailed for just 55 minutes 15 seconds, and never by more than a touchdown. Iowa didn't trail in the fourth quarter of any regular-season game.

And after being unranked from November 28, 2010, to September 27, 2015, Iowa spent the final 11 weeks in the top 25. Iowa got as high as third and finished ninth after a 16–13 loss to Michigan State in the Big Ten Championship Game and a 45–16 loss to Stanford in the Rose Bowl.

The Hawkeyes' regular-season march to perfection included road victories over No. 18 Wisconsin and No. 20 Northwestern. Only eventual national champion Alabama had more, with three. Iowa and Clemson were the only teams in the nation to make it through the regular season undefeated.

"You can't do any better than that," Ferentz said.

Here's how it happened:

Iowa 31, Illinois State 14 (Iowa City)—Iowa took a 17–0 halftime lead, including a 99-yard drive for its second touchdown of the season.

"There were a lot of good teaching moments out there, but I was really pleased with the win," Ferentz said.

Iowa 31, Iowa State 17 (Ames)—The Hawkeyes broke free from a 17–17 tie with two touchdowns in the final 2:14. Quarterback C.J. Beathard found Riley McCarron on a 25-yard touchdown connection, then Jordan Canzeri sealed the deal with an eight-yard run.

"Hopefully we can push forward," Ferentz said. "That's our mind-set now."

Iowa 27, Pittsburgh 24 (Iowa City)—The Panthers tied the game with 52 seconds remaining, but Iowa placekicker Marshall Koehn nailed a Kinnick Stadium–tying-record 57-yard field goal on the final play.

"I've had my ups and downs," Koehn said. "I'm glad I could help us out."

Iowa 62, North Texas 16 (Iowa City)—Beathard completed his first 15 passes and the Hawkeyes had it on cruise control in a hurry.

"Another very positive step for our football team," Ferentz said.

Iowa 10, Wisconsin 6 (Madison, Wisconsin)—The Hawkeyes took a 10–3 halftime lead, didn't score in the final two quarters, and won ugly.

"I think any win is a beautiful thing," center Austin Blythe said.

Iowa 29, Illinois 20 (Iowa City)—With his team rated for the first time since 2010, Canzeri gained 256 yards on a school-record 43 carries and scored twice.

"I had no idea he had 43 carries," Ferentz said. "But he never even looked at the bench."

Iowa 40, Northwestern 10 (Evanston, Illinois)—Akrum Wadley rushed for 204 yards behind a makeshift line, and Iowa's defense dominated the line of scrimmage.

"How good we are, I have no idea right now," Ferentz said. "But I do know this: this team plays extremely hard, and they've got a lot of guts."

Iowa 31, Maryland 15 (Iowa City)—The Hawkeyes took a 21–0 halftime lead, and added to it when Desmond King had a fourth-quarter 88-yard interception return for a touchdown.

"Our goal the first week of the season was to win a game," Ferentz said. "Ever since then, it's been to win the next game. We're trying to keep it as simple as that."

Iowa 35, Indiana 27 (Bloomington, Indiana)—Iowa trailed 17–14 late in the second quarter. But Beathard, playing with hip and groin injuries, went airborne on a seven-yard touchdown run 17 seconds before halftime.

"A Kodak moment," Ferentz said.

Iowa would not trail in the regular season again.

Iowa 40, Minnesota 35 (Iowa City)—The Hawkeyes scored on six of their first seven possessions and started 10–0 for the first time in school history.

"The only pressure any of us feel is to not let each other down," Ferentz said.

Iowa 40, Purdue 20 (Iowa City)—The Hawkeyes completed their first undefeated home season since 2004, as Beathard threw three touchdown passes. The victory clinched the Big Ten West Division title.

"It's a moment I'll carry for the rest of my life," Blythe said.

Iowa 28, Nebraska 20 (Lincoln, Nebraska)—The Hawkeyes defense picked off four passes, and Canzeri scored on touchdown runs of 29 and 68 yards to complete an undefeated regular season.

"To look at our players, and what they've accomplished, that's a pretty good feeling," Ferentz said.

23 Beating No. 1

Iowa's 1963–64 basketball team had an 8–15 record, including seven losses in the last eight games. It was Sharm Scheuerman's final season as head coach. UCLA, on the other hand, was coming off a 30–0 national championship season under John Wooden.

Unlikely as it sounds, that set the table for Iowa's first-ever victory over a No. 1 team the following season. It was January 29, 1965, to be exact. With first-year coach Ralph Miller calling the shots, the Hawkeyes upset No. 1 UCLA 87–82 at Chicago Stadium.

It happened again, 34 years later. And the blueprint was strikingly similar. Iowa had a first-year coach in Steve Alford. Connecticut was the defending national champion. But in Alford's first game as Hawkeyes coach on November 11, 1999, at Madison Square Garden in New York City, Iowa knocked off the Huskies 70–68.

Iowa's third victory over No. 1 came in the Big Ten opener, on December 29, 2015, an 83–70 decision for coach Fran McCaffery's team over Michigan State. It was also the Hawkeyes' first triumph over a No. 1 team at home.

Those victories came against three of the game's most successful coaches—Wooden, Jim Calhoun of Connecticut, and Tom Izzo of Michigan State.

Iowa's 1964–65 team had won nine games, one more than the previous season, when it crossed paths with a mighty UCLA team that had won 43 of their previous 44 games.

A 19–9 run to start the second half gave Iowa the lead for good, but it was a precarious advantage for much of the final 20 minutes. A three-point play by Chris Pervall, a junior-college transfer who scored 28 points, got Iowa over the top.

Five Iowa players scored in double figures. Jimmy Rodgers added 16, and his adept ballhandling helped the Hawkeyes negotiate Wooden's trademark press.

The Bruins did not lose again, finishing the season 28–2 and winning their second straight NCAA crown. UCLA would go on to win 11 NCAA titles under Wooden.

It was the Hawkeyes' second straight upset of a highly ranked opponent. In its previous game, Iowa won 74–68 at No. 5

Indiana. Miller's teams had traditionally started seasons slow and reached a peak late in the schedule. His 1964–65 team broke that stereotype.

"These kids beat Father Time," Miller said. "They beat him flat. The first time it's happened in my coaching career. Even my good clubs at Wichita State came along slowly."

But the magic season ran out of gas. The Hawkeyes lost four of their last five games to finish 14–10 overall and 8–6 in the Big Ten, good for fifth place.

The 1999 victory over Connecticut at Madison Square Garden was as equally unexpected as the UCLA triumph.

"What a way for Steve to start his program," Dick Vitale gushed. "It's incredible. When you look at what he did against Connecticut, it's unbelievable. Amazing. Phenomenal."

Crossing Paths with Wooden

Iowa's victory over No. 1 UCLA in 1965 isn't the only time the Hawkeyes got the best of Coach John Wooden, who played his college ball at Purdue.

The Hawkeyes knocked off Wooden's Boilermakers team, the defending Big Ten champs, and limited him to a single point in a 25–23 victory on January 12, 1931, in Iowa City. Purdue got a measure of revenge when the teams met on March 7 in West Lafayette. Wooden scored 11 points in a 39–19 romp.

Iowa's basketball program was involved in another footnote involving Wooden's UCLA dynasty. The Bruins stretched their winning streak to 88 games with a 66–44 victory over the visiting Hawkeyes on January 17, 1974, even though star center Bill Walton missed the game with a foot injury. His backup, Ralph Drollinger, finished with 13 points and 17 rebounds.

That was the Bruins' last victory in the streak. UCLA lost 71–70 at Notre Dame two days later. For the record, Iowa was also victim No. 17 in that 88-game run, losing a 106–72 decision at UCLA on December 4, 1971.

And just like in 1965, a junior-college transfer led the Hawkeyes in scoring. This time it was Jacob Jaacks, who had 20 points against the Huskies. "We were a bunch of nobodies, and they had everybody on their team," Jaacks said. "But this team has a lot of heart and soul."

"Iowa is certainly a better team than we are because they have five guys who play together well as a unit both offensively and defensively," Calhoun said. "We did not do that."

Iowa had a 36–21 halftime lead but had to hold on after point guard Dean Oliver got in foul trouble. After getting called for one foul in the first half, Oliver picked up three more in a three-and-a-half-minute stretch of the second half and went to the bench with Iowa in front 42–29. When he returned, with just less than seven minutes to go, the advantage had become a 55–53 deficit.

But Ryan Luehrsmann's two free throws with three seconds remaining gave Iowa a five-point lead and turned the key on the upset.

"Despite losing their best player for an extended period of time in the second half, they completely outplayed us," Calhoun said. "And hopefully Iowa gave this team a lesson in how to play basketball together."

The Hawkeyes finished the season 14–16 overall and 6–10 in the Big Ten. That night in Madison Square Garden was their one shining moment.

Iowa had lost 14 of 15 games to Michigan State, including nine in a row, entering the 2015 game. But the Hawkeyes trailed for just 44 seconds in picking up a third triumph over No. 1 behind point guard Mike Gesell's 25 points. Iowa took a 37–23 halftime lead, then shot 63.6 percent from the field in the second half to complete the upset. "We sustained effort and paid attention to detail with regard to the game plan," McCaffery said.

Students stormed the court afterward. And McCaffery tried to put the accomplishment in perspective. "It's the first game of the Big Ten season," he said. "Celebrate and get back to work tomorrow. It's one win." One win, yes. But a historical one.

24 Points and Victories Aplenty

Purdue was favored to win the 1969–70 Big Ten basketball title.

"Illinois and Ohio State could offer strong challenges in what should be a wide open race," noted a league preview from the Associated Press. Further down in the article was this:

"Iowa, Michigan, and Northwestern could knock on the title door."

The Hawkeyes knocked down that door by going 14–0 and unleashing an offense that remains unmatched in Big Ten history.

Iowa's 102.9-point scoring average in league games is still a Big Ten record. And only two teams—Indiana in 1974–75 and 1975–76—have gone undefeated since.

Four of Iowa's starters—John Johnson, Fred Brown, Chad Calabria, and Glenn Vidnovic—combined to score in double figures 55 of 56 times against Big Ten opponents. The Hawkeyes had four different players score at least 20 points in four Big Ten games. Johnson averaged 31.8 points, followed by Brown's 20.7; Vidnovic and Calabria both averaged 18.4.

Iowa reached the 100-point mark in 9 of 14 Big Ten games— 14 *victories*.

"That's pretty hard to do," Vidnovic said. "You figured you were going to lay an egg here or there."

Here's a closer look at the Hawkeyes' road to perfection:

January 3 (Iowa City)
Iowa 94, Purdue 88

After scoring 45 points against Iowa in two games the previous season, Rick Mount bettered that with a 53-point explosion in Iowa Field House. But John Johnson and Fred Brown combined for 54, and the Hawkeyes shot 57 percent from the field to give Coach Ralph Miller his 300th career victory.

Mount's 53 points did set an Iowa Field House record. Purdue played without Larry Weatherford and Bill Franklin, two starters and double-figure scorers, who had been suspended for a curfew violation.

January 6 (Ann Arbor, Michigan)
Iowa 107, Michigan 99

The Hawkeyes won their first Big Ten road game in two seasons by shooting a school-record 63.4 percent from the field.

Michigan All-American Rudy Tomjanovich scored 37 points. But Iowa came at the Wolverines from all directions. Johnson scored 34, Calabria 24, Brown 23, and Vidnovic 18.

January 10 (Madison, Wisconsin)
Iowa 92, Wisconsin 74

Brown got the opening tip and headed for the basket...the *Wisconsin* basket. His teammates corrected him before he took the shot. That was about Iowa's only miscue in the opening half.

Iowa sprinted to a 29-point halftime lead, then held off the Badgers' spirited comeback. Wisconsin closed to within 77–69 with just less than five minutes to play, but Iowa had an answer.

Johnson had 31 points and Brown and Calabria had 22 apiece. But it was center Dick Jensen—who had eight points, 10 rebounds, and played the solid defense this team depended on—that drew praise from Miller.

"Of course, I'm not complaining about Johnson or Brown or any of the rest of them," Miller said.

January 31 (Iowa City)
Iowa 100, Indiana 93

After a three-week break from Big Ten competition, with a 96–68 nonconference victory over Tennessee Tech mixed in, Iowa came out sluggish and trailed 45–44 at halftime.

But Vidnovic rallied the troops with a career-high 31 points, eight more than his previous high, and Iowa shot better than 50 percent from the floor for the sixth straight game. Johnson was limited to two field goals in the opening half but finished with 22 points. Calabria and Brown both scored 20.

February 3 (Iowa City)
Iowa 90, Minnesota 77

This victory, and Wisconsin's upset of Illinois in Champaign, put Iowa alone in first place at 5–0. The Hawkeyes did not relinquish that spot the rest of the season.

Iowa shot 56.9 percent from the field and gave the Gophers their first Big Ten defeat.

Johnson finished with 33 points. Calabria added 19, Vidnovic 18, and Brown 17. Minnesota hung around, trailing by a 75–70 margin, then Iowa put the game away with a 14–1 run.

February 7 (Bloomington, Indiana)
Iowa 104, Indiana 89

Hoosiers students greeted Iowa by throwing paper cups and coins at them. Bad idea.

"Those fans don't understand, but all they did was fire us up more," Calabria said. "Whenever people throw things and boo, we play harder."

Iowa followed a familiar script, shooting 61 percent from the field—70.5 percent the second half—and getting 33 points from Johnson on 14 of 19 shooting.

"It's always nice to come away from any road game alive," Miller said.

February 10 (Iowa City)
Iowa 119, Wisconsin 100
After watching his team set a school single-game scoring record, Miller was concerned about the defense giving up triple digits.

"Everybody is going to be up for us," Miller said.

But Iowa had plenty of offense to counter the Badgers' pile of points. Johnson and Calabria scored 29 points apiece, Vidnovic added 24, and sixth man Ben McGilmer had 20. The 7–0 start was Iowa's best in Big Ten play since 1944.

Miller took his starters out of the game, one by one, and each received a standing ovation from the Iowa Field House crowd.

February 14 (Iowa City)
Iowa 103, Michigan State 77
Behind 36 points from Johnson and 25 from Brown, Iowa clubbed Michigan State with a 63-point second half and cruised to victory.

The Hawkeyes did have to rally to reach the century mark, scoring five points in the last 12 seconds of the game and upsetting Michigan State coach Gus Ganakas.

Brown made two free throws with 12 seconds remaining, and Iowa slapped a full-court press on the Spartans. Brown made a steal and was fouled. Ganakas, upset at Iowa's tactics because the game was out of hand, called a timeout. But he didn't have any left, and was given a technical foul. Brown made the second free throw, and Vidnovic also made the free throw awarded for the technical.

February 17 (Champaign, Illinois)
Iowa 83, Illinois 81

The Hawkeyes shot less than 50 percent from the field for the first time in 11 games against a good Illini zone defense, but that was good enough to keep their unblemished Big Ten record intact.

"Our magic number is down to four," Miller told his team afterward.

Miller's best decision of the night came on the defensive end of the floor. After watching Illinois' Rick Howat score 28 points against Iowa guards Brown and Calabria, Miller put the 6'5" Vidnovic on him with eight minutes to play. Howat managed just one more field goal.

"We decided that Vid's extra height would help stop Howat's jump-shooting, and we figured he'd be quick enough to stay with him," Miller said.

Johnson finished with just 17 points—the only time he was held to fewer than 22 points in a Big Ten game all season.

"It didn't matter, as long as the other guys picked up the slack and we won," Johnson said.

February 21 (Columbus, Ohio)
Iowa 97, Ohio State 89

Johnson rebounded from his off game in Champaign by pouring in 38 points and making 16 of 18 shots in one stretch of the game.

Vidnovic, who forgot his jersey at home and had to wear No. 23 instead of his usual No. 44, added 20 points, and Calabria had 19 of his own.

With the victory, Iowa had a two-game lead over Purdue with four games to play.

February 24 (Iowa City)
Iowa 116, Northwestern 97

The Hawkeyes improved to 11–0 in record-setting style. Johnson scored a school-record 49 points in the blowout victory. He made 20 of 33 shots as Iowa moved a step closer to the Big Ten crown. Johnson eclipsed the 1,000-point scoring mark in less than two full seasons.

The victory set up a huge game at Purdue four days later. An Iowa victory would clinch the Big Ten title. A loss would cut the Hawkeyes' lead to one game over the Boilermakers with two games remaining.

February 28 (West Lafayette, Indiana)
Iowa 108, Purdue 107

Purdue's Rick Mount scored a Big Ten–record 61 points, but Iowa rallied from a nine-point deficit with less than five minutes to play to win the Big Ten title.

In four games against Iowa covering his junior and senior seasons, Mount averaged 51 points. But the Hawkeyes' balance was the winning formula.

Johnson scored 26 points, Calabria 25, Brown 23, and Vidnovic 20, including two free throws with 10 seconds remaining to cap the comeback.

Mount launched 47 shots, making 27 of them, but Iowa became the first Big Ten team to win in three seasons of Purdue basketball at Mackey Arena.

That left two games—Ohio State at home and at Northwestern—standing between Iowa and a perfect Big Ten season.

"They have been dedicated all along to the project of going 14–0," Miller said. "And for this reason, I don't believe they'll let down very much even though we have the title wrapped up."

March 3 (Iowa City)
Iowa 113, Ohio State 92

With fans in Iowa Field House chanting "We're No. 1," Iowa ended its home season with a one-sided romp over the Buckeyes. It was the final home game for seniors Johnson, Vidnovic, Calabria, Jensen, and McGilmer.

The Hawkeyes closed out the home season by shooting 58 percent from the field. Johnson had 37 points, Brown 24, and Vidnovic 22.

Iowa had a 52–36 halftime lead, then made 18 of its first 25 shots in the second half.

March 7 (Evanston, Illinois)
Iowa 115, Northwestern 101

Johnson became the Hawkeyes' single-season scoring leader with 32 points—his ninth game of 30-plus points in Big Ten play—as his team completed a perfect Big Ten campaign. Iowa shot just 41.1 percent from the field.

"We didn't play good at all," said Brown after a 20-point game. "I give Northwestern credit. They really tried."

Vidnovic added 25 points and Calabria 20. Iowa's 102.9-point average in Big Ten games erased the previous league record of 97.7 set by Purdue the previous season.

The Doctor Is In

Dr. Tom Davis returned to his native Midwest when he left Stanford to replace George Raveling as the basketball coach at Iowa in the spring of 1986. Davis was born and raised in Ridgeway, Wisconsin, located in Iowa County and just 140 miles from Iowa City.

Davis introduced himself in 1986–87 with a Hawkeyes team that won a school-record 30 games, got within a game of the Final Four, started the year 18–0, and reached the No. 1 position in the Associated Press poll for the first time in school history.

He went on to become Iowa's winningest coach during his 13-season run, going 269–140. That included 10 different 20-win seasons and nine berths in the NCAA Tournament.

Davis, who was both the Big Ten and Associated Press National Coach of the Year in 1987, is not a fan of listing his biggest wins. "I don't think back on that stuff very much," Davis said.

But there is one statistic he's proud of. He never lost a first-round NCAA game in his 11 career appearances. He was there twice with Boston College. Davis had an 18–11 record overall in NCAA play and also made it to a regional Final with Boston College in 1982.

But back to his first-round success and his 11–0 record. "I think a lot of it had to do with style of play," said Davis, who retired in 2007 with a 598–355 career record in 32 seasons at Lafayette, Boston College, Stanford, Iowa, and Drake. "And I think a lot of it had to do with our pressure defense, our fast break, and playing both zone and man-to-man [defense]. We used different forms of pressure. We'd pressure full-court, or we'd go three-quarter-court, and that's hard to adjust to."

Davis-coached teams survived the first round every time, even though they were a No. 9 seed once, a No. 8 seed twice, and a No. 7 seed once.

"When you get into the NCAA Tournament, that first game, you're so excited and you've only got three or four days to practice and prepare," Davis said. "And the style we used was hard to get used to. Teams were all excited and not paying close attention. In the NCAA, I think style has a lot to do with [my success]."

When Davis retired after the 2006–07 season at Drake, he handed the program over to his son, Keno. Keno, who was a graduate assistant at Iowa for his father earlier in his career, was named Associated Press National Coach of the Year in 2008 after leading the Bulldogs to a 28–5 record and winning the Missouri Valley Conference regular-season and tournament titles. Tom and Keno are the only father-son combination to have won the AP's Coach of the Year Award.

26 Mount Scores 61, but Iowa Wins

Iowa trailed by a point with 20 seconds remaining at Purdue, its undefeated Big Ten basketball record and a chance to clinch the 1969–70 title hanging in the balance at Mackey Arena. The fans were buzzing. Their star guard, Rick "the Rocket" Mount, had already scored 59 points.

In the huddle, Hawkeyes coach Ralph Miller drew up an elaborate play. "He had everybody moving and picking," said Glenn Vidnovic, a starting forward on that team. "And then, as we walked out on the court, Johnny said, 'Throw it to me.' And that's exactly what happened. Fred [Brown] threw it in to Johnny, [and] he dribbled to the corner and made the basket."

"Johnny" is John Johnson, whose basket gave Iowa a 106–105 lead. Purdue missed two shots at the other end, Vidnovic rebounded and got fouled. He made two clutch free throws with 10 seconds to go.

Mount raced down the floor and scored on a layup as the clock was about to expire. That gave him a Big Ten–record 61 points. But Iowa won 108–107, snapping the Boilermakers' 30-game winning streak at Mackey Arena. It was also Purdue's first loss to a Big Ten foe in an arena that opened at the start of the 1967–68 season.

"That was before they hung how many points you had on the wall," Vidnovic said. "He might have had a calculator in his head saying, 'I'm going for 61 here. I better get down there before the buzzer goes off.'"

Mount's final basket was his 47th shot attempt of the game. He made 27 of them. But his quick trigger might have been his team's downfall. "We were actually down nine points with four minutes to go," Vidnovic said. "Without a shot clock, that was pretty late in the game. But Mount kept shooting. Had he not kept shooting, we probably would have lost. We would have had to foul. And then you're going on dead luck by then."

Mount passed the previous Big Ten scoring mark of 57 set by Purdue's Dave Schellhase (against Michigan in 1966) on a basket with 6:23 to go. He didn't score again until the layup right before the buzzer.

The loss was the third in league play for the reigning Big Ten champion Boilermakers, giving undefeated Iowa its first outright title since 1956. The Hawkeyes would win their last two games to finish 14–0 in the league.

A video review of the game many years later came to the conclusion that Mount would have scored 74 points had there been a three-point shot back then. But in the end, the one great scorer couldn't keep up with Iowa's balance.

Johnson scored 26 points, Chad Calabria 25, Brown 23, and Vidnovic 20. Calabria and Vidnovic combined to make 17 of 18 free-throw attempts. Johnson made 10 of 19 shots from the floor, and Brown made 9 of 14.

A crowd of 4,000 fans greeted the newly crowned champs at the Iowa City Airport that night. Miller held the game ball over his head and said, "Here's our trophy."

27 Upset for the Ages

Forest Evashevski's first victory as Iowa football coach was also one of the biggest upsets in school history.

Evashevski's undermanned 1952 squad had lost its first four games of the season and was coming off a 42–13 dismantling by Wisconsin at home. No. 14 Ohio State came to Iowa City for homecoming the following week, and few expected a competitive game. Especially since the Buckeyes, under second-year coach Woody Hayes, had drubbed Iowa by scores of 83–21 and 47–21 in the previous two seasons, respectively.

But Evashevski, an Xs and Os mastermind, got the last laugh on October 25. In practice that week, Evashevski changed the offense from single-wing and T formations to a split T. Iowa pulled off an 8–0 upset victory that, according to *Des Moines Register* columnist Sec Taylor, "was like my 8-year-old granddaughter out-boxing Sugar Ray Robinson."

The Associated Press ranked Iowa's victory No. 3 on a list of the most startling upsets of 1952.

"We had scrimmaged Tuesday before the Ohio game and we didn't look good at all," Evashevski said. "I went to bed tired that night and was drawing circles and *Xs*, diagramming play possibilities. I knew we lacked the speed to run outside, and I was trying to figure out how we could get an inside attack going.

"I decided the only thing we could do was try to spread Ohio State out as far as possible. With the wingback left, by shifting our backfield we could put the core of the offensive strength about three yards over to the right. That would be hard to cope with, from a defensive standpoint."

Iowa got a second-quarter safety when Binkey Broeder's punt was mishandled at the 2 and then fumbled into the end zone. Broeder recorded the game's only touchdown on a one-yard run with just 2:17 left.

Iowa's defense also showed up that day. Ohio State managed just 42 yards rushing and never got deeper than the Iowa 28 the entire game.

Evashevski, who had put in the new offense at practice the Wednesday before the game, was carried off the field by his team. "Looking back, it was a historic game," Evashevski said five decades later. "Few people realize that back then, Woody was the passingest coach in the Big Ten, not the running coach he became. Shortly before he died [in 1987], Woody told me that that game made him change his philosophy."

28 An Epic Duel at Kinnick

Rob Houghtlin made the most of his second opportunity. His 29-yard field goal on the final play of the game gave No. 1 Iowa a 12–10 victory over No. 2 Michigan on October 19, 1985. Decades later, it remains one of the greatest games ever played in Kinnick Stadium.

Houghtlin, who had been short and wide-right on a 44-yard attempt with 7:38 remaining and the Hawkeyes trailing 10–9, kicked his way into Iowa football history with the game on the line.

His boot also set off a celebration that Iowa quarterback and Heisman Trophy runner-up Chuck Long will never forget. "The euphoria and elation of that crowd was never matched again in my career as a player or a coach," Long said. "You couldn't replicate it if you tried a thousand times."

Houghtlin's fourth field goal of the game is the one that will also be remembered, the final play in a game that Iowa dominated statistically. The Hawkeyes had 422 yards of total offense to Michigan's 182. Iowa had a huge edge in time of possession too, at 38 minutes and 5 seconds. Iowa ran 84 plays; the Wolverines ran just 41.

Houghtlin's first field goal of the game, a 35-yarder on Iowa's first possession of the second quarter, came after the game's most controversial play. Long had thrown an 18-yard touchdown pass to Scott Helverson. Officials ruled Helverson's foot had touched the out-of-bounds line at the back of the end zone. Television replays told a different story. But officials couldn't use replays to overturn calls back then. In an interesting side note, Helverson would go on to become an NFL official.

Michigan hadn't allowed a point in the fourth quarter all season until Houghtlin gave the Hawkeyes a 9–7 lead on a 36-yard field goal with 14:20 to play in the game.

Michigan's Mike Gillette made a 40-yarder with more than 10 minutes to go to put his team back in front and set the stage for a drama-filled stretch drive.

The Wolverines tried to milk the clock on their final possession. But on a key third-and-2, Iowa linebacker Larry Station knifed in and tackled Jamie Morris for a two-yard loss.

Houghtlin's Place in History

Rob Houghtlin transferred to Iowa from Miami of Ohio, and he made the most of his second opportunity.

Houghtlin's clutch kick to beat Michigan in 1985 was one of many dramatic moments for the native of Glenview, Illinois. There was a touch of good fortune thrown in there too.

Iowa was playing at Minnesota on November 22, 1986, the final regular-season game of the season. With the battle for Floyd of Rosedale tied 27–27, Houghtlin missed a 51-yard attempt that would have won the game. But the Gophers were flagged for having too many men on the field. With no time on the clock, Houghtlin drilled a 37-yarder to win the game 30–27.

The Hawkeyes went on to play in the Holiday Bowl that season. There, Houghtlin kicked a 41-yarder on the last play of the game for a 39–38 victory over San Diego State.

Houghtlin is also remembered for kicking a 25-yard field goal with just more than a minute to play that gave Iowa a crucial 27–24 victory at Purdue on November 16, 1985. That kick, like the one against Michigan, was instrumental in Iowa's march toward a Big Ten title and the Rose Bowl.

The 1985 Michigan thriller was one of nine games in which Houghtlin kicked three field goals. In his three-season career, Houghtlin made 54 of 85 field goals. He kicked a career-long 55-yarder against Iowa State in 1987, and made a 52-yarder in the 1986 Rose Bowl.

Michigan punted. Long converted on a trio of third downs in the final drive—two passes to tight end Mike Flagg and a run by David Hudson—to keep the ball moving toward the Michigan end zone. Houghtlin's historic kick followed.

Long completed 26 of 39 passes for 297 yards. Running back Ronnie Harmon had 32 carries for 120 yards and caught six of Long's passes for 72 more. "Long and Harmon on the same team makes it extremely difficult to shut them down," Michigan coach Bo Schembechler said after the game. "Our defense again played well, but they did a poor job on that last series." A series that set the stage for Houghtlin's historical kick.

"I remember two plays," Long said. "The No. 1 play was Larry Station's stop [of Morris]. That's the play that sticks out. It stopped their drive. And then Rob Houghtlin's field goal. I call it a Hollywood script game. No. 1 versus No. 2. We had to go on that last two-minute drive. And a kick by Rob to win the game."

Then came the celebration that is etched in Long's memory for life. "The fans hung around," Long said. "It felt like they waited around for us outside the locker room. And then we all went downtown and celebrated together."

29 Purple Heart Hawkeye

Nile Kinnick still casts a larger-than-life shadow over the Iowa football program. But one of Kinnick's Hawkeyes teammates, Erwin Prasse, is another remarkable story.

Prasse, not Kinnick, was captain of Iowa's famed Ironmen team of 1939. In the Big Ten opener that year against Indiana, Prasse caught three touchdown passes from Kinnick, a stadium record that lasted until 2005.

The last touchdown reception came with five minutes remaining in the game and the Hoosiers clinging to a 29–26 lead. Facing a fourth-and-15, Iowa could have tried to tie the game with a Kinnick dropkick field goal. But in the huddle, Kinnick told his teammates to "forget the tie" and passed to Prasse for the winning score.

Prasse averaged 26.9 yards per reception as a senior. In his final home game, Prasse caught a 48-yard touchdown pass to beat

Minnesota 13–9 and give Iowa possession of Floyd of Rosedale for the first time.

Prasse was a two-time All–Big Ten selection. And in 1939, when Kinnick was presented with the Heisman Trophy, the 6'3" Prasse was a second-team All-American. He played both offensive and defensive end.

Football wasn't Prasse's only calling. He also played basketball (1938–40) and baseball (1938–40) at Iowa, and was the second Hawkeye to earn nine letters. Aubrey Devine was the first (football, 1919–21; baseball, 1920–22; and track, 1920–22). Only six men in the history of the school have won nine letters. Prasse played second base on two Big Ten championship baseball teams for the Hawkeyes.

Inducted into the University of Iowa Athletics Hall of Fame in 1989, Prasse remained a versatile athlete once he left college.

He was selected in the ninth round of the NFL Draft by the Detroit Lions, but instead played professionally in both basketball (in the NBA-predecessor the National Basketball League) and baseball. Prasse played three seasons for the Oshkosh All-Stars. His team won a championship in 1941. Branch Rickey signed Prasse to a minor league baseball contract with the St. Louis Cardinals.

But a year into his baseball career, in 1942, Prasse was drafted into the army and went off to fight in World War II. He landed on Omaha Beach on D-Day, June 6, 1944. Later, he was shot in the arm while on a reconnaissance mission in Germany. The army discharged Prasse in 1946, and he was awarded the Purple Heart. Prasse decided to put his athletic career on the shelf and sold life insurance in the Chicago area.

30 Breaking the Bank(s)

Tavian Banks received a standing ovation from the Kinnick Stadium crowd after setting an Iowa single-game rushing record against Tulsa on September 13, 1997. Banks had 314 yards on 29 carries, including four touchdowns, in the 54–16 romp.

Banks, from Bettendorf, Iowa, erased the previous record of 286 yards established by Ed Podolak of Atlantic against Northwestern on November 9, 1968. Podolak, the color analyst for the Hawkeye Radio Network, witnessed the changing of the guard from his perch in the press box.

"When Tavian broke the record, an announcement was made," said Gary Dolphin, Iowa's play-by-play voice. "The crowd gets up, and I look over and Eddie is leaning out of the press box, clapping. Eddie was giving him his own standing ovation. One great football player applauding another. It tied the two generations together."

Back in 1968, Podolak needed just 17 carries to wipe out the previous Big Ten record of 268 yards set by Michigan State's Clinton Jones against the Hawkeyes in 1966. A position change earlier that season gave Podolak an opportunity to make history. He'd always been a run-pass threat at quarterback earlier in his career. But as the 1968 season arrived, Iowa coach Ray Nagel was looking to find ways to take better advantage of Podolak's speed. He also wanted to get sophomore quarterback Larry Lawrence on the field. That opportunity presented itself when starting running back Dennis Green was injured.

Nagel moved Podolak to running back. He gained 129 yards in just 14 carries in his first start at that position, a 41–0 victory over Wisconsin in the fifth game of the season. With Podolak as the chief ball carrier and Lawrence behind center, good things started to happen. It all came together against Northwestern.

"That is when our offense had really started to click," Podolak said. "It was the third or fourth game after I had moved to tailback [from quarterback]. We had a terrific fullback named Tim Sullivan, and ran a lot of this sweep play where I could go either inside or outside, reading his block. He was a great blocker, and there was always a lot of green space ahead of me."

Iowa toyed with the Northwestern defense all day in the 68–34 victory, rolling up 639 yards of total offense. Podolak's longest run on his record-setting day came on a 60-yard touchdown scamper. "[Quarterback Larry] Lawrence called for a pass-run option in the huddle," Podolak said. "After we lined up, Larry called an audible, changing it to a straight off-tackle play. It was a smart call." Podolak also scored on a 32-yard run during his record-setting day.

"If Eddie isn't the All–Big Ten back this season, then I never expect to have one at Iowa," Nagel said after the game. "This kid is as good an athlete as I have ever coached, besides being a great guy off the field. He's been outstanding for three seasons, but he hasn't always had strong support."

Podolak was the first-team All–Big Ten running back that season. He rushed for 937 yards on a team that finished with a 5–5 record.

At the end of the third quarter, an announcement was made over the public address system that Podolak had set a school and Big Ten single-game rushing record. Nagel took Podolak out of the game and presented him the game ball. "I still have it," Podolak said. "I'd have to look for it. It's somewhere among my memorabilia."

With the ball safely put away in a box, Podolak carried it under his arm and into the locker room after the game. Twenty-nine years later, Podolak walked back into that locker room and gave Banks a hug after he had set the record. "He was a heck of a back," Podolak said.

Banks scored on runs of 71, 14, 14, and 23 yards against the Golden Hurricane. He also had a 48-yard run wiped out by a holding call.

"It's just the same adjectives over and over again," Iowa coach Hayden Fry said. "He's a graceful, fluid runner with great, great vision."

Banks dedicated the game to his uncle, Dino Banks, who had passed away the morning of Iowa's game the previous week against Northern Iowa. "We were real close," Banks said.

A backup to Sedrick Shaw his first three seasons at Iowa, Banks passed Podolak with a nifty 29-yard run in the second half. Banks went around right end, made a sharp cut left to dodge a defender, cut back to his right, and went out-of-bounds with his name in the record books.

"He had a couple of moves on that record-breaking run that weren't part of my repertoire," Podolak said.

Two words appeared on the Kinnick Stadium Jumbotron after that run: CONGRATS TAVIAN.

Podolak's school record lasted nearly three decades. But his Big Ten record lasted only a week. Michigan's Ron Johnson rushed for 347 yards against Wisconsin on November 16, 1968.

"Shortest Big Ten record in history," Podolak said.

31 Better Waite Than Never

Iowa trailed Georgetown 46–32 three possessions into the second half of their 1980 NCAA East Regional championship game at the Spectrum in Philadelphia, Pennsylvania. And then came the most brilliant 18 minutes and 40 seconds of Hawkeyes basketball you'll ever see.

Iowa scored on 24 of its final 28 possessions of the game. Coach Lute Olson's team made 17 of its last 22 field-goal attempts, all 15 free-throw attempts, and turned it over just once. And with five seconds to play, junior center Steve Waite made one of the biggest three-point plays in school history to send his team to the Final Four.

The Hoyas' Craig Shelton tied the game 78–78, and Olson took a timeout with 1:56 remaining to play. There was no shot clock in the college game back then. Iowa milked the game clock to 1:15, when Kevin Boyle called a timeout after getting trapped near the half-court line. The Hawkeyes worked the clock to :14, when Olson called another timeout and set up a final play that didn't come off as planned.

Ronnie Lester made the in-bounds pass to Boyle, who was supposed to give it back to Lester. But the Hoyas' Eric "Sleepy" Floyd, who scored 31 points, denied Lester the ball. So Boyle turned and started to dribble toward the basket. "The play breaks down, and I think, *Oh, no, what is Kevin going to do now?*" said center Steve Krafcisin. "Then he gave it to Waite."

Boyle had clear sailing as he neared the free-throw line. "Somebody tried to stop me, and I threw it right to [Waite]," Boyle said. Waite caught the ball in the left corner, drove around Georgetown center Ed Spriggs, and made the bank shot on the left side of the basket with his right hand. Shelton got his right hand tangled up in the net as he went for the block, and he fouled Waite.

"If his hand hadn't got caught in the net, it probably would have ended up in the second row," Boyle said.

Iowa's bench exploded in celebration when Waite scored. "I was on the bench, jumping around," said Bob Hansen, a freshman on that team. "I remember screaming at him, 'Just make the free throw and the game is over.' He looked me right in the eye and said, 'Shut up, I got it.'"

Georgetown coach John Thompson called a pair of timeouts, the first to discuss strategy and the second to ice Waite. "And then he stepped up, cool as can be, and knocked it down," Boyle said.

That gave Iowa an 81–78 lead. The college game didn't have a three-point shot at the time. Georgetown threw a full-court pass, missed a shot, then scored after an offensive rebound as Iowa players backed off, not wanting to commit a foul. Less than a second remained. Ronnie Lester caught the in-bounds pass from Boyle and the Hawkeyes were headed to the Final Four for the first time since 1956.

One of the strengths of Iowa's 1979–80 team was tremendous balance on the offensive end. That was evident in the comeback from the 14-point second-half deficit.

Waite scored 13 of the final 49 points. Boyle had 10, Lester 8, and Kenny Arnold, Vince Brookins, and Hansen had 6 apiece. Many of those field goals were midrange jumpers over Georgetown's stingy zone defense. But the last one, by Waite, came from point-blank range. "My first thought was to pass it back and let a shooter shoot it," Waite said. "But I saw an opening and drove."

Waite, a 62 percent free-throw shooter entering the game, was perfect in seven attempts against the Hoyas. And the last one was the biggest free throw of his career. "I'm only a 60 percent free-throw shooter statistically, but I was 100 percent sure I'd make that one," Waite said.

Olson was inducted into the Naismith Memorial Basketball Hall of Fame in 2002 and won an NCAA title at Arizona in 1997. He was a two-time Big Ten Coach of the Year and a seven-time Pac-10 (now Pac-12) Coach of the Year. He has seen his teams play plenty of outstanding basketball. But Iowa's second half that day in Philadelphia was special.

"The second half against Georgetown has to be one of the most amazing ever in basketball," Olson said. "We played almost perfect basketball from the standpoint of turnovers, free throws, and field goals."

Olson said in 2009, on a return visit to Iowa City, that he had not watched the second half of that Georgetown game again. "That would scare me to look at [the tape of the second half] because I know one turnover in there would have cost us the game," Olson said. "That has to go down as one of the most unbelievable halves when you look at both teams as close to perfection as those two teams were. That was an outstanding Georgetown team."

Waite was a junior who never left home. He was an All-State center at Iowa City West before signing with Iowa. And he was quiet by nature. Krafcisin, from suburban Chicago, wore his emotions on his sleeve. And it wasn't hard to get him to talk. They were both centers, but were polar opposites when it came to personalities. "I left all my emotion on the floor," Krafcisin said. "Waite was very reserved. It was hard to get him to talk. He would do all the dirty work, and was not really flashy. I tried to be as flashy as I could. And we got along so well."

But with a trip to the Final Four on the line, Waite made the shot heard around Iowa. "It was great to see him get the glory, an Iowa kid," Krafcisin said. "And he certainly deserved it, because he was one of the unsung guys on our team."

32 Olympic Brand

The introductions tend to get long when you've got an accomplished wrestling résumé. Tom Brands wishes that wasn't the case. "I just wish there wouldn't be long introductions when I speak," Brands said. "Just say, 'Coach of the Iowa Hawkeyes.'"

But that's not easy. What do you leave out? A gold medalist at the 1996 Olympics in Atlanta? World Cup gold medals in 1994 and 1995? A World Freestyle Championship in 1993? A Pan American champion in 1995? Four US National titles (1993–96)? A 2001 inductee in wrestling's hall of fame? A four-time All-American at Iowa (1989–92), and a three-time Big Ten and NCAA champion? A three-time Big Ten Coach of the Year? The coach of three NCAA championship teams?

That's why introductions tend to run longer than Brands' fiery speeches.

One thing that will never be left out is his Olympic gold medal performance at 136.5 pounds in 1996. Standing on the victory stand is something Brands will never forget. "For sure," he said.

Getting to that defining gold moment wasn't easy. It was a story of perseverance. At the World Championships in Atlanta the year before, Brands was eliminated after the first day and finished ninth. And he did not place the year before that in Turkey. The most optimistic prediction heading into the Olympic games had Brands winning a silver. Others predicted no medal at all. "There is no greater satisfaction in the world than doing what people say you can't do," Brands said.

He shut out Jang Jade-Sung of South Korea 7–0 in the Finals, scoring a takedown just 25 seconds into the match and never looking back.

Tom Brands brings fire to the Iowa wrestling program.

Brands outscored his four opponents 19–1 on his way to gold. His idol and coach at Iowa, Dan Gable, surrendered no points while winning gold in Munich in 1972. Twenty-four years later, Gable was on hand to see Brands turn in a Gable-like performance.

"As far as going out and doing it, it was the greatest tournament I've ever seen, to go out and beat everybody up like he did," Gable said. Praise from Gable—there's something else to add to the introduction.

"When I think of the Olympics, it's [Arsen] Fadzayev [of the Soviet Union] and Gable," Brands said. "For the public, it's Michael Phelps. Mark Spitz. Gable. Iconic athletes. Michael Jordan."

But in the world of wrestling, the Brands name carries clout. "It's the Olympic Games, and you won an event," Brands said. "That is a big deal to a lot of people. And it's global. But I took a lot of lumps along the way."

33 The Rampaging Redhead

Iowa had one of its greatest basketball seasons ever in 1944–45. The Hawkeyes finished the season 17–1 overall, the only loss a one-point decision at Illinois. Iowa won the school's first outright Big Ten championship. Brothers Herb and Clayton Wilkinson were first-team All–Big Ten selections. Herb Wilkinson and Dick Ives were All-Americans.

A redheaded freshman guard from Muscatine played a role on that loaded team. Murray Wier averaged 7.8 points for the Hawkeyes. It was the start of something big. Coach Pops Harrison offered Wier a scholarship after watching him complete an outstanding senior season at Muscatine High School that resulted in first-team All-State honors. Wier had transferred to Muscatine from tiny Grandview for his senior season, because he wanted to play at a bigger school.

By the time Wier left Iowa, his legacy as one of the Hawkeyes' greatest players was complete. Wier spent his final three seasons at Iowa beating opponents with an assortment of moves. At 5'9" he had the size of a guard, but he could be effective all over the floor. Those moves, at times, defied description.

"He was unguardable," wrote the *Des Moines Register*'s Bert McGrane. "He'd fire 'em off his hip or up from an ankle with equal abandon, even hoisting in baskets from midair in the midst of a drive. He didn't shoot baskets. He just threw 'em, while racing, whirling, jumping and engaging in some other novel means of rapid transit."

Wier said his unorthodox approach to shooting was a byproduct of his size. As he grew up with a basketball in his hands, he realized he had to be creative to get shots off. "I had two older brothers who were a lot taller than me," Wier said. "We'd play in the backyard, and to get a shot over them, I had to throw the ball. That's really how it started. It looked goofier than hell, but it was so natural to me."

Wier led the Hawkeyes in scoring as a junior in 1946–47, averaging 15.1 points. His senior season was one of the best in the history of Iowa basketball. The NCAA recognized individual statistical champions for the first time in 1948, and Wier led the country in scoring at 21 points a game. He was a first-team All–Big Ten selection and a consensus first-team All-American as a senior, one of two the school has produced. Chuck Darling (1952) is the other. Wier was also honored as the Big Ten Player of the Year.

In one of his most memorable performances that senior year, Wier scored 34 points in a 70–61 victory over Illinois, witnessed by a crowd of 16,048 in Iowa Field House. Wier attempted 33 shots and made 15. The rest of the Iowa team attempted 33 shots, too, making 11.

"That game was one of my best memories," Wier said in 2002, when he was one of 20 players selected to the school's All-Century team.

The Illinois team had its own star in Jack Burmaster, regarded to be the best defensive player in the Big Ten that season. One of Burmaster's high school teammates, Tom Parker, was on the Iowa team. Parker went to see Burmaster at the Illinois team's hotel the night before the game. When Parker returned, Wier wanted to know what Burmaster had said. "He said, 'Burmaster is really worried,'" Wier recalled many years later. "I thought, *Uh-oh, if he's*

Distinguished Company

In conjunction with its 100th season of basketball in 2002, the University of Iowa selected an All-Century team. Wier was one of the 20 players selected.

"I don't think you could get a bigger honor," Wier said. "Just to be mentioned with all those other guys is something in itself."

The five best players from each decade were also chosen.

Iowa's All-Century team: B.J. Armstrong (1986–89); Fred Brown (1970–71); Carl Cain (1954–56); Chuck Darling (1950–52); Acie Earl (1990–93); Dave Gunther (1957–59); John Johnson (1969–70); Dick Ives (1945–47); Kevin Kunnert (1971–73); Ronnie Lester (1977–80); Bill Logan (1954–56); Roy Marble (1986–89); Don Nelson (1960–62); Bill Seaberg (1954–56); Ben Selzer (1932–34); Greg Stokes (1982–85); Murray Wier (1945–48); Herb Wilkinson (1945–47); Sam Williams (1967–68); Andre Woolridge (1995–97).

Iowa's All-Decade teams

1900s—James Barton (1905–07); Chester Buckner (1906–08); J.O. Perrine (1907–09); C.P. Schenck (1902–05); Walter Stewart (1908–10).

1910s—Edwin Bannick (1915–17); Clifford Berrien (1917–19); Lawrence Dutton (1915–17); H.L. Von Lackum (1914–16); John Von Lackum (1916–18).

1920s—Aubrey Devine (1920–22); Hector Janse (1923–25); Charles McConnell (1925–27); Forest Twogood (1927–29); George Van Deusen (1925–27).

1930s—Howard Bastian (1933–34); John Grim (1933–35); Howard Moffitt (1932–34); Ben Selzer (1932–34); Ben Stephens (1937–39).

1940s—Dave Danner (1944–47); Dick Ives (1944–47); Vic Siegel (1940–42); Murray Wier (1945–48); Herb Wilkinson (1945–47).

1950s—Carl Cain (1954–56); Chuck Darling (1950–52); Dave Gunther (1957–59); Bill Logan (1954–56); Bill Seaberg (1954–56).

1960s—Chad Calabria (1968–70); Don Nelson (1960–62); Jimmy Rodgers (1963–65); Glenn Vidnovic (1968–70); Sam Williams (1967–68).

1970s—Fred Brown (1970–71); John Johnson (1969–70); Bruce King (1975–77); Kevin Kunnert (1971–73); Ronnie Lester (1977–80).

1980s—B.J. Armstrong (1986–89); Bob Hansen (1980–83); Ed Horton (1986–89); Roy Marble (1986–89); Greg Stokes (1982–85).

1990s—Acie Earl (1990–93); Dean Oliver (1998–01); Jess Settles (1994–96, 1999); Chris Street (1991–93); Andre Woolridge (1995–97).

worried and we're in Iowa City, watch out. After about five minutes, I could do anything with him that I wanted. I remember looking at his face. He was bewildered. It was one of those games where everything went right."

Wier, who passed away in 2016, went on to play four seasons of professional basketball. Fort Wayne's NBA franchise drafted him, but he played for the Tri-Cities Blackhawks and Waterloo Hawks. He was coached in his second professional season by the legendary Red Auerbach, who would go on to fame as coach of the Boston Celtics. Wier, too, became a successful coach at Waterloo East High School in Iowa, winning a state championship in 1974 and compiling a 374–140 record.

To this day, the guy nicknamed the Rampaging Redhead is the only Iowa player to lead the nation in scoring.

34 From Hawkeye to Mongo

Long before he gained popularity as Mongo in *Blazing Saddles*, as a star in the TV sitcom *Webster*, or as part of the *Monday Night Football* lineup with Howard Cosell and Frank Gifford, from 1974 to 1976, Alex Karras was the first two-time All-American lineman in Iowa history and the 1957 Outland Trophy winner. "He was a great guy," said Karras' former teammate Randy Duncan. "And a great teammate."

Karras came to Iowa from Gary, Indiana, and coach Forest Evashevski and his staff used a little trickery to get their man. Schools like Notre Dame, Indiana, Michigan State, and Michigan were also trying to recruit Karras. But Iowa hid him for a summer in Spencer, Iowa, to keep him away from rival recruiters until he made it to Iowa City in the fall of 1954. "They figured nobody would know where Spencer was," Karras said.

After an injury-marred sophomore season in 1955, Karras decided to leave school. Not so, his mother told him. "If you quit now you'll quit again, when things get tough," she told him. So Karras stayed in Iowa City and blossomed as a standout lineman in 1956. He was a first-team All–Big Ten and All-America selection.

"He wasn't the toughest, fastest guy around," Duncan said. "But he was quick. Nobody could block him. He could spin out of a double-team, be right there and get the guy. It was just incredible how quick he was."

Karras repeated as a first-team All–Big Ten and All-America selection as a senior. He finished second to John David Crow of Texas A&M in voting for the 1957 Heisman Trophy, picking up 128 first-place votes.

The Detroit Lions took Karras with the 10th pick in the first round of the 1958 NFL Draft, and he played there for 12 seasons. Karras was suspended for the 1963 season, along with Green Bay's Paul Hornung, for gambling on games they played in. Karras was a three-time All-Pro who retired following the 1970 season.

Karras was elected to the National Football Foundation College Football Hall of Fame in 1991 and is part of the Kinnick Stadium Wall of Honor. He passed away in 2012 at 77 years of age.

35 The Steubenville Trio

This is a recruiting tale of the highest order. And it happened on the south side of Steubenville, Ohio, in August 1952. Three good friends were about to embark on their college football careers. Calvin Jones was headed to Ohio State. Frank Gilliam and Eddie Vincent, not offered by the Buckeyes, had decided to attend Iowa. And it was time to say good-bye.

"We stopped at his home just before leaving town, to say we'd see him around Thanksgiving," Gilliam recalled. "C.J. said, 'I'm going with you,' ran upstairs, packed a bag and rode to Iowa City in our car." And Iowa football coach Forest Evashevski, about to start his first season as Iowa coach, had picked up an impressive recruit.

As you can imagine, the fact that Jones landed in Iowa City instead of Columbus, Ohio, had Ohio State coach Woody Hayes none too happy. In fact, Big Ten commissioner Kenneth "Tug" Wilson investigated. As legend has it, Jones told the commissioner, "I'll tell you why I came out here. They treated me like a white man, and I like it here. I'm going to stay."

The Fainting Irish

The Steubenville Trio played in one of the most talked-about and controversial football games in Iowa history.

The program was showing progress in Forest Evashevski's second season as coach. Coming off a 2–7 record in his debut, four victories in five games gave the 1953 team a 5–3 record. The last of those victories, a 27–0 shutout over No. 15 Minnesota, moved Iowa into the national rankings at 20. The Gophers fell out of the rankings, and Iowa was assured of its first winning season since 1946.

The regular-season finale was challenging, to say the least. The Hawkeyes traveled to South Bend to play undefeated No. 1 Notre Dame as a two-touchdown underdog. But the Irish had to resort to controversial tactics to get away with a 14–14 tie.

Eddie Vincent's four-yard touchdown run gave Iowa a 7–0 first-quarter lead, and the score remained that way until late in the first half. Notre Dame had the ball at the Iowa 12 as the final seconds ticked away, with no timeouts to stop the clock. So lineman Frank Varrichione fell to the field, faking an injury, and officials stopped play. Only a few seconds remained, enough to get off one more play. Notre Dame quarterback Ralph Guglielmi threw a touchdown pass to Dan Shannon to tie the game after the extra point.

Iowa regained the lead in the second half on a touchdown pass from Bobby Stearnes to Frank Gilliam with 2:06 to play in the game. The point-after gave the Hawkeyes a 14–7 lead.

Notre Dame, again out of timeouts, started its final drive from its own 41. Guglielmi completed seven consecutive passes to move the ball downfield. Irish players Don Penza and Art Hunter took turns faking injuries and falling to the turf to stop the clock.

With six seconds remaining, Guglielmi found Dan Shannon again from nine yards out for a touchdown. A point-after later, Coach Frank Leahy's team had escaped with a tie.

The national reaction to Notre Dame's tactics was swift. Esteemed sportswriter Grantland Rice, speaking to a New York Football Writers luncheon two days later, said he considered Notre Dame's actions "a complete violation of the spirit and ethics of football, and I was sorry to see Notre Dame, of all teams, using this method. Why, in heaven's name, was it allowed?"

Evashevski wondered the same thing. On the same day that Rice was speaking in New York, Evashevski appeared at a "victory" rally in Iowa City. Evashevski took liberties with Rice's famous "One Great Scorer" poem:

When the One Great Scorer comes
To write against our name,
He won't ask that we won or lost,
But how we got gypped at Notre Dame.

Notre Dame's tactics did prove costly. The Irish dropped to No. 2 in the AP poll the following week, and stayed there. Maryland was declared the national champion. Leahy resigned as coach at the end of the season.

Iowa jumped 11 spots in the poll and finished the season ranked ninth.

Iowa was cleared of any wrongdoing, and the Steubenville Trio was back together again. But Jones, a solidly built 6'0" 220-pounder, was the real catch. Especially for a program that had enjoyed just one winning season in the previous eight. "Cal was always *the* guy…a little bigger, a little stronger, a little better," Gilliam said. "He is one of the very few stars who started four years in both football and basketball for Steubenville. He was all-everything in football."

Jones, Vincent, and Gilliam were all three-year lettermen for the Hawkeyes. Vincent was a halfback, and Gilliam was an end who was named to Iowa's All-Time team in 1989 when the program celebrated its 100th season. Jones was clearly the most decorated player. He played guard on both sides of the ball during these single-platoon days, but was considered a defensive star.

"The greatest football player I ever saw," said former Iowa All-American Alex Karras. "Calvin had phenomenal reactions. I'd never seen a man hustle like he hustled. He never stopped running in practice. Never."

Jones was named to 22 different All-America teams during his career. He was the first two-time consensus All-American in program history, and he became the first African American to win the Outland Trophy, which goes to the nation's best interior lineman, as a senior in 1955. He was also the first college player to appear on the cover of *Sports Illustrated*, on September 24, 1954, the magazine's seventh issue.

Jones, too, was named to Iowa's All-Time team in 1989. He is on the Kinnick Stadium Wall of Honor. His No. 62 is one of two retired numbers at Iowa. The other is the 24 worn by 1939 Heisman Trophy winner Nile Kinnick.

Jones was drafted by the Detroit Lions in the ninth round of the 1956 draft but signed instead with the Winnipeg Blue Bombers and played in Canada. After playing in the East-West All-Star Game in Vancouver as a rookie, Jones made plans to travel to Pasadena, California, to see Gilliam and Iowa play in the Rose Bowl. Gilliam, a senior, had missed the 1955 season with a broken leg.

Jones missed his scheduled December 9, 1956, morning flight out of Vancouver, and scheduled an afternoon flight to Calgary. Trans-Canada Air Lines Flight 810 crashed into Slesse Mountain, killing all 62 people on board. The Iowa team dedicated the program's first Rose Bowl appearance in Iowa history to Jones. After beating Oregon State 35–19, the game ball was sent to his mother in Steubenville.

36 An Unlikely Journey

An Iowa basketball team has never won an NCAA title, but one of the program's All-Americans did. And how Herb Wilkinson got to Iowa City is one of the strangest recruiting tales of all time.

Wilkinson, raised a Mormon, started his basketball career as a guard. Then he grew more than a foot between his sophomore season of high school and his freshman season at Utah. That gave Wilkinson a unique skill set; he was a player who could handle and shoot the ball in a 6'4" frame.

Utah's 1943–44 season ended with a loss to Kentucky in the first round of the NIT. But fate extended Wilkinson's freshman season. Arkansas had two players injured in an auto accident, and the school withdrew from the NCAA Tournament. Utah was selected to replace the Razorbacks in the eight-team field.

A victory over Missouri got the Utes in the Final Four, then a 40–31 victory over Iowa State got them in the championship game against Dartmouth.

Utah won 42–40 in overtime, when Wilkinson's shot from the top of the key hit the front of the rim and fell in. By then, Wilkinson already had been thinking about leaving Utah. He wanted to be a dentist, and Utah didn't have a dental school. His older brother, Clayton, also wanted to go to dental school. Clayton had played his freshman season at Utah as well, but left for a two-year Mormon mission that took him to Cedar Rapids.

Clayton was playing in a YMCA league there when he was spotted by a friend of Iowa coach Pops Harrison. So Harrison came to take a look for himself, liked what he saw, and talked to Clayton about coming to Iowa. When Wilkinson told Harrison he wanted to go to dental school, Pops told him Iowa's was top-notch. Clayton said his brother wanted to join him. Harrison, unaware that Herb was playing basketball at Utah, said that could be arranged.

Utah was playing Dartmouth for the NCAA title on the same day Harrison met with Clayton. The next day, Harrison saw a picture in the newspaper of Utah players carrying Herb off the court after he made the winning shot. Harrison called Clayton and said, "Is that your little brother?" Yes, Clayton told him. "Hell, bring him along," Harrison said.

Harrison inherited a pair of Wilkinson brothers, and both had three seasons of eligibility remaining. They joined a 1944–45 team that included high-scoring sophomore Dick Ives and freshman sensation Murray Wier and won Iowa's first outright Big Ten title with an 11–1 record. The Hawkeyes were 17–1 overall, but school officials elected not to play in the NCAA Tournament. Herb averaged 9.6 points, less than Clayton's 11.5, but was named a consensus second-team All-American. Both brothers were first-team All–Big Ten selections.

Herb, a skilled high jumper as well, also tied for fourth at the NCAA Championships in the spring of 1945.

Iowa never won another Big Ten basketball crown with the Wilkinsons in uniform. Herb went on to become Iowa's only three-time first-team All–Big Ten selection. He was also a second-team All-American as a junior and senior. Herb was also named to Iowa's All-Century team in 2002.

37 The Game That Wasn't Played

Iowa was scheduled to end the 1963 football season by hosting Notre Dame on November 23, 1963. The day before the game, a storm forced the team to practice in Iowa Field House. This group of Hawkeyes would never play together again, because of a national tragedy.

President John F. Kennedy was assassinated on November 22 in Dallas, Texas, setting off a long chain of events in Iowa City. The Notre Dame team was already in Iowa City. Representatives of the two universities met to discuss whether the game should be played or not.

Iowa's coach, Jerry Burns, was in his office that Friday, being interviewed by the *Des Moines Register*'s Bert McGrane, when his secretary walked in and told them Kennedy was dead. "Bert McGrane dropped to a knee and said a prayer," Burns said. "I've always remembered that. It was so stunning, such an unexpected thing."

Friday evening, athletic directors Forest Evashevski of Iowa and Edward "Moose" Krause of Notre Dame announced that the game would take place, as scheduled, at 12:30 PM Saturday. "I served as President Kennedy's physical fitness advisor for the Peace Corps," Evashevski said. "I know the president would have wanted the game played, because it represents the ideals which he advocated. The young men representing Notre Dame and Iowa represent the very thing in which the late President Kennedy believed."

But things changed. At 12:30 AM Saturday, Francis Graham, Iowa's business manager of athletics, announced the game had been canceled. President Virgil Hancher of Iowa and the Reverend Theodore Hesburgh of Notre Dame issued a joint statement.

Iowa officials expressed regret for the late decision. Reverend Hesburgh had been attending a meeting in Colorado, and his travel to Chicago had been delayed. That forced a meeting with Iowa officials to be moved back to late Friday night.

Several alternate dates were considered. One option, playing the following Saturday, was eliminated because the Irish were playing Syracuse two days before that. The other was to move the game to December 7, two weeks later. Iowa officials decided against that.

"Our board was unanimous in its opinion that the extending of the football season would be difficult to justify educationally," Evashevski said. "It was with regret that the board agreed that it would be unwise to prolong the season until December 7."

Saturday morning, Notre Dame's players went to St. Thomas More Catholic Church. There, the Reverend Edmund Joyce, Notre Dame's vice president, said a memorial mass for President Kennedy. The Notre Dame party left Iowa City to return to South Bend, Indiana, around noon.

Fans were offered refunds on their $5 tickets. Iowa's 14 upperclassmen never had their senior day. That included the Hawkeyes' two outstanding guards, most valuable player Mike Reilly and Wally Hilgenberg, as well as halfback-receiver Paul Krause, end Cloyd Webb, and quarterback Fred Riddle.

The Hawkeyes finished with a 3–3–2 record under Coach Jerry Burns. Reilly, nicknamed the Hammer, was an All-American and first-team All–Big Ten selection. Hilgenberg was also a first-team All–Big Ten pick. Krause and Webb made the All–Big Ten second team.

Kennedy had actually attended the November 21, 1959, game when Notre Dame won 20–19 at Iowa. Kennedy, an Irish Catholic, was on his way to a campaign stop in Carroll later that day. He was a US Senator at the time.

"I cheered for Iowa, but I prayed for Notre Dame," Kennedy said later.

38 Reaching the Pinnacle

Iowa's second-ranked basketball team was 15–0 when it traveled to Champaign, Illinois, for a Big Ten game with No. 8 Illinois on January 14, 1987. And the Hawkeyes had been living dangerously under first-year coach Tom Davis.

Five times Iowa had rallied from deficits of a dozen points or more to win. And then Illinois happened. The Illini took control of the game with a 52-point first half. Iowa trailed 61–39 with 16 minutes, 10 seconds to play. Catching up from 22 down? No problem.

The Hawkeyes started to chip away at the deficit. It was still sizeable, at 15 points, with 9:45 to go. But the Illini got hesitant on offense, while Iowa attacked the basket in desperation. And the Hawkeyes made it all the way back. "We got down a bit and just kept clawing away, and got back in it," Brad Lohaus recalled.

Iowa won the game 91–88 in overtime. Lohaus, who finished with 23 points and 12 rebounds, made a pair of clinching free throws with seven seconds left. "That game let us know we were never out of ballgames," guard Kevin Gamble said.

Iowa had never rallied from a bigger deficit to win a game in school history. And five days later, the Hawkeyes moved to No. 1 in the Associated Press poll for the first time ever. Iowa replaced Nevada–Las Vegas. The Runnin' Rebels had been knocked off by Oklahoma the week before.

"We had some good, level-headed seniors in Gamble, Lohaus, and [Gerry] Wright, so I had some good leadership," Davis said.

On the day Iowa moved to No. 1, the Hawkeyes faced another stern test. They had to play a 14–1 Purdue team at Mackey Arena. The Boilermakers were ranked fifth. The challenge grew when Roy

Marble, Iowa's leading scorer, suffered an eye injury with 11:27 remaining in the first half and didn't return.

Iowa still won the game, 70–67, as Purdue scored just two points over the last 4:48. The Boilermakers had been shooting 52 percent from the field over their first 14 games. But Iowa's defense limited Purdue to 39 percent and had a whopping 43–24 advantage on the glass to make up for Marble's absence.

Gamble scored 19 points, a career high at the time, and sophomore center Ed Horton added 14 points and eight rebounds as Iowa won its 17th consecutive game. That tied a school record set by the 1955–56 team, which had had its winning streak snapped 83–71 by Bill Russell and San Francisco in the NCAA title game.

"Beating a Gene Keady team in West Lafayette was no minor achievement," said Al Lorenzen, a junior forward on that team. "I just think we started to understand, 'Hey, we've got a good shot here.' You start to let things creep into your mind like, *We're good enough to win it all.*"

Three nights later, Iowa returned to Carver-Hawkeye Arena for a game against No. 3 Indiana. Coach Bob Knight's Hoosiers had already won at Ohio State, Michigan, and Michigan State, and would go on the win the NCAA title. But it was Iowa creating history on that night.

The Hawkeyes won their school-record 18th consecutive game, 101–88. It was the first time a Knight-coached team had ever allowed 100 points in a game. The previous high at IU was 92 in a two-point loss to Kentucky in the 1975 NCAA Tournament that ended the Hoosiers' 31-game winning streak and in a 19-point loss at Michigan on January 26, 1978.

"Coach Knight was more conservative, grinding it out," said Gerry Wright, a senior center on that team. "Tom didn't stop fast breaking, didn't stop swinging. The team that quit swinging was the team that was going to go down."

On that day, it was Indiana who blinked first. And it brought an end to arguably the best nine days in Iowa basketball history—victories over three top 10 teams, two of them on the road—establishing a school record for consecutive victories, and reaching No. 1.

"People just don't handle teams in that order," said Lorenzen, a forward. "That was special."

Two days later, Dennis Hopson scored 32 points as unranked Ohio State ended Iowa's winning streak 80–76 in Iowa City, and knocked it out of the No. 1 spot.

"Hopson was at the top of his game," Horton recalled. "He came into Carver and really put on a show. It was a wake-up call. Ohio State really opened our eyes that day."

Gary Williams was the Ohio State coach at the time. Davis had been a volunteer assistant at Maryland when Williams was a player there. Soon after, Davis became the freshman coach at Maryland and Williams served as his assistant.

When Davis got his first head coaching job, at Lafayette College in 1971, he took Williams along as his assistant with one stipulation—Williams also had to be the school's head soccer coach. They remained together for one more change of address. When Davis was hired at Boston College in 1977, Williams also joined him there. Williams later replaced Davis at Boston College when Davis took the Stanford job. And it was Williams, during his first season at Ohio State, who gave Davis his first defeat at Iowa, in the 19th game he coached. "We were so fired up for Indiana," Gamble said. "Reaching the 100-point barrier. Then we had a little letdown."

39 Two Teams, One Astronaut

The University of Iowa campus was the home to two college foot-ball teams from 1942 to 1944—the Iowa Hawkeyes and the Iowa Pre-Flight Seahawks.

As a way to prepare for World War II, the United States Navy commissioned preflight schools at the University of Iowa, the University of Georgia, the University of North Carolina, and Saint Mary's College.

Cadets received three months of training at each site—both physical training and aerial navigation and communications training. Graduates moved on to flight school or advanced flight training before being sent on to the Pacific Fleet.

The navy thought athletic endeavors—in this case, foot-ball—would be good preparation for World War II. College and professional athletes and coaches were recruited. During the war years, professional players were allowed to play for service teams. These became, essentially, all-star teams.

The Iowa Seahawks were the most powerful of all the preflight teams assembled. The coach in 1942 was Bernie Bierman, who had guided Minnesota to five national championships between 1932 and 1941. His players included Michigan standout Forest Evashevski, who would return to campus in 1952 as the Hawkeyes' head coach. Former Iowa running back Bus Mertes, who would go on to coach at Drake, played on all three Iowa preflight teams. Also on that 1942 team was John Glenn, who would go on to become the first American to orbit Earth, aboard *Friendship 7* on February 20, 1962.

The Seahawks played six teams in 1942 that had been ranked in the final Associated Press poll the year before. And 9 of their 10 games were played on the road. Only a 46–0 drubbing of Nebraska took place in Iowa Stadium because of scheduling conflicts. The Hawkeyes played seven home games that season.

The Seahawks finished 7–3 that first season, losing to Notre Dame, Ohio State, and Missouri. The AP poll included preflight school teams in 1943, and the Seahawks finished the season No. 2 in the country. Former Missouri coach Don Faurot took over coaching duties from Bierman. His assistants included Jim Tatum, who went on to coach Maryland to a national championship, and Bud Wilkinson, who later coached Oklahoma to an NCAA-record 47 consecutive victories.

The Seahawks won their first eight games that season, including a 25–0 victory over an Iowa team that managed just one first down and finished the season with a 1–6–1 record.

On November 20 the second-ranked Seahawks played at No. 1 Notre Dame. Iowa Pre-Flight had outscored its first eight opponents 232–84. Notre Dame had a 312–37 edge on its opponents. The Irish won the game 14–13. That loss cost Iowa Pre-Flight the mythical national championship.

Former Auburn coach Jack Meagher took over the Seahawks in 1944. They finished 10–1 and were sixth in the final AP poll. The only loss was a 12–7 decision to Michigan in the season opener. The last game the Seahawks ever played was a 30–6 November 25 victory over the Hawkeyes in Iowa Stadium before a crowd of 2,500.

Income from that game was $290.42. The cost to hire police and ticket sellers was $360.27. The game officials were paid $348.84. The Seahawks' share of gate receipts was $248.43. Scouting and other expenses came to $200.56. It was a loss for the 1–7 Hawkeyes in more ways than one.

40 Pickoff Artists

When Paul Krause set an NFL record with his 80th career interception in 1979, he broke Emlen Tunnell's record. Both are members of the Pro Football Hall of Fame, and both played football for the Iowa Hawkeyes.

Tunnell spent two seasons (1946–47) at Iowa, taking a long path to Iowa City. He started his career at Toledo but suffered a neck injury. Neither the army nor navy would let him enlist during World War II because of the injury, and he ended up in the Coast Guard.

There he met Jim Walker, who lettered at tackle for the Hawkeyes in 1939, 1940, and 1941. Walker talked about former Iowa players like Duke Slater and Ozzie Simmons. "So I knew blacks got a fair shake there," said Tunnell, who is from Bryn Mawr, Pennsylvania.

That's how Tunnell ended up at Iowa. One day, while fielding punts with a flair, he caught the eye of Dr. Eddie Anderson, who was starting his second term as Hawkeyes coach. "I remember [Anderson] stopping practice and calling everybody over to watch," Tunnell said. "That kind of embarrassed me. But Dr. Eddie was different. He'd let you do something your way if you didn't make mistakes."

Tunnell was a standout wide receiver as well as a kick returner, and caught three touchdown passes against Indiana in 1947. He returned home the summer before his senior season in 1948. Because his original college class had graduated, Emlen was eligible to play pro football. He received a form letter from the New York Giants, seeing if he'd be interested, and Tunnell hitchhiked his way there and asked for a tryout.

A standout at Iowa, Em Tunnell was the first African American inducted into the Pro Football Hall of Fame, in 1967.

Tunnell made the team and signed a contract—a $500 signing bonus and a one-year deal for $5,000. He was the first African American player in New York Giants history.

That was the start of a 14-season career, and a string of 158 consecutive games. He was moved to the secondary and played for the Giants' groundbreaking Umbrella defense, now known as the 4-3.

Tunnell picked off a record 79 passes for 1,282 yards. He returned 258 punts for 2,209 yards. "The reason I did so well on interceptions is that I never dropped any balls," Emlen said. "Other guys would start running before the catch. I always caught first."

Tunnell played 11 seasons for the Giants, then three more for Vince Lombardi's Green Bay Packers. "Lombardi was the only coach I knew who could give a pep talk and make you want to bust heads," said Tunnell, the first African American inducted into the Pro Football Hall of Fame (in 1967).

Krause was three years into his NFL career by then. He came to Iowa out of Burton, Michigan, where he was a four-sport star in high school. Recruited to Iowa by Jerry Burns, Krause was a three-year letterman from 1961 to 1963. He also played baseball for the Hawkeyes.

He played wide receiver and defensive back at Iowa, catching six touchdown passes as a senior. The Washington Redskins took Krause in the second round of the 1964 NFL Draft, the 18th player selected.

He made quite an NFL debut, picking off 12 passes as a rookie—including one in seven consecutive games—and earning All-Pro laurels. Krause was an eight-time Pro Bowl selection at safety during a 16-year career. Krause spent his final 12 seasons with the Minnesota Vikings, playing in four Super Bowls. He was enshrined in the Pro Football Hall of Fame in 1998.

Krause contemplated retirement after the 1978 season but came back to take a shot at Tunnell's interception record. Krause had 78 picks at the time. "I got an interception early in the season, but it began to look like I wouldn't get the record breaker," Krause said. "I had some opportunities, but some balls bounced off my chest or something happened."

But two interceptions in an overtime loss to the Los Angeles Rams, in the third-to-last game of the regular season, enabled Krause to pass another former Hawkeye and put his name in the record book.

41 Long's Second Senior Season

Iowa's magical 1985 Big Ten football season might not have happened without an assist from the NCAA. An assist, in the form of a rule change, that gave quarterback Chuck Long two senior seasons instead of one.

The NCAA did not allow freshmen to be redshirted in both 1980 and 1981, Long's freshman season at Iowa. Redshirting was brought back starting in 1982. A retroactive redshirt rule was passed at the NCAA convention in January 1984, and later approved by the Big Ten Conference in March. That new rule granted freshmen who played in no more than 20 percent of the games in either 1980 or 1981 another season of eligibility.

Long fell under that umbrella because he had taken snaps in just two games as a freshman—against Northwestern during the Big Ten season and against Washington in the Rose Bowl.

After Long passed for 461 yards and a school-record six touchdowns against Texas in the 1984 Freedom Bowl, he had a decision to make: head to the NFL or return to Iowa for another senior season. It was during practice for the bowl game that Long really began to weigh his options. "No. 1, I wanted to get my degree," said Long, who needed to complete six more hours of class work. "I knew we had a good team coming back. And my dream was always to be captain of a Rose Bowl team. So it all fell into place. I knew shortly after that bowl game that I was coming back."

Long sat on his decision for weeks, making sure it was the right one. At a news conference on February 5, 1985, he told the world he would play one more season for the Hawkeyes.

"We had high expectations," Long said. "And we lived up to them."

Coach Hayden Fry joked that Long's decision to come back "was the greatest recruiting job I ever did. But in the end the decision was his, and I think he made it for the best of reasons. He was having fun, and he wanted to be a college student one more year. The fact that we expected to have a strong football team undoubtedly played a role in his thinking, but mainly he just wanted to stay in college a while longer before embarking on a professional career. I wish more young men would follow his example."

Iowa started the 1995 season averaging 54.3 points in victories over Drake, Northern Illinois, and Iowa State, and took that momentum—and the No. 1 ranking in the Associated Press poll—into Big Ten play.

Iowa opened with a 35–31 victory over Michigan State in a game Fry had put on Long's shoulders. Iowa trailed 31–28 with the ball on the Spartans' 2-yard line and 31 seconds on the clock. Fry used his last timeout to plot strategy. "We're running a bootleg," he told his quarterback.

"I said, 'Are you sure? What if I don't make it?'" Long told his coach.

Fry said, "Charlie, don't worry about it. You're going to get in. Just run the play." Long faked a handoff the Ronnie Harmon, rolled to his right, and scored untouched.

After a 23–13 victory at Wisconsin, the Hawkeyes returned home for one of the biggest games in Kinnick Stadium history: No. 1 Iowa against No. 2 Michigan and Coach Bo Schembechler. Rob Houghtlin's last-second field goal from 29 yards gave the Hawkeyes a 12–10 victory.

A 49–10 victory at Northwestern was next, followed by a trip to Ohio State. Iowa's undefeated season and No. 1 perch in the AP poll ended in the rain, 22–13. Buckeyes fans tore down the goal posts in Ohio Stadium afterward.

"That's when you could say the Big Ten was no longer the Big Two and the Little Eight," Long said. "We had established that in 1981. But 1985 cemented it."

Iowa earned the Big Ten title after Long came back to win with victories over Illinois (59–0), Purdue (27–24), and Minnesota (31–9). The 10–2 season, and Long's career, ended with a disappointing 45–28 loss to UCLA in the Rose Bowl.

"I think that was Hayden's best opportunity to win the Rose Bowl," Long said. "We felt good going into that game. It didn't turn out the way we wanted, and that game still sticks with me. I wanted it bad for us. But more so for Coach Fry."

42 An Unlikely Title Run

Iowa limped into the Windy City, and the Big Ten Basketball Tournament, in 2001. Literally and figuratively.

Coach Steve Alford's team, 17–4 in late January, lost seven of their last eight regular-season games. A fractured right kneecap sidelined Luke Recker, the Hawkeyes' leading scorer, for the final nine games of the regular season. Ryan Hogan, one of the first guards off the bench, missed the final four regular-season games with a knee injury. Even strong play from forward Reggie Evans, a second-team All–Big Ten selection, and point guard Dean Oliver, a third-team choice, couldn't keep the ship afloat.

Iowa was the Big Ten's sixth seed, and faced No. 11 seed Northwestern in a first-round game in Chicago. "I hope you packed for the whole week," Iowa guard Brody Boyd said. "We're going to win it all." Yeah, right. Even the first-round game against Northwestern looked ominous. The Wildcats had defeated Iowa 69–61 in Evanston on February 10, ending a 32-game regular-season Big Ten losing streak. "I'm sure there are plenty of people laughing at us right now," Oliver said after that game.

That was the loss that Alford pointed to as the turning point in his team's late-season slide. "When we lost to Northwestern to break their 32-game string, I think that really took the air out of us," said Alford.

Iowa had not lost to Northwestern twice in the same season since 1958–59, but that streak appeared to be in serious jeopardy. "I'm sure, being in their home city, they're going to be confident knowing they're playing somebody they've already beaten," Alford said.

But that confidence didn't carry over to the rematch. Evans, a native of Pensacola, Florida, who grew up a fan of the Chicago Bulls, recorded his 20th double-double of the season in a 72–55 Iowa victory. The game was played at the United Center, the Bulls' home court. "It was an honor to get to play in their gym," Evans said after a 20-point, 14-rebound effort.

Turns out it was the start of a long stay for Evans and his teammates in Chicago, where every day was an NCAA elimination game.

Iowa rallied from a 11-point halftime deficit to defeat No. 24 Ohio State 75–66 in the quarterfinals. That snapped the Buckeyes' nine-game winning streak. Iowa shot 54 percent from the field the second half, compared to 25 percent shooting for the Buckeyes.

Evans was limited to six points and eight rebounds, but Oliver, Glen Worley, and Duez Henderson carried the load offensively as Iowa scored 53 second-half points. It was also the Hawkeyes' 20th victory of the season.

"We came here thinking this was a fresh start," Oliver said. "We came in trying to win the championship. Now a couple of positive things have happened."

Penn State, another team fighting for its NCAA life, was the next challenge in the semifinals. The Nittany Lions had advanced with a victory against second-seeded Michigan State. Evans scored a career-high 30 points and matched a career high with 18 rebounds in Iowa's 94–74 thumping. Penn State finished with 18 rebounds as a team.

Iowa fans greeted Evans with chants of "Reg-gie, Reg-gie" late in the game. "Whenever they chant your name, you know you're doing something good," Evans said.

Iowa shot 57.4 percent from the floor for its second victory in 19 hours. The team had won just one game over the final 31 days of the regular season. "Maybe we can win a championship and get me a ring," Oliver said.

Iowa faced Indiana, where Alford had been an All-American guard, in the title game. The Hoosiers had defeated Illinois, the No. 1 seed, by a 58–56 margin in the other semifinal.

Evans was named the tournament's most valuable player after an eight-point, 11-rebound performance against the Hoosiers. He also blocked Kirk Haston's three-pointer from the top of the key in the final seconds to secure a 63–61 victory. Evans finished with a tournament-record 51 rebounds.

"What these kids have done is truly remarkable and amazing," Alford said of a team that went from winning four games in the final four weeks of the regular season to winning four in four days. "We went from the bubble to a team that won a Big Ten championship."

Oliver added 12 points and joined Gary Grant of Michigan and Bruce Douglas of Illinois as the only players in Big Ten history to get to 1,500 career points, 500 assists, and 200 steals.

"All the hard work, the effort, the blood, sweat, and tears we put into it, I couldn't ask for anything more," Oliver said.

Before Big Ten commissioner Jim Delany presented the Hawkeyes with the trophy, he called their four-day run "an unpredictable, unprecedented championship performance."

Iowa finished the riches-to-rags-to-riches season by drawing Creighton in a first-round NCAA Tournament game in Uniondale, New York. The Hawkeyes advanced with a 69–56 victory. Evans scored 12 of his 19 points in the last five minutes to put Creighton away. A 61 percent free-throw shooter, Evans ran off nine straight at one point and finished 13 of 15 at the line. Duez Henderson added 16 points, Oliver 15, and Worley 12.

Kentucky bounced Iowa from the tournament in the second round, 92–79. Oliver scored 26 points in his final game. The Hawkeyes' late-season rally resulted in a 23–12 record.

"I've had an unreal career," Oliver said. "It has been a great experience being a Hawkeye."

43 The Best in His Field

Baltimore Ravens guard Marshal Yanda has been called the best offensive lineman in the NFL. High praise for a guy who wasn't drafted until the third round of the 2007 NFL Draft after two solid seasons at Iowa.

Marshal Yanda has enjoyed a successful career on the gridiron beyond Iowa.

"So he's really good at what he does, in terms of his job description," Iowa football coach Kirk Ferentz said. "But I always felt the thing that makes Marshal so special is what he adds to a football team, whether it's the offensive line group, or the offensive team, or the entire team. Not by the speeches he gives but just the way he goes about things."

Yanda is part of a growing tradition at Iowa. The program has produced a long list of offensive linemen who have made it in the NFL. Ferentz, a former offensive line coach himself, is proud of that tradition. And every player has a different story. Robert Gallery was the second player selected in the 2004 NFL Draft. Yanda was the 86th player taken in 2007. But these players have similar traits—they are no-nonsense players who always strive to get better. They make the most of the coaching they got at Iowa. They're universally low on fanfare, high on success.

A reporter from the *Baltimore Sun* approached Yanda in 2014, three days before a game with New Orleans, and asked him whether he was the best player in Ravens history. Yanda's answer sums up his approach to football: "It's tough, because I'm a team guy, and I don't worry about that stuff," Yanda said. "If I'm worried about that stuff, then I'm not worried about what's most important, which is blocking New Orleans. If you get in that mind-set, you're going to take steps backward. You can go from the top to the bottom in a half. Not a game, not a year. In a half."

Yanda grew up in Anamosa, Iowa, 38 miles from Iowa City. Playing for the Hawkeyes had been his dream. But the son of a fourth-generation dairy farmer had to put that dream on hold because he didn't have the required grades.

He spent two seasons at North Iowa Area Community College in Mason City, a school that dropped its football program in 2009. And then, with a little arm-twisting from Iowa assistant coach Reese Morgan, Ferentz offered Yanda a scholarship.

Ferentz's first take after seeing Yanda work out? "He wasn't very impressive," Ferentz said. "And that's being kind."

Two seasons later, Ferentz had a different impression. Yanda started every game, at left guard or right tackle, during the 2005 season. He started every game at tackle as a senior in 2006. He was named a permanent team captain and most valuable player on the offense. He also received the Hayden Fry Extra Heartbeat Award. And then Ferentz started to campaign for him with NFL scouts and general managers. "During his senior year, I told all the pro guys, "Look, your coaches are going to hate him when they see him running around in shorts, but once they see him play actual football, they'll come back and thank you for drafting him," Ferentz said.

Yanda has been a fixture in the Ravens' starting lineup since 2010, and enjoyed the spoils of a Super Bowl title in 2012. He is a five-time Pro Bowler. He was also rewarded with a four-year, $31.9 million contract extension in October 2015.

But Yanda, who returns to the Iowa football complex each off-season to train with Chris Doyle, the Hawkeyes' strength coach, didn't become successful by chasing the dollar. He became successful because he wants to be the best at his trade. Now he leads by example.

"To me, when Baltimore pays Marshal Yanda, they pay not only to block well, but it's the other things," Ferentz said. "That's why they're such a good organization. They reward that."

44 Whoa, Nellie

Don Nelson was an All-American forward at Iowa as a senior in 1961–62, averaging 23.8 points a game. He also left a few hours shy of a degree. Fifty years later, in May 2012, Nelson returned to Iowa City, donned a cap and gown, and got that degree in physical education during graduation ceremonies at Carver-Hawkeye Arena.

"When I went to college, I was the first male in my family with a chance to go," recalled Nelson, who graduated from Rock Island High School in Rock Island, Illinois, in 1958. "One thing that was important to me was to get a degree. I was in the pros for so long that I had to postpone it until now. But it was a goal of mine, and I achieved it."

Nelson, a two-time All–Big Ten forward who averaged 21.2 points for his 72-game Hawkeyes career, nearly stuck around and picked up that degree 50 years earlier. His coach at Iowa, Sharm Scheuerman, offered Nelson and Joel Novak, his high school and college teammate, $6,000 to coach the freshman team. "That was a lot of money at the time," Novak said. "Nellie was going to stay and get his degree. But all of a sudden he said, 'I'm going to go pro and finish my degree later.' I didn't blame him. He was a hot property."

Nelson, a two-time All–Big Ten selection for the Hawkeyes, was selected by the Chicago Zephyrs in the third round of the 1962 NBA Draft, the 17th pick overall. Nelson played 14 NBA seasons and was part of five championship teams with the Boston Celtics. He spent his final 11 seasons in Boston, and the Celtics retired his jersey (No. 19) in 1978. Nelson scored 10,898 points and grabbed 5,192 rebounds during his pro career.

He was then an NBA head coach for 31 seasons. He coached for the Milwaukee Bucks, Golden State Warriors, New York Knicks, Dallas Mavericks, and then returned to the Warriors for a second tour of duty. He retired after the 2009–10 season. His 1,335 coaching victories are an NBA record.

Nelson was elected into the Naismith Memorial Basketball Hall of Fame in September 2012. But four months earlier, he had realized another goal—picking up his college degree at 71 years old.

Nelson fulfilled his foreign language requirement through correspondence. His NBA coaching schedule didn't make it possible for him to return and officially get that diploma, but retirement opened the door for his memorable trip back to Iowa City in 2012.

"A lot of guys never go back and finish," Nelson said. "I thought, *By golly, when I retire I'm going to get mine.*"

45 The Norm Game

When Kirk Ferentz was hired to replace Hayden Fry as Iowa's football coach before the 1999 season, he brought in Norm Parker as his defensive coordinator. It was a wise decision. Parker was the mastermind behind some great Hawkeyes defenses before health issues forced him to retire following the 2011 season. Parker passed away in 2014.

"He impacted an awful lot of folks," Ferentz said. "It wasn't just the defensive players. That was a big part of my thinking when we hired Norm too. When we hit bumpy waters, which you always do, it's going to be pretty hard to rock his boat, just because he was one of those guys. He could put a good spin on things."

Parker, who coached college football for more than four decades at eight different schools, loved the challenge of finding a way to stop an opponent. That included Georgia Tech in the 2010 Orange Bowl. The Yellow Jackets came into the game with an effective but old-school attack. Coach Paul Johnson used the triple-option. Georgia Tech entered the game second nationally in rushing at 307.2 yards a game, 12th in total offense (442.7 yards), and 13th in scoring (35.3 points per game). Running back Jonathan Dwyer had gained better than 1,300 yards on the season, and had scored 36 career touchdowns.

"Words can't describe how exciting the offense is to be a part of—to know in any part of the game a big play is going to happen," Dwyer said.

Parker's defense was ninth nationally in scoring defense (15.5 points per game) and 10th in total defense (286.7 yards). Parker relished the challenge of unlocking the key to the triple-option. "If you're a football purist, this thing really is sort of fun," he said in the days leading up to the game. "I'm having fun preparing for it."

Parker had plenty of fun after the game too. Iowa beat Georgia Tech 24–14. The Yellow Jackets managed just 143 yards on the ground, and 12 through the air. "It's disappointing because we haven't played many games like that," Coach Johnson said.

Georgia Tech had no answer for Iowa defensive end Adrian Clayborn. He had nine tackles and two sacks, and was voted the game's most valuable player.

And Parker had another feather in his cap. In Iowa that Orange Bowl is better known as the Norm Game.

Ferentz was one of three speakers to eulogize Parker at his funeral. He singled out three games Iowa won during the Parker era.

The first game came in 2000, a 27–17 victory over No. 12 Northwestern in Iowa City. The Wildcats were averaging 38.4

points and 486.3 yards of total offense. Parker's defense held them to 17 points and 377 yards in a 27–17 Iowa victory.

"I was totally thinking one thing, and he was totally thinking another," Ferentz said. "We were 180 degrees apart on what I thought we would do in that game. And I'm glad we went with his choice. He knew our team better, he knew what to do. And that was a huge win for us."

The second game was a 34–9 victory at No. 8 Michigan in 2002. It cleared a big hurdle in Iowa's run to an undefeated Big Ten season. Iowa held the Wolverines to 171 yards of total offense. And Parker, who was from Chelsea, Michigan, was on top of the world. "Being a Michigan State and Eastern Michigan guy, that was a big win for him," Ferentz said.

The third game was the victory in the 2010 Orange Bowl. "The bowl game was pretty special," Ferentz said. The Norm Game.

46 Looking for the Ultimate Victory

This is what Fran McCaffery inherited when he became Iowa's men's basketball coach in 2010: three straight losing seasons, no NCAA Tournament bids in four years, and a Carver-Hawkeye Arena full of apathy.

An average of 9,550 fans bought tickets to Iowa's home games in 2009–10, an all-time low in an arena that opened in 1983 and seats 15,400. And that was tickets *sold*. Actual attendance averaged less than 6,000.

McCaffery left the comfort of Siena, where he had won 27 games in each of the previous two seasons, to take on the challenge of a Big Ten program with a dusty track record of success. "I wanted it from day one," McCaffery said the day after he accepted athletic director Gary Barta's offer to replace Todd Lickliter as coach.

McCaffery faced the most overwhelming rebuilding challenge for an Iowa coach since Lute Olson, who arrived in 1974–75 and took over a program that had not had a winning Big Ten record in four seasons and had won only eight games the year before he arrived.

Four seasons later, Olson's 1978–79 Hawkeyes team won a share of the Big Ten title and played in the NCAA Tournament for the first time since 1970. His 1979–80 team earned Iowa's first Final Four appearance since 1956.

Iowa had not played a fan-friendly style of basketball under Lickliter. In three seasons, his teams failed to score at least 60 points in 54 games. They didn't reach 50 points 18 times. "I let my guys play," McCaffery said on the eve of his first season at Iowa. "At the same time, there's got to be a plan behind it. You don't just turn them loose and play with reckless abandon. We can't have that. But we have to be able to understand that sometimes, when you give talented players space, it's a lot better than coming down and playing against a stacked defense every possession."

Iowa's scoring pace has increased under McCaffery. So have the victories.

McCaffery-coached teams have won at least 20 games in each of the last four seasons. That hasn't happened since Tom Davis–coached teams won at least 20 games in five consecutive seasons (1994–95 to 1998–99).

In 2015–16 McCaffery's team was ranked in the national polls for a third straight season, and made it inside the top 10 for the first time since 2001–02. His 2014–15 team won an NCAA Tournament game for the first time in 14 years. Yes, the program has a pulse again.

"I don't know that there's anything magical to it other than if you recruit good kids that work hard and believe in each other, you can win," McCaffery said. "Even against the teams in this league, which is not easy."

But the Iowa coach is on another mission that goes beyond wins and losses. He has devoted countless hours of time and energy to the fight against cancer.

The disease has hit close to home. McCaffery lost both his parents to colon cancer. And his son, Patrick, had a malignant tumor removed from his thyroid in 2014.

McCaffery and his wife, Margaret, have jumped headfirst into finding a way to beat this disease. They host a Coaches vs. Cancer outing every year in Iowa City to raise money for cancer research.

"When we started this, we never realized that our son would end up having cancer," McCaffery said. "And that, in a way, created a different level of awareness for our event."

At the 2015 Final Four, McCaffery received the Coaches vs. Cancer Champions Award. It is presented annually to a college coach who assists in fund-raising and education in the fight against cancer.

Raising money and awareness for the Adolescent and Young Adult Cancer Program at the University of Iowa is the McCafferys' pet project. McCaffery will tell you that helping beat cancer would be the most important victory of his career. "Yes, it would," he said.

47 Thunderfoot, All-American

When push came to shove, Reggie Roby had to make a decision: did he want to throw and hit a ball, or kick one?

A gifted athlete at Waterloo East High School, Roby decided to pass on baseball and pursue a college football career as a punter. Iowa coach Hayden Fry was glad he did. Roby was a two-time All-American for the Hawkeyes, and went on to a 16-year NFL career. He passed away in 2005, at age 43.

Dan McCarney, an assistant coach on Fry's staff at the time, went to the first game of Roby's senior season at East. Sitting by him was Dave Triplett, a former Hawkeyes player and then an assistant coach to Earle Bruce at Iowa State. After watching Roby put the opening kickoff through the uprights, McCarney said to Triplett, "I believe that's a Division I leg we just saw out there."

Both Iowa and Iowa State offered Roby a scholarship. Bruce made his offer over the phone. Fry did it in person. "They said he was coming and I didn't really believe it," Roby said. "When [Fry] walked into my house, I felt like I must be the most important guy in the world. I thought, *I've got to do this. I've got to follow this guy.*"

McCarney was the one who told Fry Roby had accepted Iowa's scholarship offer. "Coach Fry and I were hollering and jumping up and down," McCarney said. "That was about as high as I ever saw Coach Fry's boots get off the ground, when I told him we got Reggie."

Fry knew what a difference Roby's leg would make in the all-important field-position battle. Maybe the best example of that came in 1981, Roby's junior season. The Hawkeyes were in

All-American Reggie Roby shows his form in practice before the 1982 Rose Bowl.

contention for a piece of the Big Ten title when they traveled to Wisconsin on November 14. If the Badgers won, they'd have the inside track to the championship.

But after Iowa took a 17–0 halftime lead, Fry buttoned up the offense and rested on Roby's leg. "I told the players at halftime that we didn't want to take any chances and give Wisconsin good field position with cheap turnovers," Fry said. "So we relied on Reggie to keep booming the ball to the other end of the field, and we figured the defense could do the rest." Iowa won the game 17–7 and went on to win a share of the Big Ten title and play in the 1982 Rose Bowl.

Roby averaged an NCAA-record 49.8 yards per punt in 1981, and set Iowa records for punting average in a game (55.8 yards) and career (45.4). Roby was a first-team All-American in both 1981 and 1982.

Selected by Miami in the sixth round of the 1983 NFL Draft, Roby punted for five different franchises before retiring in 2002. He was a three-time Pro Bowl selection and had a 43.3-yard career average. Ten of his seasons were with the Dolphins, and Roby's leg left an impression on Coach Don Shula.

"Often on walkthroughs in domed stadiums the day before the game, he always would try to hit the top of the dome with a punt," Shula recalled after Roby had passed away. "He sometimes succeeded, which illustrates just how strong a leg he had. Reggie helped define the position. Even after he retired, every time I saw a long, high punt, it always reminded me of one of his kicks."

48 Shooter Extraordinaire

Purdue's Rick Mount got the lion's share of attention, but there was another dynamic scorer in the Big Ten during the 1969–70 basketball season. His name was John Howard Getty Johnson, better known as J.J. to Iowa basketball fans. Johnson averaged 27.9 points as a senior, and 31.8 points against Big Ten competition. The Hawkeyes finished 14–0 and won an outright conference title.

"John Johnson is the Big Ten's most valuable player, or there isn't one," Iowa coach Ralph Miller said after his team won 115–100 at Northwestern to finish Big Ten play undefeated. "He is the one who led us to the Big Ten title." But Mount, who averaged 57 points in two games against the Hawkeyes and 39.4 points for the season, was named the winner of the Big Ten / Chicago Tribune Most Valuable Player Award.

Johnson's scoring success is unmatched in Iowa history. He scored a school-record 49 points against Northwestern in a 116–97 victory at Iowa Field House, making 20 of 33 shots from the field and 9 free throws in 10 attempts. He broke his own record of 46 against Wisconsin-Milwaukee as a junior.

"Northwestern tried a box-and-one, and everything else, against him [defensively]," said Glenn Vidnovic, Johnson's roommate and a starting forward on that Iowa team. "Nothing worked."

Johnson also scored 38 and 37 in games against Ohio State, 36 against Michigan State, 34 against Michigan, 33 against Minnesota and Indiana, 32 in the other meeting with Northwestern, and 31 against Wisconsin. He scored less than 22 points in just one Big Ten game, a 17-point outing against Illinois.

Miller figured he'd have a good team at Iowa. But Johnson's shooting was a pleasant surprise. "I expected Johnson to have a great year, but his shooting has been close to fantastic," Miller said late in the Big Ten season. "In practice before the season he was shooting well, but it's hard to believe he's a 60 percent shooter. If I had to pick one surprise about this team, that would be it—not John's overall play but his tremendous shooting all season."

Johnson, a first-team All–Big Ten and All-America selection as a senior, finished the Big Ten season shooting 60.7 percent from the field, making 181 of 298 shots. He also shot 80.6 percent from the free-throw line. "I've never seen anyone shoot like that," said Vidnovic, one of four starters to average at least 17.3 points on a team that scored a Big Ten–record 102.9 points a game.

Johnson was a 6'7" forward who could play like a guard. "He wasn't that fast, but he could dribble," Vidnovic said. "He could freeze you just enough to get that shot off, in that little two-foot-square area. And it went in."

Johnson averaged 27.9 points and shot 56.9 percent in all games that season. He was selected by the Cleveland Cavaliers with the seventh pick of the 1970 NBA Draft, and had a 12-year career. He was a two-time NBA All-Star and played with his Iowa teammate, Fred Brown, on Seattle's 1979 NBA championship team.

49 Remember the Alamo

Nate Kaeding will always remember the 2001 Alamo Bowl. "We were all pretty geared up for that game," Kaeding said. "We were playing it like it was our Super Bowl." While this game against Texas Tech didn't have the buzz of a Rose Bowl or Orange Bowl, it was a significant moment in time for the Kirk Ferentz coaching era at Iowa.

Ferentz replaced Hayden Fry in 1999 and won one game his first season. Three wins followed in 2000, when Kaeding was a freshman. Iowa doubled its victory total in 2001 to earn its first bowl game under Ferentz. It was also the Hawkeyes' first bowl appearance since 1997. "While 6–5 wasn't the record we strived for this season, we made significant improvement as a football team and as a program," Ferentz said.

Iowa's chances of winning the Alamo Bowl didn't look promising after Ladell Betts, who had led the Hawkeyes in rushing for a fourth straight season, was injured on the first drive of the game and couldn't return. In stepped Aaron Greving, a sophomore from Ames, who had the game of his career. He was named the most valuable offensive player after rushing for 115 yards and a touchdown in 25 carries.

The game was tied 16–16 when Iowa quarterback Kyle McCann engineered his team on an eight-play, 53-yard drive that put the ball on the Texas Tech 30. With 44 seconds remaining, Kaeding came in to try a 47-yard field goal. "I was feeling pressure, absolutely," Kaeding said. "I certainly knew what it was all about."

Kaeding drilled the kick, then Bob Sanders made an interception in the end zone on the final play of the game to secure the 19–16 victory. It was Iowa's first bowl victory since 1996. "The Hawks are back," Ferentz, microphone in hand, told the 10,000 Iowa fans in attendance at the Alamodome. "Here we go."

Kaeding, who made four of five field goals that day, said the victory set the table for future success. "It was that moment where Kirk and the guys in my class were given hope and confirmation that what we were doing was right, and the program was moving in the right direction," Kaeding said. "Getting a win on a national stage was really exciting, after going through a bowl drought there for several years. Winning it gave us confidence going forward into that off-season, and the results played out over the course of the next year."

Iowa would share the Big Ten title with Ohio State in 2002, going 8–0. A 38–17 loss to USC in the Orange Bowl ended an 11–2 season. The Hawkeyes were ranked eighth in the final Associated Press poll, the program's highest finish since 1960. Quarterback Brad Banks was a runner-up in the Heisman Trophy voting, and Kaeding won the Lou Groza Award as the nation's best kicker.

Looking back, Ferentz says now that getting to a bowl game in his third season wasn't part of a master plan. "We didn't necessarily have a timetable," Ferentz said. "How could you?"

But momentum for the Ferentz era started in 2001. And it was capped off in San Antonio, with that victory against Texas Tech in the Alamo Bowl. "It was really a fun day for us," Kaeding said.

50 John Streif

Bump Elliott left Michigan to become Iowa's athletic director in 1972. He is known as the man who hired a long list of successful coaches, including Dan Gable, Lute Olson, Hayden Fry, and Tom Davis.

Elliott will tell you none of them were his best hire, however. That distinction goes to a man the casual fan might not know, a man who put others before himself for 40 years as the Hawkeyes' assistant athletic trainer, travel coordinator, and ego-free father figure. His name is John Streif. "It was the best hire we ever made," Elliott said of Streif. "I mean that sincerely."

Streif, a native of Manchester and an Iowa graduate, had been an assistant athletic trainer at West Point Military Academy when his alma mater hired him in 1972. He immediately became the student-athlete's best friend. Not every school has a John Streif. "That would be impossible," Iowa football coach Kirk Ferentz said. "I think it's fair to say that everyone who was here learned a lot from John Streif."

In 2009, when the university was doing fund-raising for enhancements to Carver-Hawkeye Arena, former star point guard Ronnie Lester donated $100,000 to the University of Iowa Foundation in Streif's name to help with the project. The arena's training room is now named after Streif. "He's so selfless, hardworking, and dedicated," Lester said. "He's just a great, great person."

In 1994 Streif was honored with the development of an endowed athletic scholarship in his name, established by former Iowa basketball players. And in 1997 Streif was named cowinner of the annual Chris Street Award. That is presented annually to "a Hawkeye player who best exemplifies the spirit, enthusiasm, and intensity of Chris Street." Street died in an automobile accident on January 19, 1993, in the middle of his junior season.

In 2010 Streif was honored at an appreciation luncheon at the Iowa Memorial Union ballroom in Iowa City.

Vince Brookins was an outstanding forward on Iowa's 1980 Final Four team. He struggled with a hand injury his first two seasons at Iowa, but Streif's unsinkable spirit kept him afloat. "The environment around John was always so encouraging," Brookins said.

Streif announced his retirement in December 2012. He did it with a press release, no fanfare. But the adulation still came. "John's service and dedication to our student-athletes, coaches, and staff members is second to none," Iowa athletic director Gary Barta said. "He has touched the lives of so many people, within the University of Iowa, the Big Ten Conference, and college athletics." Barta added, "We know he can never be replaced."

And that is the true legacy of John Streif.

51 Yes, Darling

Chuck Darling would be considered old-school by today's standards. He made a name for himself with a deadly hook shot, which has pretty much disappeared from the game of basketball.

But there's nothing old-school about this: the 6'8" center averaged 25.5 points as a senior at Iowa during the 1951–52 season. Only John Johnson (27.9 in 1969–70) and Fred Brown (27.6 in 1970–71) have averaged more points in a season for the Hawkeyes.

Darling was named a consensus All-American in 1952, the second in school history. (Murray Wier was the other, in 1948.) Also, the *Chicago Tribune* named Darling the Big Ten's most valuable player. And he was Iowa's MVP.

Darling helped Coach Bucky O'Connor's team finish 19–3 overall, second in the Big Ten (11–3), a game behind Illinois. His accomplishments went beyond his scoring in the post. Darling set an Iowa record with 30 rebounds against Wisconsin on March 3, 1952. He also had 34 points in that game, but Iowa lost 78–75 to the Badgers in the final Big Ten game of the season. The 30 rebounds wiped out Darling's previous record of 25, which he had the year before against Purdue. His rebounding average of 17.6 per game in 1950–51 remains another school mark.

A Phi Beta Kappa student, Darling was drafted by the Rochester Royals in the 1952 NBA Draft. But he elected to play AAU ball for the Phillips Oilers, a decision that led him to the 1956 Olympics in Melbourne, Australia.

In the final round of the Olympic tryouts in Kansas City, the Oilers faced a college All-Star team coached by O'Connor. The roster included All-American center Bill Russell of San Francisco, a team that had just defeated O'Connor's Hawkeyes in the NCAA title game in Evanston, Illinois.

Darling outplayed Russell, scoring 21 points and adding 10 rebounds in a 79–75 victory. "That game was the highlight of my career," Darling said.

O'Connor, who would have been the Olympic coach that year had his team won, gave Darling all the credit. "Darling beat us," O'Connor said. "He played the finest game I have ever seen him play."

Russell and Iowa's Carl Cain joined Darling on that 1956 Olympic team. They won the gold medal with an 89–55 drubbing of the Soviet Union.

52 Not a Coach, an Educator

When Iowa athletic director Bump Elliott hired George Raveling to replace Lute Olson as the men's basketball coach in the spring of 1983, he did so with no preconceived notions.

"I felt he was a good basketball coach who would be a good fit for Iowa," Elliott said. "I wasn't thinking about whether or not we should have a black coach." Raveling left Washington State to start the next chapter of his coaching life. And he was Iowa's first African American men's basketball coach.

Gems from George

George Raveling was never at a loss for words in his three seasons as Iowa's basketball coach. He majored in self-deprecating candor. Here are some gems from the 1983–84 season, his first at Iowa, when his team struggled through a 13–15 season and tied for seventh in the Big Ten (6–12).

Ohio State 65, Iowa 54 (January 26, Columbus, Ohio)
"I know there was a lot of media hype about this being their little guys going against our big guys. They might not be 6'10", but some of them jump 6'10"."

Indiana 54, Iowa 47 (January 28, Bloomington, Indiana)
"Somehow, the good Lord has got to call this off."

Illinois 54, Iowa 52 (double overtime) (February 2, Iowa City)
"This is the most disappointing loss I've ever been associated with since I started playing basketball in the seventh grade."

Purdue 48, Iowa 46 (February 4, Iowa City)
"We seem to find ways to lose. We can't hit the big shot."

Purdue 79, Iowa 58 (February 9, West Lafayette, Indiana)
"It was an extremely poor performance, and I don't know the reason for it. If I did, I wouldn't be coaching basketball at Iowa. I'd be making a million dollars somewhere."

Illinois 73, Iowa 53 (February 12, Champaign, Illinois)
Asked if he could get his team to play hard the rest of the season, Raveling responded, "To be honest, I'm not sure. I don't want to lie to you."

Indiana 49, Iowa 45 (February 16, Iowa City)
"Iowa doesn't need a coach," he said after watching his team score just two points in the final 9:54 of the game. "I'm stealing money, because the players don't listen to me."

Raveling's final two Hawkeyes teams won at least 20 games, had identical 10–8 conference records, and made it to the NCAA Tournament.

Raveling stayed just three seasons, and his last two teams won at least 20 games and made the NCAA Tournament. He also served as an assistant coach to Indiana's Bob Knight on the gold medal–winning 1984 US Olympic team.

Raveling's time at Iowa was anything but routine. The door to his office said EDUCATOR, not COACH. Raveling and his staff wore warm-up suits during games. And he coached with his heart on his sleeve. After a double-overtime loss at Iowa State in 1984, Raveling said, "This was a tragedy. I'd almost rather be dead than disappoint all the Iowa fans."

He would travel to statewide I-Club events with Iowa wrestling coach and icon Dan Gable. Raveling said Gable gave him a tip he used for the rest of his career: "Always include one kid on your team for leadership."

Raveling also drew national attention when a reporter from the *Cedar Rapids Gazette* named Bob Denney, interviewing him about being the first black coach at Iowa, discovered Raveling had an original copy of Dr. Martin Luther King Jr.'s 1963 "I Have a Dream" speech. "I was a security guard and I was assigned to the podium," Raveling said. "I was maybe three feet from him." After the speech, Raveling approached Dr. King. "I just said, 'Dr. King, could I have that copy?'" Raveling said. "And he turned and handed it to me."

Raveling had a 54–38 record in his three seasons at Iowa. When he took the job at Southern California after the 1985–86 season, Raveling left behind a stockpile of talent that his successor, Tom Davis, coached to a 30–5 season.

When Raveling left Iowa City, there was a feeling that his move had racial overtones because Iowa was a predominately white state. Raveling downplayed that in an interview more than 20 years later. "From a social standpoint, it was difficult for me to really find a comfort zone that I needed," Raveling said. "But I couldn't even tell you one racial incident that happened during my tenure there. I don't remember anyone ever putting me in an uncomfortable position or anything like that from a racial standpoint."

Raveling, in fact, regrets leaving Iowa when he did. "To be candid with you, If I had to do it all over again, I would have stayed," Raveling said. "Probably the biggest mistake I made in my coaching career was leaving Iowa."

Raveling left USC in the fall of 1994, after being seriously injured in an automobile accident, and, following two brief broadcasting stints, went to work for Nike. He was enshrined in the Naismith Memorial Basketball Hall of Fame in September 2015. "It's been a magical ride, and to have this bestowed upon me at 78 years old is an incredible experience," Raveling said. "It's humbling and it's certainly appreciated."

53 White Gold

Iowa basketball coach Fran McCaffery has made a living at mining lightly recruited prospects and watching them turn to gold during their four-year careers.

When he was coaching at Siena, the first player McCaffery signed was Kenny Hasbrouck. "We beat Jacksonville for him," McCaffery said. "We got him in June. He visited on graduation weekend." Hasbrouck started 28 games as a freshman and went on to score 1,917 career points.

But Aaron White might have been the most under-the-radar find McCaffery has had as a coach. A forward from Strongsville, Ohio, White had one offer from a Big Ten school. That was Iowa. His top two schools were the Hawkeyes and Duquesne, located in Pittsburgh, Pennsylvania, two hours from his home. White's father,

Forward Aaron White celebrates the score in a 2011 game against Boise State.

Rick, thought the Atlantic-10 school was better suited for his son. In this case, father didn't know best. "He felt extremely slighted that he didn't have any other big-time offers besides Iowa," Rick said. "He had that fire in his stomach, and he liked Fran, and it was the Big Ten. And that's what he went for. He was right."

Iowa had gone 11–20 in McCaffery's first season, and won just four Big Ten games, when White arrived on campus. He scored 19 points and grabbed 10 rebounds in his first collegiate game, against Chicago State. White became the first Iowa freshman to record a double-double in his college debut since Jess Settles did it against Drake in 1993.

The 19 points were the most for a Hawkeyes rookie in his first game since freshmen regained eligibility in the 1972–73 season. The last freshman to score 19 points in his first game was Dick Ives, against Nebraska, in a game 68 seasons earlier.

White and Settles are two of four Iowa players to record double-doubles in their first collegiate game. The others were center Michael Payne (13 points, 10 rebounds against Northern Illinois in 1981) and guard Dean Oliver (10 points and 12 assists against Chicago State in 1997).

White went on to have a very productive career at Iowa. He scored at least 20 points in six straight games late in the 2014–15 season. The final game in that streak was a 26-point outing against Davidson as Iowa won an NCAA Tournament game for the first time since 2001.

White earned first-team All–Big Ten honors in his swan song season. He finished as Iowa's second-leading career scorer (1,859 points) and third-leading rebounder (901). He made more free throws (618) than any other Big Ten player in the last 50 seasons and ranks No. 3 all-time. He was the first Iowa player to lead the team in rebounding four straight seasons. He played in 140 career games, a school record. All this from a player who had no other Big Ten scholarship offers.

A Fond Farewell

Aaron White ended his Iowa basketball career on top of his game. After reaching the 20-point mark 15 times in his first 133 games as a Hawkeye, White caught fire and led his team to its first NCAA victory since 2001.

White's hot streak started with a 29-point effort in a 68–60 victory over Illinois on February 25. That game was essentially an NCAA play-in game. He followed that with 21 points at Penn State, 21 at Indiana, 25 against Northwestern, 21 against Penn State in the Big Ten Tournament, and 26 in an NCAA first-round victory over Davidson. He scored 17 of his team's 21 points in a seven-minute stretch in the second half.

White's streak ended in his final game in an Iowa uniform, an NCAA loss to Gonzaga. He scored 19 points.

During his six straight games of 20-plus points, White shot 55.5 percent from the field, including 53.3 percent from three-point distance. He shot 84.9 percent from the free-throw line. And he averaged 9.2 rebounds.

"My career at Iowa was very special to me," said White, who was selected by the Washington Wizards in the second round of the 2015 NBA Draft and is currently playing professionally in Germany. "I loved playing for Coach McCaffery, having great teammates, and playing in front of our amazing fans. It was a lot of fun to help reenergize the program and leave it better than when our class came in. Iowa City will always have a special place in my heart."

In fairness to his other players, McCaffery is hesitant to call White the greatest recruiting find of his coaching career. But the fact that White did what he did while playing in the Big Ten makes his accomplishments hard to beat. "It's hard, at this level, to do what he did, to accomplish those numbers," McCaffery said. "When you consider who he went against, and the sophistication of the scouting, it's really hard."

54 Staff for the Ages

They posed for a picture inside Kinnick Stadium, two rows deep, dressed in matching slacks and golf shirts. With one exception: Hayden Fry, Iowa's head football coach, was dressed in a coat and tie. He stood in the back row, right in the middle. The others made up his coaching staff in 1983.

Fry was flanked by Kirk Ferentz, Del Miller, and Bill Snyder to his right. Carl Jackson and Don Patterson were to his left. In the front row were Bernie Wyatt, Barry Alvarez, Bill Brashier, Dan McCarney, and a fresh face—former Iowa player–turned–graduate assistant Bob Stoops.

"You could tell they were all pretty special on that staff," Stoops said. "And I always felt incredibly lucky and blessed that I was able to hang around them all."

Special because of how long they stuck together. Special because of what they accomplished after they left Iowa City. "I joined that staff in 1981, and we stuck together for seven years," Ferentz said. "We had great continuity. It was a really great staff to work with. And it started with Coach Fry. And then we had great people."

When Fry left North Texas State to take the Iowa job before the 1979 season, he brought five members of his staff with him. That included Snyder, his offensive coordinator, and Brashier, his defensive coordinator. He kept McCarney, a member of the previous Iowa staff. He plucked Alvarez out of Mason City High School. Jackson, Miller, Wyatt, and Patterson were also on that original staff.

"Hayden had that rare quality of finding great people on his staff," said Chuck Long, an All–Big Ten quarterback for the Hawkeyes. "And one of his great hires was Kirk Ferentz."

Needing an offensive line coach, Fry shocked members of his staff by bringing in Ferentz, who had been a graduate assistant at Pittsburgh, for an interview in the summer of 1981. "The key was hiring a veteran offensive line coach," Alvarez said. "The guys Hayden was bringing in were all veterans. And here comes this 25-year-old graduate assistant from Pittsburgh."

Long, who joined the program in the fall of 1981, benefited from the offensive lines Ferentz would mold. "No one in their right mind would have hired a graduate assistant," Long said. "You go out and hire the best possible guy, pry him away from Michigan or someplace. Coach Fry goes out and hires Kirk. It was a great hire, probably the instrumental hire he made for success."

Iowa went to two Rose Bowls in the first five seasons this staff was together. The Hawkeyes, who took a streak of 19 straight non-winning seasons into the 1981 campaign, won at least eight games in each of the next seven seasons.

Then Alvarez left after 1987 to become an assistant at Notre Dame. He later rebuilt the Wisconsin program and is now the school's athletic director. A statute of Alvarez stands outside Camp Randall Stadium, a symbol of his success in Madison.

Snyder left after the 1988 season to take over the program at Kansas State. As a testimony to his success, the football stadium is now named after him.

Ferentz left after the 1989 season to take over the program at Maine. After time as an NFL assistant coach, he returned to Iowa as Fry's successor in 1999 and has taken 13 teams to bowl games in 17 seasons.

McCarney also left after the 1989 season to join Alvarez at Wisconsin, and later was the head coach at Iowa State and North Texas.

After time on staffs at Iowa, Kansas State, and Florida, Stoops was named head coach at Oklahoma in 1999. His 2000 team won a national championship.

When the 2016 football season starts, Stoops and Ferentz will lead the nation in head coaching longevity at a single school.

55 Divine Intervention

Michigan State basketball coach Tom Izzo put the night in perspective. "If it's possible to have a rewarding loss, that one might be the ultimate," Izzo said. "Because it was way bigger than the game."

Izzo was speaking about Iowa's 96–90 overtime victory over the Spartans at the Breslin Student Events Center on January 28, 1993. Nine days earlier, Iowa star forward Chris Street had perished in an automobile accident on the outskirts of Iowa City. This was the Hawkeyes' first game following Street's death.

Iowa had a one-point lead at halftime, but the Spartans opened the second half on a 16–0 run. It was still a 70–55 deficit with 3:15 remaining in regulation. Iowa had made just two of 12 three-pointers in the game when Barnes hit one to ignite an improbable comeback. With an assist.

"You had to be totally amazed with the effort of the players, and how things turned out," said Mike Street, Chris' dad. "And you've got to believe there were more powers involved, let's put it that way."

Michigan State missed a handful of free throws, and didn't have a field goal the last 7:13 of regulation. Iowa, wearing CMS 40 patches on their jerseys in honor of their fallen teammate (who had worn No. 40), took advantage. Another Barnes three-pointer tied the game at 76–76, with 20 seconds to go in regulation.

"Once it got to overtime, we knew we weren't going to lose," the Hawkeyes' Kenyon Murray said. Iowa scored the first four points of overtime and rode that momentum to victory.

Barnes finished with 29 points, including several deep threes. "He hit one from so far out that it had to have come from above," said Izzo, an assistant to Jud Heathcote at the time. "It had to. It was just insane. The comeback was incredible."

Watching the game on ESPN back home in Indianola, Iowa, Street's parents felt the same way. "How could that happen without some help?" wondered Patty Street, Chris' mom.

A Somber Celebration

Three days after the victory at Michigan State, Iowa played its first game without Street at Carver-Hawkeye Arena against No. 5 Michigan.

A sellout crowd observed a moment of silence for their fallen star before the game. Ushers wore black buttons with Street's No. 40, in gold. Members of the athletic department wore black-and-gold ribbons or badges that included Street's number and initials. Street's parents, Mike and Patty, and his sisters, Sarah and Betsy, sat courtside for the game.

The arena was electric as Iowa broke open a close game in the final minutes to secure an 88–80 victory. "I'm amazed," Iowa Coach Tom Davis said after the game.

After the final buzzer, Iowa players ran to the Streets to celebrate with them, and presented them with the game ball. It was an impromptu moment. "We got our inspiration from Chris, and we went out and won the game for him," said Kenyon Murray, a freshman on that team. "The memory of Chris is going to be with us for the rest of our lives. We want the family to know they'll always be a part of our team."

Mike Street held the ball in the air as he walked off the court with the team. "Christopher might have given a little inspiration to these players," Mike said. "But I'll tell you what: The players did it. They deserve the credit."

Describing the events to a statewide listening audience on WHO Radio in Des Moines, Jim Zabel summed up the emotional day: "This is what being a Hawkeye is all about," Zabel said.

Divine intervention? Izzo has no doubt. "It was crushing to lose that game," Izzo said. "And yet you caught yourself saying, 'That guy got us when he was alive. And he got us after he died.'"

Tom Davis won a school-record 269 games in 13 seasons as Iowa's coach. That victory in East Lansing is one he'll never forget.

"That's how [Street] lived, and I think that's how he tried to play," Davis said. "And that's how we played in that particular game."

56 Tim and Tavian

It's been called one of the greatest football games ever played in the history of the Iowa high school playoffs.

It matched two speedsters—Tavian Banks of Bettendorf against Tim Dwight of Iowa City High. A standing-room-only crowd watched as Bettendorf won the epic 1992 quarterfinal matchup 31–28 after trailing by two touchdowns to start the game. Banks rushed for 244 yards and three touchdowns. He had two more touchdown runs called back by penalties. Dwight scored all four City High touchdowns.

Five seasons later, this happened: Banks ran for four touchdowns and Dwight caught three touchdown passes as Iowa won 63–20 at Iowa State. That is just one tasty sample of what these two Iowa prep prodigies did during their Hawkeyes careers.

Both Dwight and Banks lettered for the Hawkeyes from 1994 to 1997 before heading to the National Football League. Dwight is also regarded as one of the greatest track and football athletes in Iowa high school history. "What separated him was his explosiveness and competitiveness," said Reese Morgan, an assistant at Iowa who previously tried to slow down Dwight as the head coach at Iowa City West. "It was men against boys."

Dwight had plenty of scholarship offers out of high school but elected to stay home and play for Hayden Fry and the Hawkeyes. "I was born in 1975, and he came here in 1979," Dwight said. "I grew up in the era of Hayden Fry and the reestablishment of Iowa football in the 1980s, with the [Chuck] Longs and the [Ronnie] Harmons."

Banks, a soccer star as well, said that sport taught him the quickness, balance, vision, and agility he used with great success on the football field. Miami of Florida, Nebraska, and Washington were among the schools courting Banks for football. But he too elected to be a homegrown Hawkeye.

Dwight and Banks never shared the backfield at Iowa. Dwight instead became a star as a wide receiver and kick returner, using his speed to roll up the yards. Dwight was a first-team All–Big Ten selection and consensus All-American as a senior in 1997. He led the nation that season in punt-return yardage, averaging 19.3 yards. He also finished seventh in balloting for the Heisman Trophy.

When all the numbers were added up, Dwight eclipsed the 1,000-yard mark in three different categories. He finished with 139 catches for 2,271 yards and 21 touchdowns. Twice he had eight catches in a game. He established a Big Ten record for career punt return yardage. His 1,102 yards included five touchdowns. And he had 1,195 career yards worth of kickoff returns.

Banks had to be more patient. The running back in front of him, Sedrick Shaw, rushed for better than 1,000 yards in three straight seasons and is Iowa's career rushing leader with 4,156 yards.

Banks also earned first-team All–Big Ten honors as a senior in 1997, rushing for 1,691 yards, a school record until Shonn Greene's 1,850 yards in 2008. Banks also set a new single-game school rushing record with 314 yards in 29 carries against Tulsa.

Both Dwight and Banks were selected in the fourth round of the NFL Draft—Dwight by Atlanta, Banks by Jacksonville. Dwight played 10 NFL seasons for five different teams, and returned a kickoff 94 yards for a touchdown in Super Bowl XXXIII as a rookie with the Falcons. Banks suffered a major knee injury against Dwight's team, Atlanta, in his second season. The Falcons' Ray Buchanan delivered the career-changing hit. "I tore everything," Banks said. "I tore all three ligaments in the knee. I had a torn hamstring and a stretched nerve. All with that one hit."

Banks tried a comeback with New Orleans in 2002 but was released a year later.

57 15 Cy-Hawk Victories in a Row

Iowa running back Owen Gill had 136 yards rushing against Iowa State in a 51–10 romp in 1983. Gill had more yards that day in Ames than Iowa State backs had against Hawkeyes defenses from 1983 to 1986 combined. Cyclones ball carriers managed just 121 yards in 141 carries over that four-season stretch, when Iowa's dominance over its in-state rival was gaining momentum.

Starting with that 1983 game, the Hawkeyes won 15 straight games in the series. Over that time, Iowa averaged 39.3 points to Iowa State's 13.7. Iowa scored 50 or more points four times, and nine different running backs rushed for at least 100 yards. Eight of Iowa's victories were by three touchdowns or more.

Chuck Long quarterbacked the Hawkeyes to the first three victories in the streak. The Hawkeyes won those three games by an average score of 55.6 to 11.3. Long completed 42 of 66 passes for 644 yards, one interception, and eight touchdowns.

With Long behind center, Iowa started a streak of success over Iowa State that is unmatched in the Cy-Hawk series. Here's what 15 seasons of dominance looks like.

1983 (Ames)

Iowa 51, Iowa State 10

Iowa wasted no time in ending a three-game losing streak to the Cyclones, taking a 17–0 lead after one quarter and a 31–3 edge at halftime. The Hawkeyes rushed for 257 yards, compared to 31 for Iowa State.

"This is the most satisfying opening game I've ever had," Iowa coach Hayden Fry said. "We needed this one."

First-year Iowa State coach Jim Criner said his team played "one-eighteenth of what I think we're capable of."

Long completed 13 of 17 passes, threw for one touchdown, and ran for another.

"I think we can get better and better," Fry said. "I don't know how good Iowa State is, and I hate to see this happen to a new coach."

The best was yet to come.

1984 (Iowa City)

Iowa 59, Iowa State 21

Based on the final score, this is hard to believe: with 4:27 to play in the first half, Iowa's offense had accounted for just six first downs and negative-3 yards rushing against the Cyclones.

"We got off to rocky start, but I expected that," Long said. "Iowa State threw everything at us...blitzes and stunts. We knew we would break one sooner or later."

This game had no Rocky ending from an Iowa State perspective. Three Iowa State turnovers were turned into quick Hawkeyes scores.

Long threw touchdown passes of 68 yards to Ronnie Harmon and 63 yards to Robert Smith. Harmon also got loose for an 86-yard touchdown sprint. Iowa's first touchdown came on defensive end Dave Strobel's 38-yard pick six.

Iowa removed all doubt with three touchdowns in the final 4:41 of the opening half to make it 42–7.

1985 (Ames)
Iowa 57, Iowa State 3
Fry had predicted a close game all week. "I was wrong," he said, with a victorious smile, after the game.

Iowa took a 41–0 halftime lead on a cold, rainy day, and fans headed for the exits early. The stadium was less than half full at the start of the third quarter.

Long passed for 223 yards and three touchdowns, including a 46-yard scoring strike to Scott Helverson.

The Hawkeyes were ranked No. 3, and poised to move up after No. 1 Auburn lost 38–20 to Tennessee and No. 2 Oklahoma snuck by Minnesota 13–7.

Fry said it would be "the kiss of death" to be ranked No. 1.

"We're happy right where we are," he said.

When the Associated Press poll was released the following week, Iowa was No. 1.

1986 (Iowa City)
Iowa 43, Iowa State 7
Wide receiver Jim Mauro, who transferred to Iowa from Missouri Western, caught three touchdown passes to tie a school record shared by Erwin Prasse, Emlen Tunnell, Robert Smith, and Bill Happel.

"I wasn't supposed to be big enough or fast enough to play major college football," said Mauro, who replaced the injured Quinn Early in the lineup and made the most of his chance. Mauro caught two Mark Vlasic passes for touchdowns of 43 and 47 yards. He also caught a 17-yard scoring pass from Smith on one of Fry's "exotic" plays.

In four games against Criner, Fry's teams had a 210–41 scoring edge. Fry also passed Forest Evashevski as the winningest coach in Iowa history with the victory.

1987 (Ames)
Iowa 48, Iowa State 9

Fry said during the week that his goal was to improve the Hawkeyes' running game. With that in mind, Iowa's first seven plays from scrimmage were handoffs to running back Kevin Harmon. The senior rushed for 179 yards—nine yards less than he'd accounted for in any of his first three seasons as a Hawkeye—and three touchdowns in another rout. The Cyclones had changed coaches—Jim Walden had replaced Criner—but the results remained the same.

Iowa held a precarious 10–6 lead midway through the second quarter, but Iowa State quarterback Derek DeGennaro was intercepted twice, by safety Kerry Burt and defensive end Sean Ridley. Iowa converted both turnovers into touchdowns.

"Things just got kind of yucky after that," Walden said. "Their ability and our inability blended into a real mess."

1988 (Iowa City)
Iowa 10, Iowa State 3

Walden talked about ghosts to his team before the game. "We told our players not to worry about the ghosts—the things that happened before in the Iowa State–Iowa series."

Walden also said he thought his team, a 24-point underdog, could win. And he was almost right. Only Tork Hook's interception of a Bret Oberg pass at the Iowa 6-yard line in the final minute kept Iowa's winning streak over the Cyclones alive. That moment was the biggest thrill of Hook's Hawkeyes career.

"Especially since it came against our archrival," Hook said. "I'm from this state, and Iowa State tried to recruit me when I was a high school senior."

Iowa State had 354 yards of total offense, to 343 for the Hawkeyes. But the only number that counted was the 10–3 final score.

"In the future, you can bet there will be a fight for the state title," Iowa State tight end Mike Busch said. "They'll be good games from now on. Look out next year, Iowa."

1989 (Ames)
Iowa 31, Iowa State 21
Fry was in a celebratory mood after the game ended. "It's like I told my players," Fry said. "The state of Iowa is still a Hawkeye state, and hopefully it will remain that way."

With his dad, former Iowa basketball star and Boston Celtics coach Jimmy Rodgers, watching from the stands, Iowa sophomore quarterback Matt Rodgers won his first Cy-Hawk start.

"I loved having my dad here to watch me play," Matt said after completing 20 of 33 passes for 276 yards and three touchdowns.

Iowa State led 21–14 at halftime. Then Iowa tackle Jim Johnson sacked Oberg near his own end zone, forcing a fumble. Hawkeyes end Larry Blue pounced on the ball in the end zone for the tying touchdown.

A Rodgers touchdown pass to John Palmer, and George Murphy's 22-yard field goal—after another Iowa State turnover— gave Iowa a 17–0 second-half advantage and the victory.

"In the end, the better team won," Walden said.

1990 (Iowa City)
Iowa 45, Iowa State 35

Iowa linebacker Melvin Foster did a little bragging after this one. "This is always going to be the Hawkeye State," Foster said.

Iowa State, playing without starting quarterback Chris Pedersen or running back Blaise Bryant, still finished with more yards of total offense, more first downs, and an advantage in time of possession.

"They played with a lot of poise and heart," Foster said. "They're tired of losing to Iowa. And that freshman quarterback of theirs played a great game." That freshman QB was Bob Utter, who completed 20 of 32 passes for 235 yards and two touchdowns in his first career start.

Nick Bell rushed for 115 yards and Tony Stewart had 101 to lead Iowa. Iowa's Merton Hanks blocked a punt to set up a first-half-ending field goal to give the Hawkeyes a 17–14 lead.

"It gave us the pep we needed," Hanks said. "It turned the momentum in our favor coming out to start the second half."

Iowa scored three third-quarter touchdowns to take an insurmountable 38–14 lead.

1991 (Ames)
Iowa 29, Iowa State 10

Iowa State quarterback Chris Pedersen completed just 7 of 15 passes for 56 yards, with an interception and two fumbles. "It was offensively ugly," Walden said of his team's performance with the ball.

Rodgers completed just 6 of 15 passes for 135 yards and two touchdowns. "I wasn't satisfied with the way I played, but I was satisfied with the win," Rodgers said.

Iowa scored 17 points in its first nine plays from scrimmage on a 46-yard Rodgers–to–Danan Hughes strike, a 41-yard field goal by Jeff Skillett, and a two-yard touchdown run by Paul Kujawa.

1992 (Iowa City)
Iowa 21, Iowa State 7
This game is most remembered for the fireworks that took place afterward. Iowa senior cocaptain Bret Bielema unloaded a profane blast on Walden, using expletives to tell the Iowa State coach how much he'd enjoyed beating him every season. Walden said Bieleman's attack lacked class.

Bielema wasn't the only Iowa player fired up after the game. "They lose the game before they play," Hughes said. "They talk so much nonsense. When we get on the field with them, we have an extra heartbeat."

Iowa took a 14–0 lead after one quarter, and that was enough to extend its winning streak over Iowa State to 10 games.

"We didn't score as many points as we wanted, but I'm not being critical," Fry said.

1993 (Ames)
Iowa 31, Iowa State 28
The Hawkeyes took a 31–7 lead with 7:55 remaining in the third quarter, and then had to hold on for dear life.

Iowa State got within 31–28, then recovered an onside kick on its own 49 with 1:23 remaining. But Iowa lineman Maurea Crain knocked the ball loose from Iowa State quarterback Bob Utter, and Iowa linebacker Mike Dailey recovered to cut short the Cyclones' rally.

"There was a lot of talk all week about how Iowa State was now playing at our level, so we came here with an attitude," Iowa quarterback Paul Burmeister said. "We wanted to show that, hey, the Hawkeyes are still the best team in the state. I feel real good about that."

1994 (Iowa City)
Iowa 37, Iowa State 9

The Hawkeyes scored 17 unanswered points in the third quarter to expand on a 13–3 halftime lead and coast to another victory.

"Before the game I was scared to death," Fry said. "Iowa State has the potential to explode. Believe me, they're going to explode against someone this year." Not exactly. The Cyclones finished 0–10–1, and Walden resigned under pressure after eight seasons.

Iowa linebacker Bobby Diaco had 15 tackles, running back Sedrick Shaw added 106 yards rushing, and free safety Kerry Cooks returned a fumble 51 yards for a touchdown.

1995 (Ames)
Iowa 27, Iowa State 10

Speaking to the Iowa State Athletic Council the Tuesday before the game, school president Martin Jischke said, "I know Iowa State will win."

He should have locked Shaw out of the stadium. The Hawkeyes running back rushed for 178 yards to take the wind out of Jischke's prediction. "Everyone's been talking about Troy Davis, but no one has been talking about Sedrick Shaw," Iowa offensive lineman Matt Purdy said. "Sedrick is a great running back. Maybe it's time people start talking about Sedrick."

Davis, who entered the game ranked second nationally in rushing, had 139 yards including a 63-yard touchdown run. But Shaw and Rodney Filer, who finished with 113 yards, won the day.

"They gave a great effort," Jischke said of his team. "We had trouble controlling the line of scrimmage, but I think people saw a great game. I do wish we were winning, though."

1996 (Iowa City)

Iowa 38, Iowa State 13

This game was supposed to be Shaw-Davis II. But Tavian Banks stole top billing. Given extra carries after Shaw left the game with an ankle injury in the third quarter, Banks rushed for 182 yards and three touchdowns.

Davis, who had run for 2,010 yards and was a Heisman Trophy finalist in 1995, was limited to 50 yards in the first half while Iowa jumped out to a 24–0 lead. He finished with 152. Banks scored on runs of 89, 12, and 28 yards.

"I just had a little more opportunity," Banks said. "The line really blocked well for me. There were a lot of good holes."

1997 (Ames)

Iowa 63, Iowa State 20

The Hawkeyes took a 21–0 lead, thanks to Banks. The former Bettendorf star scored on an 82-yard run on the second play from scrimmage. He also scored on runs of eight yards in the first quarter and a yard in the second quarter.

The score only got more lopsided, thanks to another home-grown hero. Iowa City's Tim Dwight caught Matt Sherman touchdown passes of 41 and 29 yards in the second quarter and a 33-yarder in the third quarter. Banks added a fourth touchdown on a four-yard run in the third quarter as well.

"It's the Hawkeye State," Iowa fullback Michael Burger said. "It's been that way for a long time."

58 Iowa's What-If Hero

Iowa played its first men's basketball game at Carver-Hawkeye Arena on January 5, 1983. "Everyone wanted to move into it," said Bobby Hansen, a starting guard on that 1982–83 team. "It was like moving into a brand-new house. There was excitement."

Lute Olson, Iowa's coach at the time, had spearheaded fundraising efforts for the $17 million project. When it was announced that the monetary goal had been reached on December 20, 1980, officials said the new arena would open for the 1982–83 season.

But that didn't quite happen. Instead Iowa started that season in rustic Iowa Field House, a 13,365-seat building that had been hosting games since 1927. "There was nothing like Iowa Field House," Hansen said. "You'd come out of that crazy little locker room, with Father Bob [Holzhammer] on the PA. But we needed a new facility."

Iowa played the first four home games of the 1982–83 season in Iowa Field House, the last a 66–55 victory over Southern California on December 11. After playing games at UCLA and taking part in the Rochester Classic in New York, Iowa returned home to open Big Ten play.

"To me, this [Carver-Hawkeye Arena] was state-of-the-art at the time," Hansen said. This beautiful new bowl, all shiny and well lit. And we just wanted to get that first victory in there."

Iowa's wrestling team had christened the building two nights earlier, beating Oklahoma in a dual meet. Then it was basketball's turn. Iowa was favored to beat the Spartans. The Hawkeyes were No. 8 in the Associated Press poll and 8–1 on the season. Michigan State was 7–3.

The Twin Towers

They were known as the Twin Towers, a pair of shiny recruits picked off the Class of 1982 top 100 tree by Iowa coach Lute Olson.

Greg Stokes, 6'10", was Player of the Year in Ohio. Michael Payne, 6'11", was Player of the Year in Illinois. They joined veterans such as Bobby Hansen, Kenny Arnold, and Kevin Boyle for the 1981–82 season. Payne was the most decorated of the two. His Quincy High School team had gone 91–4 with him in uniform. That included a 33–0 mark in his senior season. Payne was named to the prestigious McDonald's All-American team.

Stokes, a smooth southpaw, came to Iowa from Hamilton High School in Hamilton, Ohio. Payne made an immediate impact for the Hawkeyes, but Stokes had a more productive career.

Payne started as a freshman, averaging 11.4 points and 7.4 rebounds on a team that tied for second in the Big Ten and finished 21–8 overall after a second-round NCAA loss to Idaho. Stokes averaged 5.7 points and 4.2 rebounds off the bench.

They both started in 1982–83, when Iowa made the Sweet 16 of the NCAA Tournament, went 22–9 overall, and tied for second in the Big Ten. Stokes averaged 17.7 points and 7.2 rebounds. Stokes scored 10.6 points a game and added 7.5 rebounds. Olson left after the season to take the Arizona job, and was replaced by George Raveling.

Iowa Field House had offered a noisy home-court advantage. Fans would traditionally stomp their feet in the steel balconies. Olson wondered if the 15,500-seat Carver-Hawkeye Arena would be the same. "If the crowd noise is what we've enjoyed in the Field House, or maybe even louder than that, then everything will be just fine," Olson said the day before the game.

But Michigan State upset the Hawkeyes 61–59. Iowa shot just 40 percent from the field, and missed 7 of 11 free-throw attempts. "The newness of playing here made no difference," Olson said afterward. "These are the same rims we used in the Field House, and we've shot the ball well in practice. If there was any hoopla

Stokes and Payne remained starters for two seasons under Raveling. Stokes averaged 14.9 points and 6.9 rebounds as a junior, when he was a second-team All–Big Ten selection for the second year in a row. He was a first-team All-League choice after averaging 19.9 points and 8.4 rebounds as a senior.

Payne's numbers dropped to 9.3 points and 6.7 rebounds as a junior. He averaged 7.1 points and 7.6 rebounds as a senior.

Stokes and Payne were named Iowa's most valuable players as seniors, and closed out their careers with a loss to Arkansas in the first round of the 1985 NCAA Tournament.

Payne finished with 1,118 points and averaged 7.3 rebounds over the course of his 117-game career.

Stokes was Iowa's career scoring leader at the time, with 1,768 points. He averaged 14.7 points and 6.7 rebounds over his 120-game career. His number, 41, was retired.

Stokes was selected by the Philadelphia 76ers in the second round of the 1985 NBA Draft. He played a season there, went overseas and played for teams in Italy and Spain, and then closed out his pro career with the NBA's Sacramento Kings in 1989.

Payne, selected in the third round of the 1985 NBA Draft by the Houston Rockets, played professionally in France, Italy, and Australia for nearly a decade.

surrounding the game, it shouldn't have had any effect after the first three or four minutes."

Hansen's name is etched in the story of that debut. He scored a team-high 17 points. His three-pointer, with eight seconds to play, cut the deficit to a point. He then fouled Michigan State's Sam Vincent with five seconds on the clock. Vincent made the front end of the one-and-one but missed the second.

Iowa guard Steve Carfino got the ball, raced down the left out-of-bounds line, and fired a pass ahead to Hansen, who caught it, squared to the basket, and swished a three-pointer for the dramatic victory. Hansen hadn't heard a whistle. Neither had many in the crowd. But there had been one. Official Ed Hightower, trailing the play, ruled that Carfino had grazed the out-of-bounds line with his foot before making the pass. No basket. No Iowa victory.

Three decades later, Hightower worked the final game of his 36-year officiating career. It was at Carver-Hawkeye Arena. Hansen was courtside, working as the color analyst on Iowa's play-by-play broadcast of a December 22, 2013, game between the Hawkeyes and Arkansas–Pine Bluff. And what did they talk about? The night Hightower's whistle cost Hansen his hero status.

59 Black Helmets

Iowa's football team was already in Columbus, Ohio, preparing for a game at Ohio State the following day, when news spread of a terrible tragedy on the campus in Iowa City. It was approximately 3:40 PM on Friday, November 1, 1991, when 28-year-old Gang Lu, a doctoral candidate in physics from China, went on a shooting rampage. Upset over not receiving a prestigious dissertation prize months earlier, Lu shot six people before turning the gun on himself. Five of the six died.

Lu's assault started in Room 309 of Van Allen Hall, where he shot and killed Christoph Goertz, a professor in the physics and astronomy department; Robert Smith, an associate professor; and Linhua Shan, a researcher who had been nominated for the dissertation prize Gang Lu coveted.

The gunman then went downstairs and killed Dwight Nicholson, the chairman of the physics and astronomy department, who had nominated Shan's work for the dissertation prize. Then Lu went to Jessup Hall, two blocks away, where he shot T.

Anne Cleary, associate vice president for academic affairs, and Miya Rodolfo-Sioson, her assistant. Gang Lu then shot himself.

"It's a terrible tragedy," said Iowa president Hunter Rawlings, who left Columbus and returned to campus after the shootings.

Cleary, who died the following day, was involved in a formal complaint Lu had filed after his dissertation wasn't nominated. Rodolfo-Sioson was paralyzed from the neck down. She died of cancer in 2008.

Officials from Iowa and Ohio State met and decided to play the football game the following day. "Everyone in our traveling party was stunned by this awful event," Iowa football coach Hayden Fry wrote in his autobiography, *Hayden Fry: A High Porch Picnic.* "How could this happen on our peaceful campus? After the decision was made to play the game and we had a chance to collect our thoughts, we decided to strip our helmets of the stripes and decals. We played the game with plain black helmets and black armbands on our white jerseys. It was the most fitting way we could think of to pay tribute to those who had died in a senseless act."

Iowa won the game in Ohio Stadium 16–9, on a day that was a sobering reminder that football is not life-or-death.

60 Grapple on the Gridiron

Officially it was called Grapple on the Gridiron. In reality, Iowa wrestler Sammy Brooks had a better description. "It was a perfect storm," Brooks said. "A great day for wrestling."

Holding a wrestling dual meet outdoors in Iowa, in mid-November, is asking for trouble. But Mother Nature turned her back on the norm. The temperature was mild, in the 50s, and an all-time-record crowd of 42,287 watched the Hawkeyes upset No. 1 Oklahoma State 18–16 at Kinnick Stadium.

"It was an incredible atmosphere," Iowa coach Tom Brands said. "You can't deny that. Even I can't deny that, and I'm one that likes to talk about performance. But this was a performance within itself."

In Iowa, wrestling is as much a part of the landscape as spring planting or harvest season. In other words, it's important...*very* important.

The seed of the Grapple on the Gridiron was planted by Brands back in 2008. Iowa set a dual-meet attendance record on December 6, 2008. A crowd of 15,955 saw the top-ranked Hawkeyes beat No. 2 Iowa State 20–15.

But Brands figured someone would bypass Iowa's dual-meet record. He also knew that Carver-Hawkeye Arena wasn't big enough to keep up in the race for the record. Brands had a simple solution: "It's time to go to Kinnick."

Penn State did break Iowa's record, drawing 15,996 for a dual with Pittsburgh at the university's Bryce Jordan Center on December 8, 2013. By then, the idea of wrestling at Kinnick was moving full speed ahead.

After listening to his staff discuss the event, Iowa athletic director Gary Barta gave his approval. "Let's see if it can get done," Barta said.

Iowa announced the Grapple on the Gridiron on August 6, 2015. The fact that Oklahoma State was the opponent only enhanced the event. Iowa and Oklahoma State are the sport's two most decorated programs, combining for 57 national championships. Cowboys coach John Smith was quick to agree to participate in the event. Smith, like Brands, knew the importance of thinking outside the box to make their sport grow.

Barta also knew forces outside his control—namely the weather—would play a big factor. "A lot had to happen to make it a reality," Barta said.

Turns out, a lot did happen. Fans were greeted by 50-degree temperatures, no rain, and a spectacle. The mat was put down on the south end of the field at Kinnick Stadium, where Iowa would host Minnesota in a Big Ten football game later that night. It was the first wrestling match ever held at a Division I football stadium.

The crowd nearly tripled the previous record. "We definitely set a standard," Smith said after the meet. "I don't think people are going to sit around and go, 'You can have the record.' It forces all of us to pay a little closer attention to creating greater environments for dual meets."

Dan Gable, the sport's greatest icon, attended the event and saw nothing but positives. "Our sport can always use good promotion," Gable said. "Sometimes we're on the bubble a little bit, whether it be in college or internationally. And because of that, we need stuff like this. I feel pretty good about it."

It was an unforgettable day for the sport, and an unforgettable chapter added to the history of Kinnick Stadium.

"This was an impact day for our sport," Gable said.

61 Gamble Pays Off

Kevin Gamble attempted 374 shots during his two-year career at Iowa. One stands out among them all. "I remember it like it was yesterday," Gamble said. Gamble swished a deep three-pointer from the top of the key with three seconds remaining that gave Iowa a 93–91 victory over Oklahoma in a 1987 NCAA Sweet 16 game in Seattle, Washington.

If the officials that day had used instant replay late in games to determine whom a ball went off of, like they do now, Gamble's chance to be a hero might never have happened. On the previous play, Iowa's Roy Marble missed a shot, and it looked like the ball went off the hands of teammate Brad Lohaus and out-of-bounds. But the Hawkeyes were awarded possession with 11 seconds remaining. "We called another play," Gamble said. "I think it was called Switch."

Point guard B.J. Armstrong, who would later play on three NBA championship teams with Michael Jordan and the Chicago Bulls, dribbled on the right wing and started to drive. Gamble slid to an open spot at the top of the key. "We had a couple of tries at it before, and the guy was back, almost in the paint," Gamble said. "I made up my mind that I was going to shoot."

As soon as Armstrong drew the defenders to him, he passed it out to Gamble. "I knew he was going to throw it back, because that's how the play was drawn up," Gamble said. "I was wide-open."

Gamble, second from left, is mobbed by teammates after scoring the winning basket in the Hawkeyes' overtime victory over the Oklahoma Sooners at the NCAA West Regionals.

The winning shot dropped the curtain on one of the finest games of Gamble's Hawkeyes career. He finished with a career-high 26 points and made 11 of 13 shots from the field. That included both his three-point attempts.

But one basket is remembered more than the other 10 he made that day. It is a shot that will forever be a part of Iowa basketball history. "It's a good feeling," Gamble said. "Any time I watch it, I still get goose bumps."

62 Rivalry Resumed

When the Iowa–Iowa State football series was renewed in 1977 after 42 years in hibernation, anticipation for the game was so high that Iowa governor Robert D. Ray felt compelled to release a statement.

It wasn't a State of the State address. It was an attempt to calm emotional waters as much as anything:

> The eyes of most Iowans and millions of Americans will be on Kinnick Stadium Saturday as the Big 8 meets the Big 10. Two of our most famous state universities will lock in battle on the gridiron for the first time in well over a generation.
>
> The renewal of this supreme series has been discussed for years. This game has been discussed for months. Now, we are poised to watch or listen to an exciting game. The University of Iowa Hawkeyes and the Iowa State Cyclones will seek a victory with zeal, and with a steeled determination. We would expect nothing less. Still, two teams cannot win a football game.

Thus I would ask everyone to join Coach Bruce and Coach Commings in reminding ourselves that we are all Iowans. I hope that Iowans with a keen interest in this game will match the good sportsmanship and fair play that we expect on the field from our two teams.

Let us frame our memories of this historic occasion in a positive context. Let us remember not only that this game produced a winner and a loser, but that it brought us together to more fully appreciate our talented athletes, our excellent universities, and yes, this special place we call home, the State of Iowa.

This was clearly the most hyped game in the series. Iowa State was the favorite, Iowa the underdog. "I think we'll win," Iowa coach Bob Commings said the day before the game. "I don't think either of us knows what sort of team we have. We might both be awfully good. This will help find out."

Iowa State coach Earle Bruce said he was glad the game had finally arrived, after months of hype. "I'm looking forward to a hard-hitting, hard-fought football game," Bruce said. "That's what it should be."

Motivation was not an issue, even though Bruce went the extra mile. When his team ran onto the field at Kinnick Stadium for the start of the game, they had changed jerseys. On the front were two words: BEAT IOWA.

They didn't. Iowa upset the Cyclones 12–10 in a game all parts emotional and pedestrian. All 22 points were scored in a seven-and-a-half-minute span of the first half. And there were several big plays.

The Cyclones delivered the first blow, a 63-yard punt return for a touchdown by Tom Buck. Iowa countered with a 77-yard sweep by Dennis Mosley. "It's designated for outside, but I happened to hit the seam at the right time," Mosley said.

Iowa State maintained a 7–6 lead when Iowa placekicker Dave Holsclaw missed the point-after kick. Holsclaw was forced into action because Scott Schilling, the starting placekicker, had been injured in a freak accident at the university's Finkbine Golf Course two days before the game.

After the Hawkeyes' Jim Molini and Joe Hufford stripped Iowa State quarterback Terry Rubley of the ball, Iowa converted the turnover when Jon Lazar scored on a 10-yard run. The Hawkeyes' two-point conversion was unsuccessful.

Iowa State's Scott Kollman kicked a 42-yard field goal less than three minutes into the second quarter. And that was it for the scoring.

When the clock went to zero, Iowa fans stormed the field and tore down the goal posts. And Iowa State's BEAT IOWA jerseys went down in history for all the wrong reasons.

"A helluva game," Governor Ray said afterward. "It lived up to expectations. I wondered if it could, with all the build-up."

63 Iowa Fight Song

Meredith Willson is best known for writing *The Music Man*, a Tony-winning Broadway musical that has stood the test of time.

The musical brought fame to Willson's native state of Iowa. The fictional River City is based on his hometown of Mason City. Willson won an Oscar for the movie version and the first Grammy ever presented for the best album.

But before "Seventy-Six Trombones" and "Iowa Stubborn," Willson wrote the "Iowa Fight Song" for the University of Iowa in 1950. He had been challenged to write a "spirited state song." Here's what he came up with:

The word is fight, fight, fight for Iowa
Let every loyal Iowan sing
The word is fight, fight, fight for Iowa
Until the walls and rafters ring (Go Hawks!)
Come on and cheer, cheer, cheer for Iowa
We're gonna cheer until we hear the final gun
The word is fight, fight, fight for Iowa
Until the game is won

The song was first played at a sporting event on February 12, 1951, during an Iowa-Indiana basketball game at Iowa Field House.

Known as a "walking commercial for Iowa," Willson donated papers to the Special Collections Department of the University of Iowa Libraries. Included are sheet music for the "Iowa Fight Song" and the final script of *The Music Man*. Willson passed away in 1984.

The "Iowa Fight Song" might be the official anthem of the Iowa Hawkeyes, but it may not be the most popular tune played on game days. No.1 on the charts could well be "In Heaven There Is No Beer," also known as the "Hawkeye Victory Polka," which is popular because, one, it's a catchy tune, and two, it's only played when the clock runs out on an Iowa victory. "I hear it and I know it's a good thing," Iowa football coach Kirk Ferentz said.

The Hawkeye Marching Band plays it at Kinnick Stadium, and the Iowa Pep Band plays it at Carver-Hawkeye Arena.

The lyrics go like this:

In Heaven there is no beer,
That's why drink it here,
And when we're gone from here,
Our friends will be drinking all our beer

The tradition of the victory song started in the 1960s. It was banned by university officials for a short time in 2001 over concerns that the song promoted alcohol abuse. But overwhelming public support for the ditty got the song removed from the banned list. The song is an adaptation of a 1956 German song titled "Im Himmel gibt's kein Bier."

64 A Devine All-American

When the University of Iowa released its All-Century football team in 1989, three teammates had stood the test of time. Aubrey Devine, Fred "Duke" Slater, and Gordon Locke were all on the team. The All-American trio played key roles on Iowa's undefeated football team of 1921. Devine was the senior quarterback, Slater was the senior tackle, and Locke was the junior fullback.

Devine, a three-time All–Western Conference (Big Ten) selection, was the captain of Coach Howard Jones' 7–0 team. Those victories were part of a school-record 20-game winning streak between 1920 and 1923.

Devine and his brother, Glenn, actually enrolled at Drake to start college in 1919. They lasted a week, then packed up and headed to Iowa City. Both were starters for the Hawkeyes that season. Aubrey was the left halfback, and Glenn was the right halfback and spent a majority of his career blocking for his brother.

An injury forced Jones to move Devine to quarterback three games into his sophomore season, and he never left that position again. In his first game at quarterback, Devine led Iowa to its first victory ever at Minnesota, 9–6. Iowa finished 5–2 in both 1919 and 1920. Three victories to end the 1920 season—against

Northwestern, Minnesota, and Iowa State by a combined score of 62–17—kicked off the longest winning streak in school history.

The Hawkeyes' streak also ended Notre Dame's run of 20 straight victories. The Irish came to Iowa City on October 8, 1921. Notre Dame's captain was, like Devine, an Iowa native. His name was Dr. Eddie Anderson, and he returned to Iowa City nearly two decades later to coach Nile Kinnick and the Ironmen of 1939. Devine kicked the winning field goal, a 38-yard dropkick.

But Devine's career took on legendary status three game later, at Minnesota. He passed for 122 yards and two touchdowns. He rushed for 162 yards and four touchdowns. He kicked five extra points. And he had 200 return yards in Iowa's 41–7 victory.

After the game, Minnesota Coach Henry L. Williams acknowledged Devine's 464 total yards by calling him "the greatest player who ever stepped on our field."

Devine ran for 183 yards and four touchdowns a week later against Indiana, and went on to lead the conference in scoring for a second straight season. Devine went on to become the first native Iowan (Des Moines) to be named a first-team All-American.

Jones left Iowa after the 1923 season, spent one year at Duke University, then took the job at Southern California in 1924. Devine joined his coaching staff two years later. Jones always considered Devine one of his greatest players. "He was the greatest all-around backfield man I have ever coached or seen in the modern game," Jones said. "Others may have been great in the open field running, there may have been better punters or dropkickers, but I have never known any backfield man whose accomplishments in running, punting, drop-kicking, and forward passing combined to equal those of Aubrey Devine. He was a leader and field general of the highest type."

65 Face of the Program

Dallas Clark joined Iowa's football program as a walk-on linebacker. He left as a consensus All-American and the recipient of the John Mackey Award, which goes to the nation's best tight end.

Clark, who went on to a successful 11-year NFL career that includes a Super Bowl ring with the Indianapolis Colts, embodies Iowa football under coach Kirk Ferentz. "The Dallas Clark today is the same guy he was back in 1999, when we first met," Ferentz said. "Just a very humble, high-energy, pure, great guy. So yeah, if he's on the front cover of our program, that would be a pretty good compliment. He's as good as they get."

Ferentz calls Clark a great story, and the facts bear that out. Clark actually came to Iowa City in 1998 and enrolled as a part-time student when Hayden Fry was winding up his 20-year career. He became a full-time student in January 1999, a month after Ferentz was hired as Fry's replacement.

After redshirting the 1999 season, Clark played special teams and got in for a few plays at linebacker in 2000. Then he was moved to tight end, and put on scholarship, in the fall of 2001. Clark started 10 games in 2001 and 13 in 2002, finishing with 1,281 career receiving yards. Clark entered the NFL Draft with a season of eligibility remaining and was taken in the first round by Indianapolis, the 24th selection overall.

Clark's 95-yard touchdown reception against Purdue in 2002 is a career highlight. He also caught the winning touchdown pass from quarterback Brad Banks on a fourth-and-7 play with 1:07 remaining in that same game, a 31–28 victory on October 5 that kept Iowa's momentum going. The Hawkeyes went on to an undefeated Big Ten season and played in the Orange Bowl.

Clark went on to huge success in the NFL as one of Peyton Manning's favorite targets for many seasons.

Ferentz has a different Clark memory from that 2002 season. "He's the John Mackey Award winner, and he's bugging us at every turn about playing more special teams," Ferentz said. "There aren't many great players that would do that."

Clark is one of seven players who have won prestigious national awards on Ferentz's watch. Placekicker Nate Kaeding won the Lou Groza Award in 2002. That same year, quarterback Brad Banks won the Davey O'Brien Award and was named Associated Press National Player of the Year. Offensive tackle Robert Gallery won the Outland Trophy in 2003. Running back Shonn Greene was presented the Doak Walker Award in 2008. Offensive tackle

Brandon Scherff was named the Outland Trophy winner in 2014. And cornerback Desmond King was presented the Jim Thorpe Award in 2015.

Ferentz treads carefully when asked to name his favorite player he's coached, much like a father doesn't pick his favorite child. But it's clear that Clark would be on a short list. "We've been really lucky because we've had so many guys, and it's hard to pick one over another," Ferentz said. "But what can you say bad about Dallas Clark?"

66 Hartlieb to Cook

Practice makes perfect, no matter how long the odds. And they were staggering as the November 14, 1987, football game between Iowa and Ohio State moved inside of a minute to play at Ohio Stadium.

The Buckeyes led 27–22. Iowa was facing a fourth-and-23 predicament from the Ohio State 28. The Hawkeyes hadn't won at Ohio Stadium since 1959. And quarterback Chuck Hartlieb was going against a Buckeyes secondary that hadn't surrendered a touchdown pass in 13 quarters. Mission impossible? No.

"There was a timeout, and Coach [Hayden] Fry said to me, 'Chuck, what do you want to run?'" Hartlieb said. "And I knew exactly what I wanted to do."

Hartlieb wanted to throw to his roommate, Marv Cook, Iowa's standout tight end. "I didn't hesitate when [Fry] asked me," Hartlieb said. "I said, 'Coach, we should run Lion 75 Y Trail.' And he said, 'We're going to do it. We called up [quarterbacks coach Bill] Snyder, and he said 'Go.'"

Hartlieb came to the huddle and called the play. "In the huddle you almost had to read lips, it was so loud," Cook said. "Then I went to the line of scrimmage and went through my checklists... *Are they blitzing?* things like that. And then you just run the route and try to make a play. In practice we rehearsed those things over and over again."

Hartlieb knew what to expect as he got ready to take the snap. "I knew I was going to Marv all the way," Hartlieb said. "I knew it was man coverage. So when you have man coverage you just throw it at his back shoulder, the defensive back runs by him, and [Cook] can come underneath. It worked just like we practiced."

Hartlieb's pass wasn't a tight spiral, but he threw it to the perfect spot. Cook made the back-shoulder catch at the 9-yard line and bulled his way into the end zone for the winning touchdown with six seconds to play. Iowa 29, Ohio State 27.

"Marv made more of a play than I made a throw, but it was a great, great day," Hartlieb said.

Cook has joked with Hartlieb about his throw, all in good fun. "It was a back-shoulder throw," Cook said. "If the guy is running even with you man-to-man, you just throw it to the back side. That's what we did. We practiced that a lot to the inside but never much to the outside. It just worked out perfectly."

Entering the game, Fry had won at every Big Ten venue but Ohio Stadium. That included a 22–13 loss to the Buckeyes in 1985 when Iowa was ranked No. 1 in the nation. But Hartlieb-to-Cook changed that.

Hartlieb's final connection with Cook was his 20th completion in 37 attempts, for 333 yards. None sweeter than the last 28.

"Oh, boy," an ecstatic Fry said. "I hugged everyone in that dressing room. What a game. I've been associated with some great ones in 36 years of coaching, but I've never had one that was more meaningful to a group of players."

His winning catch still comes up from time to time in conversation, Cook says, and he considers it one of the most memorable Hawkeyes games he played in. "Every Ohio State and Michigan game was great," Cook said. "The Wisconsin games were great. But to be in Columbus, in the greatest setting in college football, and to get Coach Fry his first victory there, that was pretty exciting."

67 "I Love It"

Jim Zabel always loved to tell anyone who would listen that he followed in the footsteps of Ronald "Dutch" Reagan as the sports director at WHO Radio in Des Moines.

The story got even better when Reagan became a movie star and then president of the United States. Zabel interviewed Reagan 18 times, by his account, including a famous 1950 visit that ended this way:

> Zabel: "If we talk any longer the station may want to hire you back, and I'll be out of a job."
> Reagan: "You stay out of Hollywood, and I'll stay out of Des Moines."

Zabel also loved to tell the tale of the time he once ran a race against the great Jesse Owens. But Zabel became an icon as the play-by-play voice of the Iowa Hawkeyes football team, a job he held for 49 years, until 1996.

It was a job he loved, even when Iowa's football team couldn't find its way during 19 consecutive nonwinning seasons. Zabel made three-yard gains sound like touchdowns, and his enthusiastic

"Touchdown Iowa"

The University of Iowa made a groundbreaking, and not entirely popular, decision heading into the 1997–98 athletic year.

Instead of numerous stations calling football and men's basketball games on the road, Iowa went with a single voice and sold exclusive rights. The university signed a three-year deal with Learfield Communications, Inc., for $2.85 million.

Gary Dolphin was selected as the play-by-play voice of the statewide Iowa Radio Network. That silenced the microphones of three legends in the state. Bob Brooks, who watched the great Iowa running back Nile Kinnick play when he was a kid, had called games for the previous 50 years on WSUI in Iowa City and KCRG and KHAK in Cedar Rapids. Jim Zabel had done games for 49 consecutive seasons for WHO in Des Moines. And Ron Gonder had called games for the previous 32 years for KRNT in Des Moines and WMT in Cedar Rapids.

Zabel, Brooks, and Gonder all contributed to the new network's pregame and postgame shows for a few years. And all three were in the booth with Dolphin when the 1997 football season started with a 66–0 victory over Northern Iowa in Kinnick Stadium.

Dolphin jokes he had to pry the headset off Zabel's head to start the call of that September 6 game. "Break a leg," Zabel told Dolphin as a new era kicked off.

Dolphin didn't have to wait long for something good to happen. "It was a simple off-guard running play," Dolphin said. On the first scrimmage play of the 1997 season, Iowa's Tavian Banks scampered 63 yards for a touchdown: "Tavian Banks the single setback, [Chris] Knipper in motion to the wide side...pitch to Banks...Tavian cuts it back against the grain...40, 30, 20...put it in the banks...touchdown, Iowa."

And a new chapter in Iowa radio was off and running. "Kind of a mundane start to a season," Dolphin joked.

Dolphin has become known for his "Touchdown, Iowa" call, replacing the "I love it, I love it, I love it" line Zabel made famous when WHO's signal gave him a following across the state and beyond.

"That's kind of grown its own life," Dolphin said. "I've never gone into anything looking for a signature call. When you're doing something live, you're not sure how you're going to express yourself. I just try to be fair and accurate and simple."

pregame shows left even the most hardened skeptic thinking, *Iowa might win today.*

Zabel called the great games under Coach Forest Evashevski, and later Hayden Fry, bookmarked by those 19 underachieving seasons.

One of Zabel's trademark lines was "I love it, I love it, I love it." In fact, that was the title of his autobiography. "Kiss and hug those radios" was another Zabel mainstay during crucial moments in a game.

In one 1985 football game between No. 1 Iowa and Michigan State, with the Hawkeyes trailing 31–28 in the late stages, Zabel got fooled. He fell for quarterback Chuck Long's fake to running back Ronnie Harmon near the goal line, when in truth Long ran a bootleg to the right for the winning touchdown.

"You know, 11 Michigan State defenders a lot closer to the ball than I was missed it too," Zabel explained, in a comeback line for the ages.

Each spring, Iowa's head coaches travel the state to appear at I-Club functions, a chance to interact up close and personal with the fans. Zabel was often the master of ceremonies at these events, and he was usually the night's biggest star, because his voice was the fans' connection to the Iowa Hawkeyes more than the coaches'.

Zabel rooted for Iowa, his alma mater, and was never shy to admit that. "He knew his audience," said Gary Dolphin, who replaced Zabel as the voice of the Hawkeyes. "He knew who was listening to the games. He was just as much a fan as they were."

Zabel was Mr. Positive, with wit and charm thrown in. His Homeric Hawkeyes voice left us in May 2013, when he passed away at 91 years of age.

Zabel isn't remembered for accuracy; he is remembered for unbridled passion and enthusiasm. He became as big as the game itself to a loyal band of statewide listeners. He remains an icon to this day. "If you want to know what to put on my tombstone," Zabel said in 1994, "just three words: I HAD FUN."

68 Small-Town Star, Big-Time Success

Marv Cook was in his sixth season in the NFL when he got to experience *Monday Night Football* for the first time.

He was playing for the Chicago Bears in 1994 when they visited Philadelphia for a game with the Eagles. The Bears had a walk-through at the stadium the day before the game. As the team was boarding the bus for the ride back to the team hotel, Cook turned around, took another look at the field, and yelled, "West Branch!"

"Sounds corny," Cook said in telling the story.

But that's where the tale of Iowa's consensus All-American tight end and two-time Pro Bowler starts. In the small town of West Branch, Iowa.

"I always felt a connection with the people there," Cook said. "The ones who, when I was in fifth, sixth, seventh, and eighth grade, missing a front tooth, and I told them what I wanted to do, they didn't laugh."

West Branch is only a dozen miles from Iowa City, a short journey for the multisport star to travel to play football for Coach Hayden Fry at Iowa. It seemed like an easy transition for Cook, an outstanding athlete. It wasn't. "It was hard, a grind," Cook said. "I mean, it was tough. And there were a lot of times I had choices I could have made that would have moved me in different directions. But there was always something that kept me on the path of, 'I'm

The Pride of West Branch

When Iowa celebrated its 100th season of football in 1989, fans were asked to vote on an All-Century team. Marv Cook, the pride of West Branch, made the roster. Nile Kinnick was named the program's most outstanding player.

Offense

End—Marv Cook (1985–88); Jim Gibbons (1955–57)

Offensive line—Mike Enich (1938–40); Calvin Jones (1953–55); Jerry Hilgenberg (1951–53); John Niland (1963–65); Fred "Duke" Slater (1918–21)

Quarterback—Chuck Long (1982–85)

Running back—Ozzie Simmons (1934–36); Aubrey Devine (1919–21); Ronnie Harmon (1982–85)

Placekicker—Rob Houghtlin (1985–87)

Special Mention

Offensive line—Dave Croston (1984–86), Joe Devlin (1973–75); quarterback—Randy Duncan (1956–58); running back—Larry Ferguson (1959–62); Joe Laws (1931–33); Ed Podolak (1966–68); Bill Reichardt (1949–51); end—Erwin Prasse (1937–39)

Defense

End—Frank Gilliam (1953–56); Andre Tippett (1979–81)

Defensive line—Mark Bortz (1979–82); Dave Haight (1985–88); Alex Karras (1956–57)

Linebacker—Mike Reilly (1961–63); Larry Station (1982–85)

Defensive back—Craig Clemons (1969–71); Willis Glassgow (1927–29); Gordon Locke (1920–22); Ken Ploen (1954–56)

Punter—Reggie Roby (1979–82)

Special Mention

End—Lester Belding (1918–21); linebacker—Wally Hilgenberg (1961–63); defensive back—Devon Mitchell (1982–85); defensive end—Joe Mott (1985–88); linebacker—Brad Quast (1986–89); defensive back—Bill Reichardt (1949–51); Bobby Stoops (1979–82); Mike Stoops (1981–84) going to try to do everything I can today to get better and keep moving in the direction of my dreams and goals.'"

Two things highlighted his redshirt freshman season. The first was the fact that Cook was allowed to dress for home games after four or five weeks. The second came at the Freedom Bowl. Cook said, "As we were swarming onto the field, one of the guys, who I thought hated me, actually said something to the effect that, 'If you keep doing what you're doing, you're going to be okay.' That was the highlight of my first six months of Iowa football. I wasn't in the newspaper, I wasn't on TV, I didn't see the field at all, and that's tough on some kids. You have to understand that you have to be able to push through tough times."

Push he did, becoming one of the greatest tight ends in Iowa football history. His 126 catches are the most for a tight end in program history. He led the Big Ten with 63 receptions as a senior in 1988.

Cook was a two-time first-team All–Big Ten choice and was twice named Iowa's most valuable player. He was also a consensus All-American as a senior. He was named to Iowa's All-Century team in 1989 and has also been enshrined in the National Varsity Club Hall of Fame.

Cook was selected by New England in the third round of the 1989 NFL Draft and played seven NFL seasons with the Patriots, Bears, and St. Louis Rams before retiring following the 1995 season. He was selected to the Pro Bowl in 1991 and 1992.

Cook has now turned to coaching, where his teams at Iowa City Regina have won six straight state titles. Marv got to coach his son, Drew, now a quarterback for the Hawkeyes. "My son has grown up a Hawkeye fan," Cook said. "For him to have the opportunity to be on campus and experience some of the things I experienced, and to be with Coach [Kirk] Ferentz and his staff, the way they mentor young men…as a parent, what more can you ask for?"

69 One Shot, a Lifetime of Memories

The internal clock in Luke Recker's head was about to expire. He knew he had to pull the trigger, even though Indiana's Jared Jeffries and his intimidating seven-foot wingspan stood between him and the basket. "I didn't know if I had enough time to get it to the rim," Recker said. "It was kind of an unorthodox shot. It was like a shot-put. Thank goodness it went in."

Recker's 10-foot floater from the right baseline, released with two-tenths of a second remaining, gave Iowa a 62–60 victory against Indiana in the semifinals of the 2002 Big Ten Tournament in Indianapolis, Indiana.

But there was so much more to this story line. Recker was a high school basketball star in Auburn, Indiana, winning the state's coveted Mr. Basketball Award as a senior in 1997. He signed to play for Coach Bob Knight at Indiana but became a villain in that hoops-crazy state when he transferred after his sophomore season.

Recker decided on Arizona. But his involvement in a tragic auto accident changed his career path again. He ended up at Iowa, where he played for former Indiana All-American guard Steve Alford.

Recker was a junior, and in his first season at Iowa, when he played against Indiana for the first time. It was January 27, 2001, to be exact, at Carver-Hawkeye Arena in Iowa City. The contest was televised nationally by CBS. The Hoosiers led 43–26 at halftime, but Recker scored 17 of his game-high 27 points the second half to lead Iowa to a spirited 71–66 victory.

That was the last time Recker played that season, because he fractured his kneecap in that victory. He missed the Hawkeyes'

63–61 victory over the Hoosiers in the championship game of the Big Ten Tournament in Chicago.

The 2001–02 Hawkeyes were a top 10 team in the preseason poll, but they didn't live up to expectations. There was a 77–66 home loss to Indiana and a 79–51 defeat in Recker's return to Bloomington, Indiana. He was booed and heard chants of "Recker sucks!" the entire game.

But there was one more meeting, in Indianapolis: the semifinals of the Big Ten Tournament. Recker got a big measure of revenge for that day in Bloomington by scoring 17 points and hitting the game-winning shot. More than a decade later, Recker said that winning shot was one of the greatest memories of his college career. Also on that list was the 2001 game in Iowa City. "Because if there was one thing I wanted to do, it was to beat Indiana," Recker said. "But that game in the Big Ten Tournament was huge. To do it in Indianapolis, after going to Bloomington and, for lack of a better term, getting worked by the crowd. That was definitely a sweet memory I'll always have."

The internal clock in Recker's head got some help before his game winner. The clock froze with 2.2 seconds remaining, then started again after a delay of approximately half a second. Borrowed time to get the shot off.

"Maybe that's one time where things were on my side there," Recker said.

Recker is now the married father of two, and a successful business professional. "I have a pretty good life now, and I enjoy what I do," Recker said. "But there's no comparison to that feeling [of making a winning shot]. When you experience it as a team, it's so much more special."

The day before scoring against Jeffries, Recker's 15-foot fall-away buzzer beater over Devin Harris had given the Hawkeyes a 58–56 victory over top-seeded Wisconsin. "I tell those guys I'd trade those shots for their NBA careers," Recker said.

Iowa lost to Ohio State in the 2002 Big Ten Tournament title game, ending its dream of the NCAA Tournament. But the victory over Indiana was a pretty good consolation prize for Recker.

"Outside of the birth of my children, there's probably been no greater feeling I've ever had," Recker said.

70 A Wonderful Life

This is a story of life imitating art. Donna Reed grew up in Denison, Iowa, and became a big star in Hollywood. One of her most memorable roles is as Mary Bailey in the 1946 Frank Capra classic *It's a Wonderful Life*.

Reed is the most famous resident the town of Denison has ever produced. But nearly seven decades later, she has competition in the form of Brandon Scherff. "She was a good actress," Scherff said. "If I ever do that, it will be a great honor. It's a wonderful life back there."

Scherff left Denison to become one of Iowa's most decorated football players of all time. As a senior left offensive tackle for the Hawkeyes in 2014, Scherff was the fourth Iowa player to receive the Outland Trophy that goes to the nation's best interior lineman. He was also named winner of the Rimington-Pace Offensive Lineman of the Year in the Big Ten. And he was a consensus All-American.

Scherff got some attention after his junior season when he skipped an opportunity to enter the NFL Draft, even though scouts had him projected as a first-round pick. When Scherff made his intentions clear, Iowa coach Kirk Ferentz offered up some perspective. "He made his decision for the right reasons," Ferentz said. "And the reasons that prompted that decision give me confidence that he's thinking about the right things now. He's not trying to be a big man or anything. He just wants to be a great player at Iowa."

Scherff did just that. His portrait hangs in the All-American Room of the Hansen Football Performance Center at Iowa. Only consensus All-Americans are included.

Scherff is a big man, tipping the scales in excess of 300 pounds. But he is a gentle giant when it comes to self-promotion. He sticks to his small-town roots when he becomes the subject of questions. For example, when Scherff decided to return to Iowa for his senior season, he didn't have a news conference. He gave the story to radio station KDSN in Denison. "You've got to remember where you're from," Scherff said.

Brandon Scherff squares up against the Minnesota Golden Gophers in 2012.

On the eve of the 2015 NFL Draft, Ferentz was asked about Scherff. "He doesn't act like he's anything special," Ferentz said.

The Washington Redskins thought Scherff was something special. They selected him with the fifth pick of the first round. Scherff became the fourth Iowa player selected in the first round at that position since 2004, joining Robert Gallery, Bryan Bulaga, and Riley Reiff.

Scherff also became the fifth player in Iowa history to go in the first five picks, and the first since Gallery in 2004. He was also the seventh Ferentz-coached player to go in the first round.

Scherff played quarterback as a sophomore at Denison High School. He was moved to tight end, then the line, where he made a name for himself at Iowa (and made himself into a first-round draft pick). "I never would have imagined this," Scherff said on the night of the draft, as he thought back to his days in Denison. "It just shows what can happen if you go out, work hard every day, and try to improve."

The Redskins moved Scherff from tackle to guard, and he started all 16 games at right guard in 2015, missed just one play from scrimmage, and was selected to the NFL's All-Rookie team.

A wonderful life, indeed.

71 Renaissance Man

Andre Tippett's arrival on the Iowa campus coincided with the start of a football renaissance.

Hayden Fry took over as coach in 1979, determined to put an end to 17 consecutive nonwinning seasons. And Tippett, from

New Sheriff in Town

When Hayden Fry took over as Iowa's football coach in 1979, he decided to model the uniforms after the four-time Super Bowl–champion Pittsburgh Steelers. That way, Fry said, the Hawkeyes would look like a winner "until we broke the huddle."

The Fry era started with a $45,000 annual salary and three straight losses, but it was obvious to everyone there was a new sheriff in town.

Iowa took a 26–3 halftime lead in the season opener against Indiana, coached by future *ESPN College GameDay* fixture Lee Corso. Kinnick Stadium had a pulse for the first time in years. And then the Hoosiers rallied in the second half to win the game 30–26. The winning touchdown came on a 66-yard touchdown pass from Tim Clifford to running back Lonnie Johnson with 58 seconds remaining in the game. Johnson became wide open when a member of Iowa's secondary blew the coverage.

Iowa was a five-touchdown underdog the next week at No. 3 Oklahoma. The Hawkeyes trailed 7–6 heading into the fourth quarter, before the Sooners tacked on two late touchdowns.

When Fry heard his players being praised for a valiant effort, he unloaded. "I just told the team that if I see one single man with a smile on his face, I'm going to bust him in the mouth," Fry said. "Losing is losing, and we didn't play well. These kids have been

Newark, New Jersey, arrived after a season at Ellsworth Community College in Iowa Falls.

Three seasons later, Tippett played his final game in a Hawkeyes uniform at the Rose Bowl and Iowa football was nationally ranked.

"We didn't know what to expect when Hayden came in," Tippett said. "It was a transition period. Iowa began spending money to improve the facilities that allowed us to lift, run, and work out year-round. Hayden wanted us to have a certain look. He had an idea, and he got it done."

Tippett, a defensive end, became a star for the Hawkeyes. He was a two-time All–Big Ten selection and a unanimous babied and pampered so much when they lose that it makes me sick. Losing and looking good is a bunch of crap."

Iowa was a three-touchdown underdog the next week against No. 7 Nebraska at Kinnick Stadium. And the Hawkeyes were without starting quarterback Phil Suess, who was sidelined with a kidney injury. "Let's bow our heads and pray together," Fry joked the day before the game.

It was Big Red fans who were praying for a comeback heading into the fourth quarter, because Iowa was holding a 21–14 lead. Nebraska rallied for a 24–21 victory. "I'm all right, except for the three bullet holes in my chest," Fry said the following week.

Fry's first victory as Iowa coach came in Week 4, 30–14, against an Iowa State team that had been favored by a field goal. Iowa officials had taken down the traditional steel goal posts and replaced them with wooden goal posts for the game. Iowa students tore both of them down after the victory.

Someone handed Fry a piece of one of the goal posts as he headed to the locker room. Fry was asked if it was okay for his players to smile after the victory, a reference to his postgame comments at Oklahoma. "I'm going to take this up to the dressing room right now," Fry said, holding the chunk of goal post, "and I'm going to smack any player who is not smiling."

All-American after a 1981 season that saw Iowa put together its first winning season since 1960, with an 8–4 record; earn a share of the school's first Big Ten title since 1958; and go to the Rose Bowl and finish the season with a No. 18 national ranking in the Associated Press poll. "We changed an attitude and an environment in the state of Iowa," said Tippett, a captain in 1981. "We changed how everyone perceived the Hawkeyes."

That 1981 season was dominated by Iowa's suffocating defense. With Tippett creating havoc from his end position, nose guard Pat Dean putting up a wall, and linebacker Mel Cole racking up tackles, opponents averaged just 11.7 points, 86.9 yards rushing, and 253.6 yards of total offense in 1981.

Tippett was drafted in the second round of the 1982 NFL Draft by the New England Patriots, the 41st player selected, and played linebacker for 11 seasons. He had 12.5 sacks or more in three different seasons and ended up with 100 in his 151-game Patriots career. From 1985 to 1987, Tippett was named Linebacker of the Year by the NFL Players Association. He was also honored as a first-team All-NFL choice in 1985 and 1987 by the Associated Press and a second-team choice in 1986 and 1988. He played in five Pro Bowls.

Tippett was named to Iowa's All-Century football team when the program celebrated its 100th season of football in 1989. He was also elected into the University of Iowa's Varsity Hall of Fame in 2007.

Tippett was enshrined in the Pro Football Hall of Fame on August 2, 2008. During his induction speech, Tippett touched on his days as a Hawkeye. "When I arrived at Iowa, Hayden Fry delivered on his promise to turn the program into a winner," Tippett said. "We went from a laughingstock of the conference to winning the Big Ten championship and being the Rose Bowl representatives. I owe a debt of gratitude to the University of Iowa and my teammates, some who are here today… Thank you for the opportunity."

72 Michelle "Ice" Edwards

Michelle Edwards figured she'd play college basketball at Southern California or Virginia. The Trojans had a superstar in Cheryl Miller, quite the recruiting tool. Geno Auriemma, who could later take Connecticut to incredible success, was an assistant at Virginia at the time and was recruiting Edwards.

But then C. Vivian Stringer came into the picture, selling this native of Boston, Massachusetts, on an opportunity at Iowa. "I really had no idea where it was," Edwards said. "I had to pull out a map."

Edwards came, and helped put Iowa basketball on the map during a career that ran from 1984 to 1988. An athlete who grew up dreaming about becoming the first African American downhill skier in the Olympics found a home during Iowa's snowy winter months. "It was like a clean slate," said Edwards, a 5'9" guard. "Let's see what could happen."

Big things, it turned out. Before long, Edwards earned the nickname Ice. "She was Ice," teammate Jolette Law said. "She had ice water in her veins. She was calm under pressure and just money. As a point guard, I knew that every game we played we had a chance with Michelle. I knew if I got her the ball in the right place, we'd be money. She was our go-to player."

Iowa enjoyed uncharted success under Stringer, with Edwards right in the middle of it all. With Edwards in uniform, the Hawkeyes won two Big Ten titles and went to three NCAA Tournaments. Edwards was a three-time All–Big Ten selection and the player of the year as a senior. She was also an All-American and was named Champion National Player of the Year in 1988, then the highest honor in women's collegiate basketball.

Edwards was remarkable as a senior. She averaged 20 points, 4.8 rebounds, 4.5 assists, and 2.9 steals. In December 1987 Iowa defeated No. 2 Auburn, No. 6 Virginia, and No. 1 Texas in Miami, Florida. The Hawkeyes' reward was moving to No. 1 in the Associated Press poll for the first time in school history.

Iowa finished that season 29–2 overall and 17–1 in the Big Ten, losing to Long Beach State on the 49ers' home court in the West Regional Finals.

That was also the final game of Edwards' incredible Iowa career. She remains the program's No. 4 career scorer (1,821 points) and third in both assists (431) and steals (235).

Edwards went on to play professionally in Italy for nine seasons. And after the WNBA arrived in 1997, she played in that league for five more seasons.

Edwards was inducted into the University of Iowa's Athletics Hall of Fame in 2000. And in a testimony to her nickname, she is the only Hawkeye women's player to have her number—No. 30—retired.

She was also enshrined in the Women's Basketball Hall of Fame in 2014. Not bad for someone who wanted to ski instead of weaving her way through defenses on a basketball court.

73 A Select Group of Hawkeyes

Their names and uniform numbers are on display at Kinnick Stadium. Nine players—a select club. The University of Iowa athletic department created the Kinnick Stadium Wall of Honor in 2013. To gain membership, a Hawkeyes football player has to be a member of the University of Iowa Varsity Club Hall of Fame and meet one of three criteria: being a member of both the National

Football Foundation & College Football Hall of Fame and the Helms Athletic Foundation Hall of Fame; being a member of one of the two halls of fame and a consensus All-American; or being a two-time consensus All-American. The Helms Athletic Foundation is no longer active, so that part of the criteria doesn't exist for future players.

These names and numbers appear on the Paul W. Brechler Press Box, facing the stands:

No. 1, Aubrey Devine (1919–21)
He was quarterback and captain of Iowa's 1921 Big Ten title team. In both 1919 and 1920 he led the Hawkeyes in rushing, passing, and scoring. His dropkick beat Notre Dame 10–7 in 1921, and Iowa earned a share of its first mythical national title.

No. 25, Randy Duncan (1956–58)
He was the Heisman Trophy runner-up and Big Ten MVP after quarterbacking the Hawkeyes to a Big Ten title in 1958 and victory in the Rose Bowl. Iowa won the Grantland Rice Trophy from the Football Writers Association of America after being voted the national champion. He was a two-time All–Big Ten pick and earned the Walter Camp Award as a senior. He was the first player selected in the 1959 NFL Draft.

No. 62, Calvin Jones (1953–55)
He won the Outland Trophy in 1955 and was named to 22 different All-America teams during his Hawkeyes career. He was Iowa's first two-time consensus All-American. His number is retired.

No. 77, Alex Karras (1956–57)
He was the first two-time Associated Press All-American in Iowa history. He also won the Outland Trophy and was a runner-up for the Heisman Trophy in 1957.

No. 24, Nile Kinnick (1937–39)

He became Iowa's lone Heisman Trophy winner, in 1939, after leading the famed Ironmen. He also won the Maxwell and Walter Camp Awards as a senior. He was the Big Ten MVP and also a Phi Beta Kappa scholar and senior class president. The University of Iowa stadium was named for him in 1972. His number is retired.

No. 1, Gordon Locke (1920–22)

He was the Walter Camp All-American quarterback as a senior, after playing fullback earlier in his Hawkeyes career. He scored 72 points as a senior, a Big Ten record at the time. He was presented with the Big Ten Medal of Honor in 1923.

No. 16, Chuck Long (1982–85)

He led Iowa to a Big Ten title as a senior and was a runner-up for the Heisman Trophy. He became the first player in NCAA history to pass for more than 10,000 career yards. He completed 22 consecutive passes against Indiana as a junior, an NCAA record at the time. And he was a three-time All–Big Ten selection and league MVP as a senior.

No. 15, Duke Slater (1918–21)

He became the first African American player elected to the College Football Hall of Fame in 1951. He won seven letters at Iowa in football and track, and received All-America honors in both sports. He was a three-time All–Big Ten selection as a tackle.

No. 36, Larry Station (1982–85)

He was a consensus All-American at linebacker as a junior and senior. He's the only player in school history to lead the team in tackles four straight seasons. He was a three-time All–Big Ten honoree and finalist for the Lombardi and Butkus Awards as a senior.

The Diagonal Dagger

The small town of Diagonal was an Iowa high school basketball powerhouse when Dick Ives played there in the early 1940s. But his talent stood out. "Pops Harrison, the Iowa coach, had heard of me," Ives said. "He knew I was out there in Diagonal, and we started corresponding by mail."

Harrison didn't offer Ives a scholarship. Drake did. "But I'd always wanted to play for Iowa, so I went there and even paid my $65 tuition fee," Ives said.

Ives covered that tuition fee by mowing lawns and sweeping the floors in the athletic department offices at Iowa Field House.

"I was jealous that I wasn't given an athletic scholarship," Ives said. "I'd go out with Pops and help him recruit other players, but I wasn't given a scholarship myself."

But you can't put a price on opportunity. And Ives got one at Iowa. Freshmen were eligible for athletic competition when he arrived in Iowa City in the fall of 1943, because of World War II. Ives was one of three freshman starters that season. He was joined in the lineup by Dave Danner, a first-team All–Big Ten selection that season, and Jack Spencer. The first three reserves off the bench were also freshmen. None of them made the immediate impact that Ives did.

In his very first varsity game, a 50–33 victory over Nebraska at Iowa Field House, Ives scored 19 points (nine field goals and a free throw). The game story in the *Des Moines Register* read like this: "Iowa launched its basketball season here Friday night by walloping Nebraska, 50–33, behind the 19-point scoring of Dick Ives, the freshman scoring sensation from Diagonal."

Only one other freshman in Iowa history has scored that many points in his debut. That was Aaron White, who had 19 against Chicago State on November 11, 2011, at Carver-Hawkeye Arena.

Ives, it turned out, was just getting warmed up. And in a 103–31 victory over the University of Chicago on February 5, Ives scored a Big Ten–record 43 points. His 19 field goals was another Big Ten mark. To put 43 points in perspective, Iowa scored 37 points as a team in a pair of victories over Minnesota, and scored less than 50 points in seven other games.

Iowa was 12–0 after that victory over Chicago, in its last season as a Big Ten member. The Hawkeyes finished 14–4 and tied for second in the league at 9–3. A 42–41 loss to Northwestern in the season's final game cost the Hawkeyes a share of the championship with Ohio State.

Ives finished that season by scoring a then-school-record 327 points, earning the nickname the Diagonal Dagger. His 18.1-point average is still a school record for a freshman. His 43-point outburst ranks third all time. Ives' record stood until John Johnson scored 46 points against Wisconsin-Milwaukee on December 7, 1968.

Ives, who passed away in 1997, was a three-time All-American and helped the Hawkeyes win a Big Ten crown in 1944–45. He was one of 20 players selected to Iowa's All-Century team when the school celebrated its 100th anniversary of basketball in 2002.

"I have no regrets about anything that happened to me at Iowa," Ives said. "Well, I guess they still owe me that $65 in tuition money."

75 A "Super" Scorer

Sam Williams' path to Iowa was unique, to stay the least. After graduating from Northern High School in Detroit, Michigan, Williams got a job at a cold storage facility, hauling beef. Deciding that wasn't something he wanted to do for the rest of his life, Williams thought about playing college basketball.

He ended up at Burlington Junior College, then joined the Hawkeyes starting in 1966–67. A dynamic scorer, he had quite a major-college debut. Williams averaged 22.6 points and 9.4 rebounds a game. Iowa went 16–8 overall and 9–5 in the Big Ten, good for third place.

Williams had earned a nickname—fans called him "Super" Sam Williams—heading into his senior season. But the 1967–68 campaign got off to a rocky start. A loss to Northwestern in the Big Ten opener left Iowa with a 5–5 record. And then Williams lived up to his nickname, and Iowa ultimately won its first Big Ten Championship in 12 years.

Williams averaged 25.3 points and 10.9 rebounds as a senior. As Iowa started winning games, Williams kept filling up the score book. He registered at least 25 points in eight straight games. "What I like to do best on offense is drive, then pull up and take the shot," said Williams, a 6'3" guard who scored 632 points and squeezed off 475 field goal attempts that senior season.

Iowa won 11 of its next 13 games after that 5–5 start. But the Hawkeyes had to share the title after losing their final regular-season game of the season. Iowa fell 71–70 to Michigan at home, in a game in which the Hawkeyes were forced to play catch-up after falling behind 15–2 at the start. The Wolverines had entered the game with a 5–8 Big Ten record, and had lost to Iowa 99–86 in Ann Arbor earlier in the season.

Michigan's upset victory left Iowa 10–4 and tied with Ohio State for the Big Ten crown. A playoff was required to determine the Big Ten's representative in the NCAA Tournament. Ohio State beat the Hawkeyes 85–81 in West Lafayette, Indiana.

Sophomore starters Chad Calabria and Glenn Vidnovic averaged double figures that season, and were important pieces on Coach Ralph Miller's undefeated Big Ten championship team two years later. But this year belonged to Williams, who was voted the Big Ten's most valuable player by the *Chicago Tribune* in 1968 after he led the league in scoring. Williams was also an All-American for the second straight season.

Williams scored 1,176 points in his two-year career. That 24-point career average in 49 games is a school record. He also had a career rebounding average of 10.2.

Williams was drafted by the Milwaukee Bucks in the third round of the 1968 NBA Draft, the 35th selection overall. He played two NBA seasons, averaging 3.9 points.

76 The Real No. 1?

LSU's football team was declared the national champion in 1958. Iowa fans wanted another vote.

Back then, the final Associated Press poll came out before the bowl games were played. The media voted LSU No. 1. Iowa was No. 2. The United Press International coaches poll also had the Tigers at No. 1.

LSU had defeated two teams in the AP's final top 10 that season—No. 11 Mississippi and No. 14 Florida. Iowa beat No. 7 Wisconsin, No. 10 Texas Christian, and No. 17 Notre Dame; tied with No. 6 Air Force; and lost to No. 8 Ohio State.

The Hawkeyes' case for No. 1 increased when they dominated No. 16 California in the Rose Bowl 38–12. LSU completed an 11–0 record by beating No. 12 Clemson 7–0 in the Sugar Bowl.

"We played in the best bowl game you could ever play in," said Iowa halfback Bob Jeter, who had been the game's most valuable player. "But what made me mad is how in the world could they have [picked] the No. 1 team before we played in the Rose Bowl. I could not believe that."

Iowa was declared the national champion by the Football Writers Association of America, and received the Grantland Rice Trophy. That balloting was done after the bowl games.

It was Jeter who put Iowa in position to be considered the best team in the land with a scintillating performance in Pasadena. He rushed for 194 yards—a school and Rose Bowl record at the time—on just nine carries. That included an 81-yard touchdown scamper in the third quarter. That broke the Rose Bowl record of 71 yards set by Frank Aschenbrenner of Northwestern against California in 1949. Jeter also got loose for a 41-yard run, setting up another Iowa touchdown.

Iowa rushed for 429 yards on the day. Jeter was named MVP in a unanimous vote. Jeter led Iowa in rushing with 609 yards the next season in just 108 carries.

Jeter, who passed away in 2008, did get a taste of No. 1 before his football career ended. He was selected in the second round of the 1960 NFL Draft by the Green Bay Packers, the 17th player selected. The Los Angeles Chargers took him in the first round of the AFL Draft. But he decided to play in the Canadian Football League for the British Columbia Lions, then joined the Packers two years later.

After getting a look at Jeter at wide receiver, Coach Vince Lombardi moved him to the secondary. Jeter became a starter in 1965 and played on teams that won three straight NFL titles, including the first two Super Bowls. A two-time Pro Bowler, Jeter was traded to the Chicago Bears in 1971. He retired in 1973 with 26 career interceptions.

Jeter was inducted into the Packers Hall of Fame in 1985, the Rose Bowl Hall of Fame in 1994, and the Iowa Athletics Hall of Fame in 2010.

77 Greene Means Go

Shonn Greene's climb to the top of Iowa's single-season rushing list was not a straight line.

The native of Sicklerville, New Jersey, was part of Iowa's 2004 signing class. But he came up short of the required test score and headed to Milford Academy in Connecticut for a season.

Greene arrived in Iowa City in 2005 and saw limited duty for the next two seasons. Then another bump in the road. Greene left school to get his academic life in order. He spent the 2007 season attending classes at Kirkwood Community College and moved furniture for a living while rooming with Iowa running back and fellow New Jersey native Albert Young.

Then it was back to Iowa for a record-setting 2008 season. Greene rushed for 109 yards in 22 carries in his first career start, against Maine in the season opener. He went on to break the 100-yard barrier in all 13 games that year, the first player in Iowa history to accomplish that. Greene needed 307 carries to set Iowa's single-season rushing record of 1,850 yards. He broke the previous mark of 1,691 yards set by Tavian Banks in 1997.

Greene's biggest game came in a 38–16 victory over Wisconsin. He tied a school record with four touchdowns, on runs of 12, 34, 34, and 52 yards. He finished with a career-high 217 yards.

"I don't know if anyone could have exceeded expectations as well as he has been playing," Iowa coach Kirk Ferentz said. "We

Shonn Greene proves his mettle in the 2009 Outback Bowl against South Carolina.

thought he would be a real good back, but he is playing as well in the backfield as anyone that I have been around."

Greene also had 211 yards in 30 carries against Purdue in the 11th game of the season. That matched the most carries he had in any game.

Iowa won its last four games that season, starting with a 24–23 upset of No. 3 Penn State on November 8. Greene had 121 yards in a 31–10 victory over South Carolina in the Outback Bowl. After the game, he announced his intentions of skipping his final season of eligibility and putting his name in the NFL Draft. "My performance this season is why—the 100 yards every game—I don't think there's a whole lot more I can do here," Greene said. "People talk about the Heisman thing, but I think that's a lot of politics."

Greene would have been a strong Heisman contender in 2009. He finished sixth after his record-breaking 2008 season, behind four quarterbacks and a wide receiver. Greene won the Doak Walker Award, which goes to the nation's leading running back. He was also a consensus All-American, the first Iowa running back to accomplish that since 1939 Heisman Trophy winner Nile Kinnick.

Greene was the only back in the country to break the 100-yard mark in every game in 2008, and he finished second nationally in rushing yards. He was also awarded the Chicago Tribune Silver Football Award, which goes to the most valuable player in the Big Ten.

"This is as good as it gets," said Greene, selected in the third round of the 2009 NFL Draft by the New York Jets. "Winning the bowl game, winning the Doak Walker Award, MVP of the Big Ten—I don't think you can do any better than that."

78 Five on a Side

Men's basketball became a sanctioned sport at the University of Iowa in 1901. Coach Ed Rule's team won their first 10 games and finished that debut season 10–2. The Hawkeyes wouldn't join the Big Ten Conference until the 1908–09 season.

But there was a basketball game of historical significance played on the Iowa campus six years before Rule's first team put on a uniform, and five years after Dr. James Naismith invented the game of basketball itself.

On January 18, 1896, Iowa played Chicago in what is called the first intercollegiate game using the modern rule of five players on a side. The Chicago team was coached by Amos Alonzo Stagg. Best known as a football coach—Stagg coached Chicago to national football championships in 1905 and 1913. He's also enshrined in the Naismith Memorial Basketball Hall of Fame.

Stagg learned the game of basketball from Naismith at Springfield College in Springfield, Massachusetts, where Naismith invented the game in 1891. Stagg also played in the first public game of basketball at the Springfield YMCA on March 11, 1892. He scored the only basket for his team.

It was Stagg who popularized the use of five players on a side, though he got an assist from Iowa physical education professor H.F. Kallenberg, who graduated from Springfield College the year before Naismith invented the game. Kallenberg wrote Naismith asking for a copy of the rules and introduced the game to his Iowa students.

Stagg coached his team to victory on that milestone day in Iowa City in 1896, which took place a month before the Intercollegiate

Conference of Faculty Representatives (now known as the Big Ten) was founded.

Chicago won the game. The Big Ten says it was by a 13–12 score, but University of Iowa records had it a 15–12 game. Neither team used a substitute.

The game was played at Iowa Armory, before 400 fans. Anywhere from seven to nine players were originally on the floor at the same time when the game was in its nascent stages. Kallenberg and Stagg agreed to reduce that to five a side.

There is some dispute over whether or not this was the first true game between two intercollegiate teams. Some say this honor goes to an 1897 game between Yale and Penn, because the Iowa team that faced Chicago the year before was made up of University of Iowa students but wasn't officially representing the university.

But there is no debate over this—five on a side became part of the game that night in Iowa City.

79 Lisa and Logic

Lisa Bluder is the winningest basketball coach in University of Iowa history, female or male. Hired by Dr. Christine Grant in 2000 after a successful stint at Drake, Bluder's ability to coach is not in question. Neither is her ability to recruit program-changing players such as Samantha Logic.

A 5'9" guard from Racine, Wisconsin, Logic was a junior when Bluder set the coaching milestone with her 270th victory as Iowa coach on February 10, 2014. Logic went on to become one of the most decorated players in Hawkeyes history and a first-round draft

Guard Samantha Logic scores big against Ohio Sate in a 2015 game.

pick in the WNBA. She joined Toni Foster (1997) as the program's only first-round selections.

"Watching Sam Logic in action is worth way more than the price of a ticket," Bluder said during Logic's senior season. "You better not take your eyes off her, or you will miss a magical pass or an unbelievable hustle play."

By the time Logic had completed her career in March 2015—with a Sweet 16 NCAA Tournament run—the numbers backed up Bluder's descriptions. Logic became the first player in NCAA history to total at least 1,500 career points, 800 rebounds, 800 assists, and 200 steals. She had six career triple-doubles, one shy of the Division I record, and 33 double-doubles.

"I don't think that I have had the opportunity to coach an all-around player such as Sam, someone who excels in so many different areas of the game and who is such a tremendous leader on and off the court," said Bluder.

Logic was named to the All–Big Ten first team for the second straight season as a senior, and was also honored as a third-team All-American. She helped Bluder set a new victory standard by emulating her leadership on the floor.

"Sam is the leader of this team by virtue of being our point guard, but also by the way that she plays and leads our team," Bluder said during Logic's senior season. "She is the coach on the floor and is so intuitive about what is going on on the court."

Logic started 135 games at Iowa, finishing with 1,546 points, 922 rebounds, 898 assists, and 260 steals. She also played on four straight NCAA Tournament teams, scoring in double figures in seven of eight games. Iowa's Sweet 16 run in Logic's senior season was the first for the program since 1996.

80 Dishing and Dunking

Andre Woolridge, who transferred to Iowa from Nebraska after his freshman season, had a motor for basketball that always ran. "At the beginning of our sophomore year, Coach [Tom Davis] told Andre and I that we needed to slow down in practice," Jess Settles recalled. "He'd make us take the rest of practice off because we were going too hard. About an hour later, after everyone else had cleared out, I knew the coaches would still be around. So I'd sneak over to Iowa Field House. And there was Andre, working out."

Woolridge established some history during the 1996–97 season. Iowa's senior point guard became the first player in Big Ten history to lead the conference in scoring and assists in the same season. "You've got to be unselfish and be able to take it yourself," Davis said. "It's hard to put those two things together."

But that's what Woolridge did as a senior. He averaged 20.2 points a game. He also led the league in assists for a second straight season with 6.0 per game.

"He was one of those rare guys who had some explosiveness to him, too," Davis said. "He could take it down the lane and dunk. But he had finesse on the perimeter with the jump shot. He had some speed up and down the court, yet had a good handle."

Woolridge led the team in scoring 23 times as a senior. Seventeen times he scored 20 points or more. He scored 31 or more three times.

"Woolridge would get my vote without any question," Indiana's Bob Knight said when asked who deserved to be Big Ten Player of the Year.

Davis felt the same way. But the award went to Minnesota point guard Bobby Jackson, who averaged 15.3 points, 6.1

rebounds, and 4.0 assists for a team that won the Big Ten with a 16–2 record. Iowa tied for second with Purdue, four games back.

Minnesota made the Final Four, but an academic fraud investigation was uncovered. Jackson was later stripped of his Player of the Year honor, and the Gophers had to vacate their Big Ten title and Final Four appearance.

Woolridge shared Iowa's most valuable player honor as a sophomore and junior and won it outright as a senior, after Iowa won 22 games and reached the second round of the NCAA Tournament. He was a first-team All–Big Ten selection his final two seasons, and was an Associated Press third-team All-American as a senior.

Woolridge went on to play 12 seasons of professional basketball overseas before retiring in 2009.

81 The Hit Man Is No. 1

Kirk Ferentz was hired in December 1998 to replace Hayden Fry as Iowa's football coach. His Hawkeyes teams lost 18 of their first 20 games under his watch. "It was well-documented," Ferentz said. "It was like a body count."

Since then, five Ferentz teams have been ranked in the top 10 of the final Associated Press poll since that 2–18 start. There are a multitude of reasons for the turnaround. But one player, more than any other, played an instrumental role.

His name was Demond Sanders, but he was better known as Bob. At 5'8" and 200 pounds, Sanders earned the nickname Hit Man during a career that saw him named to the All–Big Ten first team three times as a defensive back.

Sanders had been seeing most of his duty on special teams as a true freshman in 2000. But Ferentz gave him his first career start in an October 28 game at Wisconsin. It was a program-changing decision.

"That kind of gave us a little spark," Ferentz said. "It didn't make us a great defense. They still had 400-some yards against us, but they ended up with 13 points. Our demeanor changed a little bit. And sometimes you need a little catalyst, a guy helping you out a little bit." A guy from Erie, Pennsylvania, named Bob Sanders.

Wisconsin won that game 13–7, but Iowa won its next two—a 26–23 two-overtime thriller at Penn State and a 27–17 upset of No. 12 Northwestern at home. Iowa's winning streak ended in the 27–24 season finale at Minnesota. The Gophers rallied after Sanders was knocked out of the game with a concussion with eight minutes remaining in the third quarter. But his play had left an impression on his teammates.

"That kid's a human highlight film, a battering ram," Anthony Herron said after the loss to the Gophers. "His potential is…I can only imagine."

Iowa got to a bowl game for the first time under Ferentz a season later, going 7–5 in 2001 and beating Texas Tech in the Alamo Bowl. A Sanders interception in the end zone sealed the deal.

The Hawkeyes finished in the nation's top 10 in Sanders' final two seasons, winning a Big Ten title in 2002 and finishing 11–2 after a loss to Southern California in the Orange Bowl and going 10–3 in 2003 after clubbing Florida in the Outback Bowl.

Sanders was named an Associated Press second-team All-American as a senior. He shared Iowa's most valuable player award with offensive tackle Robert Gallery. Sanders finished with 348 career tackles, including 25 against Indiana during his sophomore season.

The Indianapolis Colts took Sanders in the second round of the 2004 NFL Draft. Indianapolis Coach Tony Dungy gave him a new nickname, Eraser, because he had a knack for erasing his teammates' mistakes with his relentless style of play.

Sanders was twice named an All-Pro and played in the 2005 and 2007 Pro Bowls. He was also named the NFL's Defensive Player of the Year in 2007.

Injuries dogged Sanders for much of his NFL career. Only twice did he play in more than six games in a season, in 2005 and 2007. His pro career ended after the 2011 season.

When it comes to listing the most important player in the Ferentz coaching era at Iowa, Sanders is No. 1.

82 Father-Son Grand Celebration

Roy Marble opened his Iowa basketball career in paradise. It was a miserable experience. He failed to score a single point, missing once from the field and once from the free-throw line in a victory against the University of Hawaii–Hilo to kick off the 1985–86 season.

Twenty-five seasons later, his son, Devyn, started his Hawkeyes career by scoring seven points in a loss to South Dakota State in the 2010–11 opener.

Not exactly headline-grabbing debuts for either one of them. But the end of their careers told a much different story. They became the first father-son tandem in Big Ten history to both reach the 1,000-point plateau.

Roy became the first player in Iowa history to reach 2,000 points during a career that ended after the 1988–89 season. He is the Hawkeyes' No. 1 all-time scorer with 2,116 points, an average of 15.8 points per game.

An off-guard, Roy was an average shooter. But he used his athleticism to slash and score. He averaged in double figures all four seasons. He was recruited to Iowa by George Raveling, who left after one season to take the job at Southern California.

Tom Davis left Stanford to become the new coach, and Marble was an inheritance gift. His skill set fit perfectly with the fast-break, full-court-press style Davis employed.

"Him, more than anybody else," Davis said. "He was a guard who could play forward. He could handle the ball, but he could dunk it."

On top of that, Davis inherited a coachable player willing to adapt to a different coaching philosophy.

"You can be a great athlete, but a lot of them aren't willing to do what has to be done to be on a winning team, or be a winning player," said Davis, whose first Hawkeyes team set a school record with 30 victories. "Roy was certainly that."

Roy scored in double figures in 105 of the 134 games he played for Iowa. He scored at least 20 points in 39 games, with three of 30 or more.

Devyn was recruited to Iowa by Todd Lickliter, who was fired after the 2009–10 season. After signing a letter of intent with the Hawkeyes in the fall of 2009, Devyn contemplated looking for a new school. But Fran McCaffery, who left Siena to replace Lickliter, successfully recruited him all over again. "I definitely made the right choice," Devyn said.

Devyn played in 136 games for the Hawkeyes, scoring in double figures 84 times. He scored 20 points or more 26 times, with three games of 30 or more.

When Devyn's career ended, he and his father had scored 3,810 points in an Iowa uniform. That was the second-highest total ever for a father-son combination playing for the same NCAA Division I school.

Roy scored more points, but his son got the final word. Devyn was a first-team All–Big Ten pick in 2014. Roy was twice a second-team choice.

83 Major League Legacy

Jack Dittmer came to Iowa on a football scholarship, but baseball took him to the big show. Dittmer played six major league seasons for Boston/Milwaukee and Detroit, after a rich and rewarding college career that saw him letter nine times for the Hawkeyes in football, baseball, and basketball, his favorite sport as a kid growing up in Elkader, Iowa.

Being a multisport star was nothing new to Dittmer. He won 12 letters in high school before moving to Iowa City, and was All-State in basketball and football. During the summer of 1945, Dittmer was nominated to play in the US All-American East-West baseball game in New York City. Dittmer's coach on the East team was Ty Cobb. Babe Ruth coached the West team.

Dittmer was first-team All–Big Ten and second-team All-American and cocaptain of an Iowa baseball team that won a conference title in 1949. He was a second-team All–Big Ten end on the football team in 1949 and the Hawkeyes' most valuable player after setting a Big Ten single-season record for receiving yards. He had six touchdown catches as a senior and left behind five school receiving records. "If the quarterback could get the ball to me, I could catch it," Dittmer said. "If I got into the open, no one caught me from behind."

The Boston Braves signed Dittmer to a professional baseball contract in 1950, and two years later he had reached the major leagues playing second base, when he made his major league debut on June 17, 1952. His best professional season came in 1953, when he hit .266 with nine home runs, 22 doubles, and 63 RBIs.

In one memorable game against the St. Louis Cardinals at Busch Stadium in 1954, Dittmer tied the game with a ninth-inning single. The Braves went on to win 7–5 in 14 innings, and the game saw Henry Aaron hit his first career home run.

"I got a $6,000 bonus when I signed with the Braves," said Dittmer, who passed away in 2014. "The minimum major league starting salary then was $6,000 a year, and the most I earned was $13,000 in my one season with Detroit."

After leaving baseball, Dittmer returned to Elkader and took over his father's automobile dealership. Dittmer was elected to the Iowa Baseball Hall of Fame in 1978 and the Iowa Athletics Hall of Fame in 1993.

84 Roger, Rodgers

Jimmy Rodgers was named the most valuable player of Iowa's 1964–65 basketball team as a senior. Matt Rodgers shared the most valuable player award on Iowa's 1991 football team as a senior. Two sports, one family. Jimmy is Matt's father, and the chief reason why his son left the East Coast to follow in his father's footsteps.

Parade magazine named Matt the No. 2 quarterback in the nation during his senior season at Walpole High School in Walpole, Massachusetts. *USA Today* and Gatorade named him the Massachusetts Player of the Year.

Matt got a lot of recruiting attention. He made official visits to Pittsburgh, Boston College, and Michigan State. And then, at his dad's request, he visited Iowa. "I didn't expect to go there, but I liked the atmosphere, and the people were nice," Matt said.

Jimmy was an assistant coach for the NBA's Boston Celtics at the time. Iowa basketball coach Sharm Scheuerman had recruited Jimmy out of East Leydon High School in Franklin Park, Illinois. Rodgers was also Iowa's MVP as a junior and a double-figure scorer for three straight seasons. He played for both Scheuerman and Ralph Miller, who was hired in 1964.

Iowa finished 14–10 overall and 8–6 in the Big Ten under Miller, the only winning season Rodgers experienced. The biggest victory came against No. 1 UCLA, 87–82, at Chicago Stadium. Rodgers scored 16 points in that game, the program's first victory against a No. 1 team, and was instrumental in handling the pressure defense that Bruins coach John Wooden used.

Jimmy decided he wanted to coach, and Bill Fitch hired him at North Dakota. Rodgers then followed Fitch to the NBA when Fitch became head coach of the Cleveland Cavaliers, and later the Boston Celtics. Rodgers was part of three Celtics World Championship teams, and was elevated to head coach in 1988. Matt was a redshirt freshman at Iowa in 1988.

Larry Bird missed most of that 1988–89 season and Boston finished 42–40. The Celtics improved to 52–30 in 1989–90, but Rodgers was fired after a first-round playoff loss to the New York Knicks.

Matt Rodgers, who used to hang out at Boston's practices and games as a kid, became a former Celtics fan after his father was let go. He became Iowa's starting quarterback in the fall of 1989, passing for 2,222 yards.

Asked in November 1990 how he was doing, Jimmy told the *Chicago Tribune*, "I'm watching Iowa football games, that's about it."

Jimmy saw his son lead the Hawkeyes to an 8–4 record in 1990, a share of the Big Ten title, and the Rose Bowl. Matt was named first-team All–Big Ten and shared the league's offensive MVP award.

Jimmy was named head coach of the Minnesota Timberwolves in the fall of 1991. Matt was again the first-team All–Big Ten quarterback in 1991, despite missing two games with an injury, as Iowa finished with a 10–1–1 record.

Matt finished his career with 6,725 passing yards. He passed for 200 yards or more 17 times, and threw a touchdown pass in 25 of his 32 career starts. His football career ended after a short stint with the NFL's Buffalo Bills.

Jimmy was fired by the Timberwolves after two seasons. But then Phil Jackson, who had played at North Dakota when Jimmy was coaching there under Fitch, added him to his Chicago Bulls staff. Jimmy was on the bench for three of the Bulls' world championship runs, in 1996, 1997, and 1998.

85 In Kinnick's Shadow

Chuck Long didn't have a victory speech prepared. That dawned on him as he took the elevator to the 1985 Heisman Trophy presentation at the Downtown Athletic Club in New York City.

"I had never expected to get that far, and all of a sudden I'm in the elevator going to the ceremony," said Long, Iowa's record-setting quarterback. "I started to put some thoughts together in my head."

Recalling the anticipation as the final minutes ticked away before the announcement, Long said, "Those last five minutes, my heart was beating out of my chest."

Unfortunately, this story doesn't have a happy ending. Long, who had led Iowa to a Big Ten title, finished a runner-up to Auburn running back Bo Jackson. The 45-vote difference was the closest finish in Heisman Trophy history at the time. It now ranks No. 2. (In 2009 Alabama running back Mark Ingram finished 28 votes in front of Stanford running back Toby Gerhart.) Long settled for the Maxwell Award and the Davey O'Brien Award.

Nile Kinnick remains the only Heisman Trophy winner in Iowa football history. He finished 246 votes ahead of Michigan's Tom Harmon for the nation's most prestigious football honor in 1939.

Long is one of four Hawkeyes—three quarterbacks and a defensive tackle—who have come very close to walking in Kinnick's footsteps Only Stanford and Oklahoma have produced more Heisman runner-ups, with five each.

Alex Karras finished a distant second to halfback John David Crow of Texas A&M in 1957. It matches the best Heisman finish ever for a lineman. Karras did receive a nice consolation prize—the Outland Trophy, which goes to the nation's top interior lineman.

A year later, Iowa quarterback Randy Duncan was a runner-up to halfback Pete Dawkins of Army. Dawkins finished with 1,394 votes, compared to 1,021 for Duncan, who had just led Iowa to a Big Ten title. Duncan was named the Walter Camp Player of the Year. "Listen, I was a quarterback playing with a bunch of talented guys," Duncan said. "Being in the right place at the right time probably was more important than my ability."

Brad Banks was Iowa's other Heisman runner-up. Banks was second to quarterback Carson Palmer of USC in 2002 after leading the Hawkeyes to an undefeated Big Ten season. Palmer had 1,328 votes, compared to 1,095 for Banks, who was named Associated

Press National Player of the Year and also won the Davey O'Brien Award.

Banks was considered the Heisman front-runner until Palmer's scintillating performance on prime-time national television against Notre Dame two weeks before the trophy presentation. Palmer completed 32 of 46 passes and had four touchdown passes in a 44–13 victory over Notre Dame; 67 percent of the ballots were filed after Palmer's big game.

"I think that gave me a big boost," Palmer said after accepting the Heisman Trophy. "I think if Brad Banks had played against Notre Dame that late in the season with so many people around the country tuned in that he would have won it. We were fortunate to be in such a big game that late in the season, and I think that might have put me over the top."

86 Krafcisin's Piece of History

As a senior at St. Laurence High School in suburban Chicago, Steve Krafcisin was a coveted basketball recruit. He made one of his official visits to Indiana. "Bob Bender was my host when I visited," Krafcisin said. "And I stayed with him in his dorm, because Coach [Bob] Knight didn't believe in putting kids up at hotels."

That turned out to be a crazy coincidence, because Krafcisin and Bender share an impressive distinction: they are the only two players in the history of college basketball to play in two Final Fours with different teams.

Bender was a reserve guard on Indiana's undefeated national championship team in 1975–76. The Hoosiers beat Michigan in the national title game. Bender then transferred to Duke and was

Lute's Total Performance Chart

Lute Olson was a high school basketball coach in California when he came up with the Total Performance Chart, his own unique way of measuring what a player brings to his team.

"I didn't like the fact that the player scoring the most points always seemed to get the most credit," Olson explained. "So I created a system that would give me a much more complete picture of player performance. That included rebounding, playing defense, forcing the other team to make mistakes, and taking high percentage shots. By this point I was using phrases like 'high percentage shots.' The box score lists steals, for example, but it's just as important when you force an opponent to travel or double-dribble or throw the ball out-of-bounds."

Olson had a point system that charted a player's performance that went beyond the total points column. A field goal was worth +2, for example. A missed field goal was –2. Being called for a foul was –1, and turning the ball over was –2. A block was +1, and drawing a charge was +3. Managers would chart games using this point system.

Olson brought the TPC with him to Iowa, where he turned around a program that had slipped from the upper echelon of the Big Ten standings.

"My number one pet peeve when I was in California was when a kid wanted to look at the score book after the game," Olson said when he was at Iowa. "It's such a meaningless statistic. Our players want to look at the chart after the game. To me, it's a hundred times a better indicator of what a player does."

Olson's former Iowa players still talk about the Total Performance Chart. "That dang Total Performance Chart," said Steve Krafcisin, who played center at Iowa from 1978 to 1981. "Next to the Bible, that was 1-A the most important document to mankind. And you know what? You ended up believing it."

Said Kevin Boyle, one of Krafcisin's teammates, "It was always something to look at."

on the 1977–78 team that lost in the national championship game to Kentucky.

Krafcisin ended up signing with Coach Dean Smith and North Carolina out of high school. The 1976–77 Tar Heels lost to Marquette in the national championship game. Krafcisin had a field goal.

He then transferred to Iowa, where he played for Coach Lute Olson's 1979–80 team that lost to Louisville in the national semifinals. Krafcisin scored 12 points and had three rebounds against the Cardinals.

"It's definitely a conversation starter," said Krafcisin, now the women's basketball coach at Des Moines Area Community College in Boone, Iowa.

Krafcisin's piece of history sometimes comes up in conversation. He was at the Iowa State Capitol in Des Moines in January 2016, standing in the rotunda on the second floor, when he was approached by a gentleman. The man was a Secret Service agent assigned to presidential candidate Dr. Ben Carson. The agent, noting Krafcisin's 6'10" frame, asked if he had played basketball. Krafcisin gave him a synopsis of his career, including the two Final Fours. "He was flabbergasted," Krafcisin said.

Coach Smith remained in contact with Krafcisin, even thought he left the program. Smith made a habit of sending a North Carolina basketball media guide to every one of his former players each season, along with a handwritten note. "He'd always say, 'Say hello to your mom and aunt and brother, Jack,'" Krafcisin said.

Krafcisin and Bender remain a two-man club, although others have come close to joining them. Most recently, Kyle Wiltjer came within a game of becoming the third member. Wiltjer was a freshman on Kentucky's 2012 NCAA championship team. He then transferred to Gonzaga. The Bulldogs got within a game of the 2015 Final Four but lost to Duke.

"It's hard to believe it hasn't happened since, because of all the people who transfer now," Krafcisin said. "Back then, it was such a rare thing."

So as it stands now, Krafcisin and Bender share the distinction of being the only two players to wear two different uniforms in the Final Four. "Kind of a cool thing," Krafcisin said.

87 Pulling a Fast One in Chapel Hill

It was the most memorable sleight of hand in Iowa basketball history. No. 9 Iowa and No. 6 North Carolina were tied at 97, with 11 seconds to play in an epic duel on January 7, 1989, at the Smith Center in Chapel Hill, North Carolina. The whistle blew. The Tar Heels' Steve Bucknall was called for a foul on Iowa's Ed Horton. Or was he? Officials sent Roy Marble to the foul line to shoot two.

"It was me," Marble had hollered to the Big Ten officiating crew of Eric Harmon, Sid Rodeheffer, and Ed Hightower. It was a successful sales job, but the Smith Center crowd didn't agree. Neither did North Carolina coach Dean Smith. "I'm not sure Marble is the one who should have gone to the line," Smith said.

Television analyst Billy Packer, working the game for CBS, had the same opinion. "It should be Horton on the line, not Marble," Packer said. Added Tim Brant, the play-by-play voice that day, "It's a great selling job by Marble."

Horton had missed three of four free throws to that point in the game. Marble had made all eight of his attempts. Marble went to the line and promptly missed the first one. "I stepped off the line too early and didn't follow through," Marble said. "Before the second one, I told myself, 'I can't miss. This has got to go in.'"

It did, and that proved to be the winning point after Ray Thompson blocked a shot by the Tar Heels' King Rice right before the buzzer.

Asked about the play after the game, Iowa coach Tom Davis said, "We don't teach that. We don't switch intentionally, because I don't believe in that."

Marble still claimed after the game that he had deserved to shoot the free throws, even though the television replay told a much different story.

Marble stuck to his story for years. He finally came clean in May 2014. "It was deliberate," said Marble, who died of cancer in September 2015 at 48 years of age. "I knew what I was doing. This had nothing to do with Coach Davis or the rest of them."

Marble said that after the foul was called, he made eye contact with Horton. As Marble went to the line, Horton walked to the other end of the court. "Ed knew he was struggling," Marble said. "He looked right at me and hurried up and walked away."

88 You Can Go Home Again

Nate Kaeding retired from the NFL in 2013. In nine seasons, he made 86.2 percent of his field-goal attempts. That made him the second-most-accurate kicker in league history when his career ended.

Before that, Kaeding was an All-American kicker at Iowa. After making just 7 of his first 15 field-goal attempts as a freshman in 2000, he made 60 of his last 68. That included 24 of 29 from 40 yards and beyond. "When I sit in the stands now and watch someone kick, or watch on TV, it looks so easy," Kaeding said. "I have to remind myself of the different elements that go into it.

Hometown hero Nate Kaeding celebrates kicking the winning field goal in the 2001 Alamo Bowl.

But on the inside, doing it and understanding how fragile it is, I appreciate it."

No matter how many kicks Kaeding made as a Hawkeye, or in NFL stadiums across the country, he knew he could never rest on his laurels. "There's always tomorrow," Kaeding said. "You never know what can get thrown your way. You learn from mistakes and can't let adversity get you down. You have to pull yourself together and go from there. The old adage that your most important kick is the next one is something you learn to appreciate as a field-goal kicker at the collegiate and professional level."

Kaeding was an All-American at Iowa as a junior in 2002, helping his team win a Big Ten title and earn a berth in the Orange Bowl. He also won the Lou Groza Award that goes to the nation's top kicker after making 21 of 24 field goals and 57 of 58 point-after kicks.

Kaeding earned consensus All-America honors as a senior, making 20 of 21 field goals and 40 of 41 point-after kicks. He was also one of three finalists for the Lou Groza Award.

Selected in the third round of the NFL Draft by San Diego, he made 181 of 210 field-goal attempts for the Chargers. He received first-team All-Pro honors in 2009 and was a two-time Pro Bowler.

Kaeding returned to Iowa City, his hometown, and got his MBA from the University of Iowa's Tippie College of Business. In 2015 the three-time All–Big Ten academic honoree was hired as the Iowa City Downtown District's retail development coordinator. He tackles his new job with the same approach he did as a kicker.

"There are things you can certainly apply to life," Kaeding said. "It doesn't matter what happened in the rearview mirror. All you can control is the next chapter of life, or the next day, or the next challenge. You learn from what you've done in the past and apply those things moving forward. That forward-thinking mentality is something I've been able to apply to my new profession."

89 Big Risk, Big Reward

Dean Oliver and Ricky Davis took similar paths to get to Iowa, and then much different ones once they became Hawkeyes basketball players.

Oliver, a 5'11" point guard from Mason City, and Davis, a 6'5" forward from Davenport North, both committed to play for Iowa in November 1994 before the start of their sophomore seasons. They announced their intentions at separate news conferences in their hometowns. "We just decided to make the decision together," Davis said.

At the time, they were the earliest commitments in the history of Iowa basketball, breaking the standard Chris Street of Indianola established when he committed before his junior season. Another Mason City product, Jeff Horner, later became the earliest commitment when he picked the Hawkeyes after his freshman season.

Oliver, who was 16 years old when he accepted Iowa's scholarship offer, was a semester shy of getting his driver's license. "I wanted to get it over with," Oliver said.

Davis had turned 15 two months earlier. Both would have to wait two calendar years to sign their letters of intent with Iowa, and it would be 18 months before either could accept phone calls from college coaches. Tom Davis, the Hawkeyes' coach at the time, couldn't comment on Oliver or Davis for 24 months.

It was a bit of a gamble by the Iowa coaching staff, offering scholarships to players so young. But it was a gamble that paid off. "I had confidence in them as individuals and in their talent," Tom Davis said. "You assume they're going to come along as projected, but it doesn't always happen. But there were so many positives about them beyond their basketball-playing abilities."

Both joined the Hawkeyes after receiving All-State laurels as high school seniors. And both showed people what all the fuss was about as college freshmen. Oliver averaged 8.8 points and had 131 assists, a school record for a freshman, and started 30 of 31 games. Davis set a school freshman scoring record with 464 points. He started 26 games, and his 15-point average led the team.

But this is where their playing careers took different paths. Davis declared himself eligible for the 1998 NBA Draft. Charlotte took him with the 21st pick of the first round. Davis played 12 NBA seasons for six different teams, averaging 13.5 points over 736 career games.

Oliver stuck around at Iowa for four seasons, becoming one of the school's best point guards of all time. He scored 1,561 points (12.4 average) between 1997 and 2001. He finished with 561 assists and 205 steals. Both those figures rank in the top three on Iowa's career charts.

Oliver, who led the Big Ten in assist-turnover ratio as a senior, was a third-team All–Big Ten selection three straight seasons. Undrafted, he played two NBA seasons with Golden State and also played in several other professional leagues before going overseas. He played for teams in Slovenia, Croatia, Poland, the Netherlands, and France before retiring.

90 America Needs Farmers

Iowa's football team had a banner year in 1985. The Hawkeyes won the Big Ten championship, played in the Rose Bowl, reached No. 1 in the Associated Press poll, and had the Heisman Trophy runner-up, Chuck Long, at quarterback.

It was not a banner year for farmers, however, in a state where agriculture plays a huge role in the economy. In fact, farming was in a crisis state as collapsing commodity and land prices bankrupted thousands of farmers.

According to Emmanuel Melicher, a senior economist with the US Federal Reserve, more than a third of America's commercial farmers were facing serious financial challenges at that time. The state of Iowa told a sobering story of its own. There were an estimated 121,000 family farms in the state before the crisis hit hard in 1985. By the time it ended, nearly 20,000 of them were gone.

Hayden Fry, Iowa's football coach, was aware of the crisis in the state and decided to offer a helping hand. That's when America Needs Farmers was born.

When Iowa went to Ohio State as the nation's top-ranked team to play the Buckeyes on November 2, 1985, Iowa players wore ANF decals on their helmets as a way to show support and bring attention to the farm crisis. "I knew I had to try and help them in some way," Fry said. "I had no idea putting a decal on the headgear of the Iowa football players would have such an impact across the nation."

But the move resonated with the farm community. Among those touched was Bill Northey, now Iowa's secretary of agriculture. "I was one of those young farmers in the 1980s, and I remember what a challenge that was," Northey told Fry during an event marking the 30th anniversary of the inception of ANF. "I'm not sure it's possible to describe what putting an ANF decal on the helmets of your players meant."

The ANF sticker disappeared for a while, but it returned to the helmet in 2012 and remains as much a part of the headgear as the Tigerhawk. "Actually, ANF today may be more important than it was then," Fry said when the ANF decal returned. "There are less farms today. More people have moved to the city and have given up farming. They've lived a hard life, but those who have hung in there do a great job. They need to be recognized for what they've done, by America and the world."

An ANF Wall of Honor is located in Kinnick Stadium. It honors former Hawkeyes football student-athletes "who exemplify the tenacity, work ethic and character of the Iowa farmer, qualities that have helped Iowa remain the leading agriculture state in the nation."

The Wall of Honor includes Iowa players Casey Wiegmann, Jared DeVries, Bruce Nelson, and Robert Gallery, who all went on to play in the NFL.

Gallery was raised on an 800-acre farm near Masonville. He was an All–Big Ten offensive tackle at Iowa and won the Outland Trophy as a senior in 2003. He was the second player selected in the 2004 NFL Draft. "I enjoy farming," said Gallery, now retired from the NFL. "It's my parents' life and it's a big part of Iowa. It's a huge honor when that ANF sticker goes on the helmet. I try to represent what that stands for to the men and women who still farm."

91 An Assist with History

The history of college basketball bows to Texas Western. In 1965–66, the Miners defeated powerhouse Kentucky 72–65 to win the NCAA title. Coach Don Haskins started five African American players for the first time in NCAA history. "There will be a lot of teams that win a championship, a lot of great teams," said Nevil Shed, one of the Miners' starters, during the 50-year celebration of that milestone victory. "But will they stand in the history of basketball like this one? I'm not sure we will ever see a championship with so much magnitude."

Books have been written and movies have been made about that team. And none of it might have happened had Texas Western (now Texas–El Paso) not beaten Iowa late in the nonconference season. They met in the Sun Bowl Tournament in El Paso on December 30, 1965. Iowa had gotten the season off to a surprising 8–0 start, and came into the game ranked No. 4 in the Associated Press poll.

The Hawkeyes promptly got crushed, 86–68. The Miners jumped out to a 21–4 lead and took a 21-point advantage into halftime. Iowa went scoreless for a stretch of more than 10 minutes in that opening half. "There was no chance of them coming back at that point," said Willie Cager, another Texas Western starter. "We blew them out. Big time."

Iowa cut the deficit to 10 points late in the game. But the Hawkeyes had four starters—Gerry Jones, George Peeples, Dennis Pauling, and Tom Chapman Jr.—foul out.

"We came down here thinking our high national ranking would carry us through," Iowa coach Ralph Miller said. "It didn't, and it is obvious to me that we have been building up to this defeat. We were outdefensed and outhustled. I guess the lucky victory over Arkansas [the night before, 77–75] didn't do the job of waking us up."

Haskins said years later that the victory over the highly ranked Hawkeyes was instrumental in creating momentum for his team's title run. "I'll always remember that Iowa game," said Jerry Armstrong, a member of the Texas Western team. "It opened the eyes of the media. It set the tone for what kind of season it could be."

Miller took a philosophical approach to the first defeat of the season. "If we've got to lose, it's nice to lose in December," Miller said. "Remember, we've got 14 tough conference games ahead."

But the momentum Texas Western gained with the victory was momentum lost for the Hawkeyes. Iowa promptly lost two of its first three Big Ten games, on the road at Wisconsin (69–68) and

Indiana (73–61). Miller's team finished 17–7 and tied for third in the Big Ten at 8–6, even though they had five players average in double figures offensively. Chris Pervall led the way at 19.1 points a game, and Peeples was next at 17.8.

Iowa dropped to No. 7 the week after losing to the Miners, and fell out of the poll the following week.

A week after beating Iowa, the Miners were ranked No. 9 and remained in the top 10 for the remainder of the season. Texas Western finished with a 28–1 record. The only loss was a 74–72 decision to Seattle in its final regular-season game.

Texas Western beat Oklahoma City 89–74 in its first-round NCAA game, and went on to the Midwest Regional title by dispatching Cincinnati 78–76 and Kansas 81–80. At the Final Four, Haskins' team beat Utah 85–78 in the semifinals to get to the title game…and a date with history.

The final AP poll was conducted before the NCAA Tournament back then. The Miners were No. 3 in that last poll. Duke was second, and Kentucky was No. 1. The mighty Wildcats received 39 of 48 first-place votes. The Miners got one first-place vote.

"It was so much fun," Willie Cager said. "We were just playing basketball and having some fun."

92 Eddie Robinson

Eddie Robinson, the second-winningest coach in NCAA Division I football history, passed away in 2007 at 88 years of age. But the legacy of Grambling State's coaching giant lives today.

Each year, the Football Writers Association of America and the Allstate Sugar Bowl present the Eddie Robinson Coach of the Year

Another Historic Iowa Grad

John B. McLendon Jr. was the first University of Iowa graduate to be enshrined in the Naismith Memorial Basketball Hall of Fame.

McLendon's mentor was none other than Dr. James Naismith, the inventor of basketball. McLendon, a native of Hiawatha, Kansas, got a degree from Kansas in 1936 but couldn't play basketball because the school didn't allow African American players at the time.

Naismith was retired but still a member of the faculty, and McLendon asked him to be his advisor. McLendon was the first African American physical education student ever at Kansas. "Dr. Naismith taught me far more than was found in textbooks," McLendon wrote three years before his passing in 1999. "Very often he would put aside his books and teach us lessons in life from his world experiences. And that always included how he happened to invent the game of basketball in 1891. There is no question that my life would not have been anywhere near what it has become if I had not had Dr. Naismith as my advisor."

After he left Kansas, McLendon went on to Iowa City and got his master's degree. The University of Iowa honored McLendon by presenting him with a Distinguished Alumni Award in 1988.

McLendon's first head coaching job in college came at North Carolina College (now North Carolina Central University) in 1940. He later coached at the Hampton Institute (now Hampton University), Tennessee A&I (now Tennessee State), Kentucky State, and Cleveland

Award. The winner of the 2015 award was Iowa's Kirk Ferentz, and there's a connection there you might not know.

Robinson earned a master's degree in physical education from the University of Iowa in 1954, while he was coaching at Grambling.

And in 1979 Iowa athletic director Bump Elliott interviewed Robinson for the Hawkeyes football job that would go to Hayden Fry.

Ferentz first met Robinson at a coaching clinic in St. Louis, Missouri, in the mid 1980s. "I asked him about the Wing-T," Ferentz said. "I was curious why Grambling would be running

State. He became the first coach to win three consecutive national titles (NAIA) at Tennessee State. At Cleveland State, he became the first African American to coach at a predominantly white university.

He also became the first African American coach in professional sports when he was hired in 1961 by the Cleveland Pipers of the American Basketball League. The team owner was George Steinbrenner, who later dominated headlines as the owner of the New York Yankees.

"He was an outstanding technician," Steinbrenner said of McLendon. "He had the respect of all his players and produced nothing but winners."

McLendon also coached the Denver Rockets of the American Basketball Association (now the Nuggets).

Over a seven-decade coaching career, McLendon is best known for popularizing the fast break and using full-court pressure to his advantage. Legend has it he would have his players run three miles a day to get in superior physical condition. McLendon called them "championship miles."

McLendon is also known as the father of the four-corner offense, which Dean Smith popularized at North Carolina before the arrival of the shot clock.

John McLendon was enshrined in the Naismith Memorial Basketball Hall of Fame as a Contributor in 1979 and as a Coach in 2016.

the Wing-T. That's when I found out he studied here and got a master's at Iowa. He told me about his visits with Coach [Forest] Evashevski."

Evashevski was the football coach at the time Robinson was doing his postgraduate work at Iowa, building a program that would win Big Ten titles in 1956 and 1958 and go to the Rose Bowl.

Ferentz was an assistant coach for the Cleveland Browns when he had a second encounter with Robinson. In April 1993, shortly before the NFL Draft, Ferentz was trying to get some information on Grambling offensive lineman Herman Arvie.

Ferentz called the Grambling football office at 6:00 PM on a Friday night. Robinson answered the phone. They spoke for 40 minutes. And the Browns selected Arvie in the fifth round of the draft.

Robinson retired in 1997 with a record of 408–165–15 in 55 seasons (1941–42; 1945–97). Only the late Joe Paterno of Penn State coached more victories. Robinson's teams were voted National Black Champions nine times, and the Tigers won 17 Southwestern Athletic Conference titles. Robinson was inducted into the College Football Hall of Fame in 1997. Robinson also received a Distinguished Alumni Award from the University of Iowa in 1986.

"Just a special man," Ferentz said. "I had two personal interactions with him, so that was pretty neat."

93 Six Seasons of Success and Agony

When he discusses his Iowa basketball career, Jess Settles comes back to the same word. "Unfulfilled," Settles said. It was a career that started with bold promise and expectations and ended in back pain and discouragement.

Settles came to Iowa from a small school, Winfield-Mount Union, where he was Iowa's Mr. Basketball in 1993. "When you come from a small school, it's a crapshoot," said Settles, a 6'7" forward. "I remember my dad telling me, 'I've taught you everything I can teach you, but I'm just a farmer who loves the game.'"

Settles was not the most gifted athlete in the Big Ten, but no one outworked him. As a youngster he had read books about Iowa wrestling coach Dan Gable, a true icon in his sport. Settles was motivated by Gable's words. "Every time I went to stop, I could hear Gable in my head saying, 'Don't you want to be great?'" Settles said.

Settles scored 13 points and grabbed 11 rebounds in his first collegiate game, against Drake on November 30, 1993. He would go on to score a freshman-record 414 points. He started all 27 games, had six double-doubles and was named Big Ten Freshman of the Year. He was the team's second-leading scorer at 15.3 points a game, and averaged a team-best 7.5 rebounds. His thirst to get better was unquenched.

"When I first came to Iowa, I didn't think it was intense enough," Settles said. "After practice [as a freshman], I would go up and work out in the wrestling room. The wrestlers were competing at the level of intensity that I craved. I remember sitting on a [stationary] bike next to Gable a few times. He would never say this, but he would always try to beat me on the bike. He would try to go harder, and I would try to go as hard as him. It was the craziest thing."

Iowa had an 11–16 record in 1993–94. But the next season Settles was joined in the starting lineup by another sophomore guard, Chris Kingsbury, and point guard Andre Woolridge, a transfer from Nebraska. "I'm thinking, *Man, we're going to be great…we're going to have three years of greatness ahead of us*," Settles said. "And then I got injured."

Iowa played an exhibition game against Marathon Oil in the Quad Cities on November 20, 1994. Settles felt pain in his back. It was pain that would linger for the rest of his career. "It was kind of a cruel, slow death by injury," Settles said. "It wasn't like I blew out a knee."

Settles earned third-team All–Big Ten honors as a sophomore, even though he missed seven games and didn't start seven more because of his back. He averaged 15.6 points and 6.2 rebounds. He fought through the pain to play in all 32 games as a junior, and was named to the All–Big Ten first team after averaging 15.1 points and 7.5 rebounds. The Hawkeyes also returned to the NCAA Tournament for the first time in three seasons.

But Settles knew he was on borrowed time because of his back injury. In May 1996 he announced he was going to bypass his final season at Iowa and enter the NBA Draft. He attended the pre-draft camp in Chicago that June, and the feedback was mixed. "A business decision enters into the process, where before it didn't," Settles said. "I wasn't sure I was going to get guaranteed money. So I made another decision to come back [to Iowa]. And then it just fell apart after that."

Settles had slipped discs in his back. He had arthroscopic procedures and took injections that were positive, but only in the short term. "I could never get it under control, so it was tough," Settles said.

He was voted the preseason Big Ten Player of the Year in 1996–97 but played in just three games and used his medical red-shirt. Settles missed the entire 1997–98 season. He applied for a sixth season of eligibility, which the NCAA granted.

He averaged 9.8 points and 4.8 rebounds and was the team's co–most valuable player in 1998–99. It was also the 13th and final season at Iowa for Coach Tom Davis, and that team made it to the Sweet 16 of the NCAA Tournament.

"Physically, the sixth year wasn't the right thing to do, and I paid the price for it," Settles said. "As far as Tom's last year, all that was a pretty special six months. But if I had to do it over again, I probably wouldn't [request a sixth year]."

Settles finished his career with 1,611 points and 747 rebounds. But it was not the career he envisioned. "I always wonder what could have been," Settles said. "I still struggle with that when I think about it. I went too hard and I didn't listen to my body enough. I wanted to make it so bad."

94 Bo, Hayden, and a Goose Egg

Bo Schembechler was hired to replace Bump Elliott as Michigan's football coach after the 1968 season. In 1979 Elliott was Iowa's athletic director when he hired Hayden Fry to be his new coach.

Fry's Iowa teams met Schembechler's Michigan teams nine times. Bo had a 5–3–1 edge on Fry in those games, but that doesn't tell the whole story.

Iowa had a 4–25–3 record against Michigan before Fry arrived. In the first meeting between the two coaches in a Big Ten game, on October 17, 1981, visiting Iowa upset Michigan 9–7. "Our chances for the Big Ten title are now zero to none," Schembechler said. "We won't play too many teams as good defensively as Iowa."

It was the Hawkeyes' first victory over Michigan since 1962, and first in Michigan Stadium since 1958. That victory was instrumental in Fry's team ending a string of 19 consecutive nonwinning seasons. It also paved the way for the Hawkeyes' first trip to the Rose Bowl since January 1, 1959.

Schembechler's Wolverines won the next two games—29–7 in Iowa City in 1982 and a 16–13 nail-biter in Ann Arbor in 1983. Michigan went on to the Rose Bowl in 1982 and the Sugar Bowl in 1983.

One of the highlights of the Fry era at Iowa came on October 20, 1984. Iowa shut out the visiting Wolverines 26–0. The only other time a Hawkeyes team shut out Michigan was a 0–0 tie in 1929. "Nobody ever dreamed we could goose egg Michigan," a delighted Fry said afterward. It was the worst defeat of Schembechler's 20-year Michigan career. "This was one of the most satisfying wins that I've ever been associated with, against one of the best football programs in America," Fry added.

RICK BROWN

Iowa's Devon Mitchell intercepted a pair of Russell Rein passes. Rein started at quarterback in place of the injured Jim Harbaugh. Mitchell returned his second pick 75 yards. Nate Creer also had an interception. "I think everybody on the defense should be MVP," Iowa quarterback Chuck Long said.

Schembechler was not particularly pleased after the game. "Iowa has the best defense we've played this year," Schembechler said. "They're good, but not good enough to shut us out. We felt we couldn't turn the ball over to have any chance, but we did."

Fry's most memorable victory over Schembechler also came in Kinnick Stadium the following season. Iowa was ranked No. 1, and Michigan was ranked No. 2. The Hawkeyes won 12–10 on Rob Houghtlin's walk-off 29-yard field goal. Iowa also represented the Big Ten in the Rose Bowl.

That tug-of-war for the nation's No. 1 ranking was the last time Fry beat Schembechler. Michigan won in Ann Arbor in 1986, 20–17, and went to the Rose Bowl. The Wolverines also beat Iowa in Michigan Stadium in 1987 by a 37–10 margin. The teams tied in 1988 in Iowa City, 17–17. And Schembechler bested Fry 26–12 in their final meeting, at Kinnick Stadium in 1989. That was Schembechler's final season as Michigan's coach.

95 Changing In-State Uniforms

Adam Haluska's decision to transfer from Iowa State to Iowa to finish his basketball career was a hot topic of conversation in his home state for several weeks back in 2003.

But he wasn't the first, or last, player to change in-state uniforms. Meet Tom Norman. Twenty-eighty years before Haluska became a household name, Norman followed the same path. Like Haluska, Norman played for the Cyclones as a freshman, then transferred to Iowa. "I heard a few people call me a turncoat, a traitor, stuff like that," Norman said. "But it was a very small minority."

Norman was recruited to Iowa State by Coach Maury John but never got to play for him. John died of cancer on October 15, 1974. Norman, a guard, played for Ken Trickey. He saw action in 15 games, averaging 6.2 points. "I really liked Iowa State," Norman said. "It was just the coaching situation at the time."

Norman transferred to Iowa after the 1974–75 season. His brother, Ron, had lettered for the Hawkeyes in 1966–67 and 1967–68. After sitting out the 1975–76 campaign to meet NCAA transfer requirements, Tom played three seasons for Coach Lute Olson. He averaged 4.9 points as a sophomore, 7.6 points as a junior, and 7.7 points as a senior, when Iowa won a share of the 1978–79 Big Ten title and played in the NCAA Tournament for the first time since 1970.

Stacy Frese also changed schools, playing for Iowa in 1995–96 and then finishing her career at Iowa State from 1997–98 to 1999–2000. Making a similar change was Alex Thompson. He played for the Hawkeyes in 2004–05 and 2005–06, then transferred to Iowa State for the final two seasons of his career.

Haluska started all 31 games for Iowa State coach Larry Eustachy's team in 2002–03, averaging 28.6 minutes and 9.2 points and being selected to the Big 12 Conference All-Freshman team.

But Haluska, who had committed to Iowa State before the start of his sophomore season at Carroll High School, decided to leave. And a coaching change was involved in that decision. Eustachy had been replaced by Wayne Morgan.

Haluska announced on May 28, 2003, that he had asked for and received an unconditional release from his scholarship at Iowa State, meaning he was free to transfer with no restrictions.

Rumors swirled that Iowa, where his friends and former AAU teammates Jeff Horner and Greg Brunner had just completed their freshman seasons, would be his destination.

On the night that Haluska was granted his release, Iowa coach Steve Alford appeared at a Carroll County I-Club gathering in Arcadia, just 10 miles from Haluska's home in Carroll. Alford declined to comment on the Haluska situation to reporters. But he got a big cheer when he told the crowd, "Our spring recruiting is going very well."

A day later, Haluska officially contacted Iowa to discuss a possible transfer to the school. He made a visit to Iowa City on May 31 and announced his intentions of becoming a Hawkeye shortly after.

After sitting out the 2003–04 season as a transfer, Haluska started three seasons for Iowa. He averaged double figures every season, and 16.1 points for his 98-game Hawkeyes career. That included a career-best 20.5 points as a senior, when he was a first-team All–Big Ten performer and Academic All-American.

Haluska scored at least 20 points in 17 of 31 games as a senior, including back-to-back games of 33 against Indiana and 34 at Minnesota.

96 Let's Talk Hawks (and Politics)

There's not a dining spot in Iowa City that can match the pomp and political savvy of the Hamburg Inn No. 2. Located at 214 North Linn, it's been around since 1948. That means history, lots of history. In addition to being a place where Hawkeyes fans gather to discuss the game just played or the next one to come, this cozy landmark also has a rich political past.

Political candidates frequent the Hamburg Inn No. 2, especially during the months leading up to the Iowa Caucus. There's a booth dedicated to former president Ronald Reagan, and pictures and stories of politicians cover the walls of the restaurant. There's the smiling face of Iowa governor Terry Branstad, the longest-serving governor in the history of the United States, on one wall.

Both the Clintons—Bill and Hillary—have a presence too. Barack Obama was here, campaigning his way to the presidency.

Drinking In History

Standing at the intersection of Clinton Street and Iowa Avenue puts you in the heart of downtown Iowa City.

Across the street is the Pentacrest and Old Capitol, two fixtures on the University of Iowa campus. But there are two more historical stops just footsteps away in both directions. Walk down Iowa Avenue and you'll run into Joe's Place, a watering hole for students since 1934. Make your way down Dubuque Street and you'll find the Airliner, another student hangout since 1944.

Both Joe's Place and the Airliner are more than bars. They're traditions, the places where today's generation walks in the footsteps of others—yes, even their parents—who walked there decades before. And they have stood the test of time.

Both establishments have unique identities, but they share one thing: fans congregate there to watch Hawkeyes games on television. The Airliner even has a link to Iowa's schedule on its website. Both places have more than 20 TVs. And the walls are decorated with Hawkeyes history. According to the Joe's Place website, "There's no question who the favorite team is at Joe's: the Hawkeyes rule."

Joe's Place has pool tables, foosball, and video games, as well as a beer garden.

This is not your father's Airliner. It has transitioned to a restaurant as much as a drinking and social establishment. The Airliner's pizza has an A+ reputation. It even offers full-menu delivery service to campus locations.

Both offer drink specials and a relaxed and casual atmosphere for students, alums, and anyone else who wants to drink in some Iowa City history.

There's a US flag on one wall, with the words UNITED WE STAND. That may not be an appropriate moniker when you consider the diverse viewpoints of the politicians this restaurant draws every four years for the caucus.

The restaurant was also featured in an episode of NBC's *The West Wing* in 2005. Now there's status for you.

Passion for Iowa sports is united. On one wall is a framed picture honoring Iowa's 1958 football team. The Football Writers Association of America named the Hawkeyes national champions. And there's a picture of the Grantland Rice Trophy to prove it.

Discussions in this cozy establishment usually have a Hawkeyes-related theme, often over breakfast. Because breakfast is as popular as the Hawkeyes here. Bring your patience if you want to chow down on weekend mornings. The good news is that breakfast is served all day, and it's worth the wait. Breakfast options include the Hawkeye Hog omelet.

Hamburg Inn No. 2—No. 1 no longer exists, for the record— is also famous for its pie shakes: a milkshake blended with a piece of pie.

So bring your hunger—and your knowledge of the Hawkeyes— with you to this slice of America.

97 Holy Toledo

Iowa's dreams of winning a share of the Big Ten basketball title went up in smoke when it lost 61–53 to Michigan at home in the second-to-last game of the 1978–79 season.

Earlier that day, Lute Olson had announced he would remain at Iowa as coach after being romanced by Southern California. He

No matter how much time passes, Iowa fans will remember "Lute! Lute! Lute!"

had been greeted by chants of "Lute! Lute! Lute!" as he walked to the bench before the game. The Wolverines weren't impressed, jumping out to a 16–2 lead.

But two days later, a miracle arrived. Wisconsin's Wesley Matthews made a 55-foot shot at the buzzer to upset Magic Johnson and Michigan State 83–81. All Iowa had to do was beat last-place Northwestern that night at home to earn a share of the title with the Spartans and Purdue at 13–5.

And that's just what happened. The Hawkeyes made quick work of the Wildcats, 95–64, for a share of the school's first league crown since 1970. The sold-out Iowa Field House crowd of 13,365 celebrated as the players cut down the nets. Inside the Hawkeyes locker room, "We Are the Champions" was playing.

Soaking Up Some History

They posed in front of the Old Capitol, this band of overachieving Hawkeyes. Star point guard Ronnie Lester was in the middle, flanked by Dick Peth, Kevin Boyle, and Steve Krafcisin to his right, and Tom Norman, William Mayfield, and Steve Waite to his left.

The picture was taken after Iowa had won a share of the 1978–79 Big Ten title. So why not stand in front of the Old Capitol, the University of Iowa's timeless symbol? The Old Capitol was there before Iowa was a state or Iowa City was home to a state university.

When many look at the Old Capitol and its gold dome, anchoring the Pentacrest, they think about the University of Iowa. The university's logo is a graphic representation of the dome.

The Old Capitol is rich in history. The cornerstone was laid on July 4, 1840, and it was the state's first permanent capitol. Inside this building, Iowa made its transition to statehood in 1846. Ansel Briggs, Iowa's first elected governor, was inaugurated there the same year. The state constitution was drafted there.

Fifty-nine days after Iowa became a state, legislation was passed inside the Old Capitol to form Iowa's first public university, the State University of Iowa.

Iowa had been picked to finish eighth in the Big Ten that season. But seniors William Mayfield, Tom Norman, Dick Peth, and Kirk Speraw went out on a much higher note. "This is the pinnacle for me," Norman said. "We've been struggling for a couple of years, and even I didn't think we could finish first. It's just the zenith of my career. We couldn't turn down the second chance Wisconsin gave us."

Even with a share of the title, an NCAA bid wasn't a certainty. After the game, Olson did some campaigning. "No question about it," he said. "Michigan State and Iowa should be the Big Ten representatives in the NCAA."

Purdue (23–7) had a better record than Iowa (20–7), but the Hawkeyes had swept the Boilermakers during the regular season.

Old Capitol was the home of state government for a decade, then state officials decided to move to a more centrally located spot in Des Moines. When that move was made in 1857, the Old Capitol building was given to the University of Iowa. In fact, it became the first building the university owned.

From 1857 to 1863, the building housed most of the university. University presidents had their offices there until 1970. Soon after, a six-year renovation took place to restore the Old Capitol to its original condition. The building was declared a National Historic Landmark on January 7, 1976. It was reopened to the public on July 3, 1976, as the United States celebrated its bicentennial.

During another renovation in 2001, contractors accidentally set the cupola that supported the gold dome on fire. The bell at the top of the Old Capitol was damaged, the dome was destroyed, and there was lots of water damage. A new bell was installed in 2002, and a new gold-covered dome was put in place in 2003. The Old Capitol was reopened to the public in 2006.

A museum, including exhibits about the history of the Old Capitol, the university, and Iowa's journey to statehood, are on the main floor. For history buffs, this is a can't-miss stop in Iowa City.

Iowa was assigned to the NCAA's Mideast Regional the next day, with a Saturday game in Bloomington, Indiana. The Hawkeyes drew Toledo after the Rockets beat Central Michigan in a playoff to determine the Mid-American Conference's representative.

The first half was to Iowa's liking. Ronnie Lester's 30-footer at the buzzer gave the Hawkeyes a 41–29 lead. But Toledo rallied and won the game 74–72 on a 20-foot jump shot by Stan "the Man" Joplin at the buzzer.

Joplin, who later became the Rockets' head coach, said many years later that the shot against Iowa is one he'll never forget. "What every kid dreams about while shooting a basketball in his driveway," Joplin said. "Three…two…one…it was unbelievable."

So was Iowa's quick exit. And Michigan State? The Spartans beat Larry Bird and Indiana State to win the 1979 NCAA title.

98 A Ringing Endorsement

John Johnson and Fred Brown were two of the greatest offensive players in Iowa basketball history. Johnson, a senior, averaged 27.9 points a game. Brown, a junior, averaged 17.9. Together, they helped the Hawkeyes to an undefeated Big Ten season in 1969–70. Brown went on to average 27.6 points as a senior.

They became teammates on another championship team nine years later, helping the Seattle SuperSonics beat the Washington Bullets in five games to win the 1979 NBA title.

And strange as it sounds, Johnson was talking defense in the winning locker room. "Defense always beats offense," Johnson said. "Offense is like the weather. It comes and goes."

Johnson's Iowa teammates would get a chuckle out of that. He was an offense-first player for the Hawkeyes, and never saw a shot he didn't like.

Johnson scored 11 points and also added five rebounds in the championship-clinching 97–93 victory against Washington. Brown, Seattle's team captain, had 14 points on 7-of-10 shooting. He poured champagne over the head of NBA commissioner Lawrence O'Brien afterward.

"We're the Rodney Dangerfields of the NBA," Johnson said after the game. "But if they don't respect us, we don't care because we are champions."

Johnson finished his NBA career with 11,200 points, a 12.9-point average. He also had 4,778 career rebounds (5.5 per game). Brown, who earned the nickname "Downtown" because of his deep shooting skills, scored 14,018 career points in the NBA, a 14.6-point average.

Johnson and Brown are two of seven former Hawkeyes to earn NBA championship rings.

Don Nelson leads that parade, playing for five title teams with the Boston Celtics (1966, 1968, 1969, 1974, and 1976). Nelson, who played at Iowa from 1959 to 1962, retired after that last title. His No. 19 was retired.

Nelson scored 10,898 points in his NBA career. Two of his most important points came in Game 7 of the 1969 Finals again the Los Angeles Lakers. With Boston clinging to a 103–102 lead and just more than a minute to play, Nelson fired up a jumper from the free-throw line that hit the back of the rim, popped straight up, and fell through the basket.

Nelson averaged 10.3 points for his NBA career, and also snagged 5,192 rebounds while earning a reputation as one of the best sixth men in the game.

Another multiple NBA champion was point guard B.J. Armstrong, who played at Iowa from 1985 to 1989. Drafted by the Chicago Bulls in the first round of the 1989 draft, the 18th selection overall, Armstrong eventually joined Michael Jordan and Scottie Pippen in the starting lineup and was part of three straight championship teams (1991–93).

After stints with Golden State, Charlotte, and Orlando, Armstrong ended up back in Chicago for his final season in 1999–2000. Armstrong finished with 7,320 career points and 2,479 assists.

Ronnie Lester, who played at Iowa from 1976 to 1980, was also a first-round draft pick. He was the 10th player selected in 1980, by Portland, and his rights were traded to Chicago. A knee injury limited his effectiveness with the Bulls. He was later a member of the Los Angeles Lakers' 1985 championship team.

Matt Bullard transferred to Iowa from Colorado and played two seasons for the Hawkeyes (1988–89 and 1989–90). Undrafted, he played 11 NBA seasons. The highlight came in 1994, when the Rockets beat the New York Knicks, four games to three, to win the championship.

Bobby Hansen got his NBA ring in his ninth and final season. Drafted by the Utah Jazz in the third round of the 1983 draft, Hansen became an important member of that team during his seven seasons there. He also played one year with the Sacramento Kings and then called it a career following the 1991–92 season with the Chicago Bulls. There, Hansen backed up Jordan.

"It was not an easy year, when you're the 12th guy on the team and you're guarding Jordan every day in practice," Hansen said. "The Bulls practiced hard, harder than any NBA team I'd ever been on. They challenged you each and every day. It was a great team, and everybody got along. There was incredible leadership with [Coach] Phil Jackson and Michael."

The Bulls played Portland in the 1992 Finals. And Hansen had his shining moment in the clinching Game 6. Chicago was leading the series 3–2 but trailed by 15 points heading into the fourth quarter. Jackson inserted Hansen to rest Jordan for the stretch run. Hansen hit a three-pointer, then stole the ball from the Trailblazers' Jerome Kersey, which led to a Pippen basket. That changed the momentum and the Bulls closed out Portland 97–93. After the game, Jordan told Hansen, "I told you I'd get you that ring." It's a ring that Hansen still wears proudly.

"It meant everything to me professionally, at that stage of my career, to be able to do that," Hansen said.

99 Diamond Revival

Jim Sundberg was a two-time All–Big Ten catcher at Iowa. In 1972, his final season with the Hawkeyes, Sundberg helped his team win the Big Ten title with a 13–3 record and advance to the College World Series.

And it took some late-season magic to do it. Iowa had to win its final 10 conference games for the school's first Big Ten baseball title since 1949 and first outright crown since 1939.

After leaving Iowa following his junior season, Sundberg had a 16-year major league career. That included a 1985 World Series title with the Kansas City Royals. Sundberg played in 1,962 major league games, earning a reputation as a defensive whiz behind the plate. He ended his career with a .993 fielding percentage. He won six Gold Gloves and was a three-time All-Star.

Sundberg moved to the front office, and retired as senior executive vice president for the Texas Rangers in 2014.

A year later, Iowa won its first NCAA Tournament game since Sundberg was in uniform. Coach Rick Heller led the resurgence in his second season at Iowa. The 2015 Hawkeyes won 41 games, the second-most in school history, including a 19–5 mark in Big Ten play. Iowa was ranked for the first time since 1990.

The Hawkeyes advanced to the Springfield Regional and won their first game there with a 3–1 decision over Oregon. "Knowing that we hadn't won a regional game since the College World Series team in 1972, that was special to win that first game," Heller said.

The 1972 team, coached by Duane Banks, lost its first postseason game to Central Michigan. Facing four straight elimination games, Iowa beat Northern Illinois, Central Michigan, and Bowling Green twice to advance to the College World Series in Omaha, Nebraska.

The Hawkeyes drew top-ranked Arizona State in their opener and lost 2–1, even though starting pitcher Mark Tschopp allowed just three hits. Temple ended the Hawkeyes' season 13–9.

The 2015 Hawkeyes, the Big Ten runner-up, earned the program's first NCAA berth since 1990. Iowa was awarded the No. 2 seed in the Springfield Regional. Tyler Peyton allowed just one run over seven and a third innings in the 3–1 victory over Oregon, which got Iowa to the 40-victory mark for the first time since 1985.

Top-seeded Missouri State defeated the Hawkeyes 5–3. Iowa stayed alive by bouncing Oregon 2–1 in an 11-inning duel, before seeing its season end with a 3–2 loss to Missouri State.

The 2015 team will be remembered for bringing a dormant program back to life, and bridging Sundberg's era with their own.

100 Enjoying a History Lesson

The Roy G. Karro Athletics Hall of Fame and Visitors Center celebrates decades of Hawkeyes success. Opened in 2002 and located at 2425 Prairie Meadow Drive in Iowa City, just west of the University of Iowa's Finkbine Golf Course, the Hall of Fame is a good way for fans to rub elbows with Hawkeyes greatness. The building tells the story of Iowa's great teams, individuals, and coaches.

Items on display include Nile Kinnick's 1939 Heisman Trophy. A Kinnick exhibit includes a football signed by Kinnick and his teammates on the famed 1939 Ironmen team. The ball was purchased and donated in 2013 by the Kappa Psi fraternity at Iowa. Kinnick was a member of that fraternity in 1938 and 1939.

The 1958 Grantland Rice Trophy, presented to Iowa by the Football Writers Association of America after that organization declared the Hawkeyes national champions, is also on display. So are the 23 NCAA wrestling championship trophies the Hawkeyes have won on the mat. The trophy for winning the 2001 Big Ten men's basketball tournament is also there. And that's a small sample size of what you'll find inside. Exhibits for all 22 varsity sports at Iowa are also part of the attraction.

There are also interactive activities, including shooting baskets on a floor that was once in Iowa Field House, and kicking field goals.

Historic moments can be watched on computer screens, and athletic highlights can also be viewed in a theater setting. Databases chronicling former athletes are available as well.

In addition, the building honors members of the National Varsity Club Hall of Fame. To be included, a student-athlete must have won at least one major letter. Candidates are eligible for induction 10 years after earning a varsity letter. Coaches and administrators are also eligible for induction.

The building is named after the late Roy G. Karro, an alum who donated $3 million to fund the home of Hawkeyes sports history.

Acknowledgments

Narrowing down decades of history to 100 items is, in a word, challenging. Then the fun begins. Putting a number value, 1 through 100, is subjective at best. This is one man's opinion. Feel free to disagree.

Before I get too far down the road, I must thank my wife, Karon, for her patience and support during this project. Without it, this book would not have been completed.

I would also like to thank my children, both University of Iowa graduates. I gave my son, Ben, a passion for sports that rivals mine. And my daughter, Blair, is the most gifted writer in the family. Both offered their support along the way, and I appreciate it greatly.

I also need to thank those who granted me interviews or shared insight into memorable moments in Hawkeyes history. You can't do better than going to the source.

Thanks, too, to the people at Triumph Books, namely Adam Motin and Josh Williams, for giving me the opportunity to write this book.

I spent nearly four decades collecting a paycheck from the *Des Moines Register*. Sports editor Gene Raffensperger hired me right out of graduate school in 1978. One of my first assignments was covering an Iowa basketball game with Raff in the Iowa Field House. That sentence alone dates me, because several generations go back no further than Carver-Hawkeye Arena when they think of Iowa basketball.

Working for the *Des Moines Register* was my lifetime goal, and I am fortunate enough to say I reached it. As I've spent hours in microfilm reliving Iowa history from the pages of the *Register* in preparation for this book, I am reminded of all the great writers and reporters who have called that paper home. Your stories provided wonderful insight to some of the stories included in this book.

I would also like to thank the University of Iowa Media Relations Office, especially Steve Roe and Matt Weitzel, for the information they provided and their trust in me to dig into their files and put everything back in order. I'd also like to thank Steve's predecessor, Phil Haddy, who has been a friend and supporter of my work since we first met in 1974.

A tip of the cap, too, to a long list of journalists who have treated me with respect down this path I called a career. Cedar Rapids broadcasting icon Bob Brooks was a kid when he watched Nile Kinnick play football for the Hawkeyes. I wish everyone was as fortunate as me to listen to Brooksie spin tales about Kinnick, Forest Evashevski, Pops Harrison, Ralph Miller, Chris Street, and many more. Your friendship means the world to me, sir.

The same goes for Randy Peterson, my friend and colleague at the *Des Moines Register*. We took turns keeping each other afloat, through impossible deadlines and the ever-changing world of newspapers.

I also want to thank many who are no longer with us. That includes George Wine, who hired me as a student assistant in the sports information office when I arrived on the Iowa campus in the fall of 1974. George took me under his wing and gave me keen insight into Hawkeyes sports, one of the loves of his life. I will never forget his kindness.

And my father, Bob, a four-decade newspaperman whose footsteps I walked in. He passed away on January 10, 2012. I had just filed my game story on an Iowa–Michigan State basketball game in East Lansing, Michigan, when I got a phone call telling me he had passed away. His final act, I'm sure, was to hold on until I made my deadline.

Sources

Books

Cedar Rapids Gazette. *Greatest Moments in Iowa Hawkeyes Football History*. Chicago: Triumph Books, 2006.

Finn, Mike and Chad Leistikow. *Hawkeye Legends, Lists & Lore*. Champaign, IL: Sports Publishing, LLC, 1998.

Fry, Hayden and George Wine. *Hayden Fry: A High Porch Picnic*. Champaign, IL: Sports Publishing, LLC, 1999.

Gable, Dan. *Coaching Wrestling Successfully*. Champaign, IL: Human Kinetics Publishers, 1998.

Grady, Al. *25 Years with the Fighting Hawkeyes*. Iowa City, IA: University of Iowa Athletic Department, 1989.

Lamb, Dick and Bert McGrane. *75 Years with the Fighting Hawkeyes*. Iowa City, IA: University of Iowa Athletic Department, 1964.

Olson, Lute and David Fisher. *Lute! The Seasons of My Life*. New York: St. Martin's Press, 2006.

Schrader, Gus and Fred Thompson. *Lute, Lute, Lute*. Minneapolis: Jostens American Yearbook Co., 1981.

Turnbull, Buck. *Hoop Tales: Iowa Hawkeyes Men's Basketball*. New York: Globe Pequot Press, 2006.

Zabel, Jim and Rich Wolfe. *I Love It! I Love It! I Love It!* Covington, KY: Clerisy Press, 2010.

Websites

Airliner (www.theairlinerbar.com)

Amateur Athletic Foundation Sports Library (www.la84.org)

Big Ten Conference (www.bigten.org)

Britannica (www.britannica.com/sports/basketball)

Cedar Rapids Gazette (www.thegazette.com)

Chicago Bulls (www.nba.com/bulls)

City of Iowa City (www.iowacity.com)

College Football Hall of Fame (www.cfbhall.com)

Des Moines Register (www.desmoinesregister.com)

El Paso Times (www.elpasotimes.com)

ESPN (www.espn.go.com)

George Raveling (www.coachgeorgeraveling.com)

Hawk Central (www.hawkcentral.com)

Heisman Trophy (www.heisman.com)

Helen Wheelock (www.fullcourt.com)

Iowa Farm Bureau (www.iowafarmbureau.com)

Iowa Public Television (www.iptv.org)

JockBio (www.jockbio.com)

Joe's Place (www.joesplace-ic.com)

Naismith Memorial Basketball Hall of Fame (www.hoophall.com)

National Collegiate Basketball Hall of Fame
    (www.collegebasketballexperience.com)

National Football League (www.nfl.com)

NCAA (www.ncaa.org)

Neal Rozendaal (www.nealrozendaal.com)

Old Capitol Museum (www.oldcap.uiowa.edu)

Pro Football Hall of Fame (www.profootballhof.com)

Quad City Times (www.qctimes.com)

University of Iowa Alumni Association (www.iowaalum.com)

University of Iowa Athletics (www.hawkeyesports.com)

University of Iowa Libraries (www.lib.uiowa.edu)

USA Today (www.usatoday.com)

News Service

Associated Press (Chuck Schoffner)

United Press International (Carrie Muskat)

Other Sources

Hawkeyesports.com (Darren Miller, James Allan, Matt Weitzel, Jil Price)

Intermat Rewind (Mark Palmer)

Minnesota Public Radio (Mark Steil)

National Register of Historic Places Nomination, Old Capitol, July 1975 (Carol Pitts)

Sports Capital Journalism Program (Frank Gogola)

University of Iowa Athletic Media Guides

University of Iowa Media Relations (Steve Roe, Matt Weitzel, Chris Brewer, Jil Price, James Allan)

Newspapers

Anamosa Journal-Eureka (Jim Johnson)

Baltimore Sun (Childs Walker, Jeff Zrebiec)

Cedar Rapids Gazette (Gus Schrader, Mike Hlas, Mark Dukes, Jim Ecker, Marc Morehouse, Scott Dochterman, Jeff Linder)

Chicago Tribune (Robert Blau, Robert Becker, Sam Smith)

Columbus Dispatch (Julie Fulton)

Daily Iowan (Evelyn Lau)

Des Moines Register (Bert McGrane, Bill Bryson, Tony Cordaro, Maury White, Ron Maly, Buck Turnbull, Rick Brown, Marc Hansen, Bob Dyer, Randy Peterson, Ken Fuson, Tom Longden, Andrew Logue, Chad Leistikow, John Naughton, Kyle Munson)

Hartford Courant (Lori Riley)

Iowa City Press-Citizen (Susan Harman, Pat Harty, Matt Cozzi)

Keokuk Daily Gate City (Brad Cameron)

Los Angeles Times (Mal Florence)

New York Times (Pat Borzi, Richard Goldstein, Neil Admur, Steven Lee Myers)

Philadelphia Inquirer (Ray Parrillo)

Quad City Times (Steve Batterson, Don Doxsie, Matt Coss)
Sioux City Journal (Steve Allspach)
USA Today (Roxanna Scott)

Personal Interviews
Kirk Ferentz (December 22, 2015)
Gordy Bohannon (January 20, 2016)
Tom Davis (January 22, 2016)
Glenn Vidnovic (January 22, 2016)
Bill Seaberg (January 22, 2016)
Bobby Hansen (January 23, 2016)
Bump Elliott (January 31, 2016)
Fran McCaffery (January 31, 2016)
Gary Dolphin (January 31, 2016)
Luke Recker (February 1, 2016)
Aaron White (February 2, 2016)
Steve Krafcisin (February 3, 2016)
Chuck Long (February 3, 2016)
Marv Cook (February 3, 2016)
Mark Ironside (February 5, 2016)
Kevin Boyle (February 6, 2016)
Tom Brands (February 9, 2016)
Nate Kaeding (February 10, 2016)
Ed Podolak (February 12, 2016)
Jess Settles (February 14, 2016)